www.wadsworth.com

www.wadsworth.com is the World Wide Web site
for Thomson Wadsworth and is your direct source
to dozens of online resources.

At *www.wadsworth.com* you can find out about
supplements, demonstration software, and student
resources. You can also send email to many of
our authors and preview new publications and
exciting new technologies.

www.wadsworth.com
Changing the way the world learns®

FOUNDATIONS OF MUSIC AND MUSICIANSHIP

THIRD EDITION

with CD-ROM

DAVID DAMSCHRODER
THE UNIVERSITY OF MINNESOTA

THOMSON

SCHIRMER™

Australia • Canada • Mexico • Singapore • Spain • United Kingdom • United States

Publisher: Clark Baxter
Assistant Editor: Anne Gittinger
Editorial Assistant: Emily Perkins
Executive Technology Project Manager: Matt Dorsey
Executive Marketing Manager: Diane Wenckebach
Marketing Assistant: Rachel Bairstow
Marketing Communications Manager: Patrick Rooney
Senior Project Manager, Editorial Production: Kimberly Adams
Executive Art Director: Maria Epes
Print Buyer: Doreen Suruki
Permissions Editor: Sarah Harkrader

Production Service: Stratford Publishing Services
Text Designer: Lee Anne Dollison
Copy Editor: Carrie Crompton
Autographers: Ernie Mansfield, Mansfield Music-Graphics; and A-R Editions
Cover Designer: Lee Anne Dollison
Cover Image: Ferruccio Sardella/marlenaagency.com
Cover Printer: Phoenix Color Corp.
Compositor: Stratford Publishing Services
Printer: Edwards Brothers, Incorporated

Printed in the United States of America
1 2 3 4 5 6 7 09 08 07 06 05

For more information about our products, contact us at:
Thomson Learning Academic Resource Center
1-800-423-0563

For permission to use material from this text or product, submit a request online at
http://www.thomsonrights.com.
Any additional questions about permissions can be submitted by email to
thomsonrights@thomson.com.

Library of Congress Control Number: 2005921444

ISBN 0-534-59552-9

Thomson Higher Education
10 Davis Drive
Belmont, CA 94002-3098
USA

Asia (including India)
Thomson Learning
5 Shenton Way
#01-01UIC Building
Singapore 068808

Australia/New Zealand
Thomson Learning Australia
102 Dodds Street
Southbank, Victoria 3006
Australia

Canada
Thomson Nelson
1120 Birchmount Road
Toronto, Ontario M1K 5G4
Canada

UK/Europe/Middle East/Africa
Thomson Learning
High Holborn House
50-51 Bedford Row
London WC1R 4LR
United Kingdom

Latin America
Thomson Learning
Seneca, 53
Colonia Polanco
11560 Mexico
D.F. Mexico

Spain (including Portugal)
Thomson Paraninfo
Calle Magallanes, 25
28015 Madrid, Spain

CONTENTS

CHAPTER 3

CHAPTER 4

CHAPTER 5

PART II: Chords and Chord Progression 151

CHAPTER 7

PREFACE FOR STUDENTS

To the Student:

When you studied English, you learned how to use the twenty-six letters to spell words, and how to use successions of words to form sentences. This text follows a similar path for music. Individual pitches (such as those that are activated by the eighty-eight keys of a piano) combine to form chords, whose successions form phrases and periods. It doesn't matter if you've never sat down at a piano before, or have never encountered musical terms such as *pitch* or *chord*. We start at the beginning and proceed gradually in a process that should unleash your musical talent and inspire you to make music by singing or by playing an instrument. I assume that you enjoy music, that you sometimes sing along with others or with a radio for fun, and that you are curious about how music works. I do not assume that you've had any formal training in music. Of course, some students who enroll in a music fundamentals course have sung in a choir, or have taken piano lessons, or have taught themselves how to play the guitar. Though such activities might make studying this text a bit easier, they are in no sense a prerequisite for success.

In today's musical culture, you often are expected to be passive—a member of an audience or a consumer of recorded performances. In this text, in contrast, you are expected to be an active participant. Learning how to read music notation would be pointless if you did not put your new skill to use. Your instructor will assign various activities that will help you develop your talent for making music from written notation. You need no special equipment to clap rhythms, and likely you will sing during class. Maybe your school has a keyboard lab (or a computer lab equipped with keyboards) so that you can learn to play melodies and chord progressions. Regardless of what activities are offered within your course, the knowledge and skill that you gain should motivate you to continue your active participation in music for years to come.

There are, of course, many kinds and styles of music, representing the world's diverse cultures. This text focuses on key-based music from the European and North American heritage, encompassing not only the work of numerous classical composers but also many popular styles. With this foundation, you will be well equipped to expand and diversify your musical explorations in the years ahead.

Don't be surprised that learning about music requires effort. Though music fills a role as entertainment in modern culture, those who succeed in entertaining us have enhanced their natural talent through extensive training and practice. Though this text is intended more for avocational than vocational music-makers, it guides you through the sorts of activities that professional musicians complete early in their development. Yes, learning music should be fun. And yes, I've tried to make the presentations in each chapter as clear and efficient as possible. But as in any other subject, if you neglect to master the content of the early chapters, it is likely that you will not make much sense of the later ones.

To get the most out of your course, make sure that you use the CD-ROM enclosed in the pocket attached to the back cover, and also visit the text's website: http://music.wadsworth.com/damschroder_3e. Take a moment now to explore the text to see what is included. All the chapters follow a similar format, with an introduction to pitch and rhythm topics, followed by a variety of activities and exercises. I've supplied the solutions to practice exercises and a glossary of musical terms at the end of the book, and you can find the solutions to selected exercises, highlighted with asterisks, on the text's website. I've also provided appendices of auxiliary information that, though not part of the chapter-by-chapter flow of the text, you might find interesting or useful.

It is my sincere hope that, as you complete this text, you will decide to become a lifelong participant in music.

PREFACE FOR INSTRUCTORS

To the Instructor:

The primary audience for this text is students of the liberal arts and sciences who elect a course in music fundamentals to fulfill a fine-arts requirement. This diverse group of students will likely include some who have a considerable background in music, and others who are relatively inexperienced. The text is written with the latter group in mind. I have made an effort to offer clear explanations of basic concepts and to provide abundant activities that will help even the most reluctant potential music-makers find joy and success in active participation. It usually turns out that students whose experience includes years of piano lessons or extensive choral singing haven't devoted much attention to anything beyond reading music notation. This text will offer them information that will make their participation in music all the more vibrant and satisfying.

A secondary audience for this text is first-term music majors. Many harmony texts provide a lamentably abbreviated coverage of music fundamentals, assuming incorrectly that music majors can establish a secure foundation in the fundamentals of music with minimal explanation or exercise. Skimping in the early stages may lead to problems as more complicated materials are introduced. Adopting this text for use during the first term of tonal harmony should rectify that situation.

Improvements for the third edition include the following:

- Students are offered three separate layers of written exercises to assist in mastering new material: (1) abundant practice exercises integrated into the presentations of new material, encouraging students to pause for some "hands-on" experience with a concept before proceeding to the next section; (2) a set of written exercises, suitable for submission, at the end of each chapter; and (3) self-grading practice examinations after Chapters 6 and 12.
- Many keyboard, singing, and aural activities have been added, along with a new section on improvisation in each chapter.
- The distribution of topics into chapters has been extensively revised, so that each of the text's twelve chapters covers about the same amount of new material, with all supplementary materials appearing together in the Appendix.
- Nearly 100 "Tips for Success," designed to help students work efficiently in mastering the course content and to alert them to pertinent materials beyond the confines of the chapter at hand, have been added at numerous points throughout the text.
- A "Scores for Music Analysis" section has been added, including chapter-keyed questions for discussion.
- The CD-ROM has been expanded, with many new exercises in aural skills.

Before beginning the term, assess the extent to which you will be able to make use of the Laboratory exercises in keyboard performance, singing, rhythm, and improvisation. To get the full benefit from these materials, students should have at least one hour of supervised instruction in a keyboard laboratory every week, with additional time available for those who proceed slowly or who want to be especially thorough in their practice. Though all of the Laboratory activities are optional—the text will stand on its own even if only the Pitch and Rhythm sections and their homework exercises are used—they play an important role in developing a student's musical capacities. If you do not have access to a keyboard laboratory, you should devote some class time to group performance of the singing and rhythm exercises.

Likewise, the activities in ear-training are optional, though I strongly encourage their use. Students will find all of the Audio Exercises performed on the CD-ROM that accompanies the text. These exercises should be reinforced by in-class practice and discussion.

I find that the full content of the twelve chapters is about the right amount of material for a fifteen-week, three-credit course at the University of Minnesota. We proceed at the rate of about one chapter per week, with extra time reserved for review before each exam. If you have an exceptionally able group of students or elect not to use all the laboratory content, your course could include coverage of materials from the Appendix or instruction in the harmonization of melodies, using materials available for free download from the publisher.

The text's website, http://music.wadsworth.com/damschroder_3e, offers registered instructors a solutions manual for all the textbook's exercises.

PART I

Intervals, Scales, and Triads

CHAPTER 1

The Piano Keyboard

Musical sounds come about in many ways. You carry one source of music within you: your voice. But watching yourself sing in a mirror provides no clue regarding how musical sounds are organized. For that purpose we instead draw upon the piano keyboard, whose keys are arranged in a meaningful way. We begin by exploring sounds activated by some of the piano's white keys. These sounds have names derived from the alphabet (the letters A through G) and correspond to symbols of music notation that you will learn to read. After exploring this notation, we will build some combinations of two pitches, called intervals, and a succession of eight pitches, called a scale.

Pitch and Its Notation

Musical sounds, called **pitches**, result from vibrations made on an instrument or by vocal cords engaged in singing. They can also be generated electronically. We distinguish pitches from one another according to their positions within a range from low to high. The piano's white and black keys assemble eighty-eight different pitches in an ascending order from left to right. Though your voice has a more limited range than the piano, it likely extends wide enough so that you could sing a melody after you have heard it a few times.

The strings of a piano or guitar vibrate, the air inside a trumpet or flute vibrates, and your vocal cords vibrate. Most pitches vibrate hundreds or even thousands of times per second. The fewer the vibrations per second (corresponding to longer, thicker vibrating bodies, such as the strings on the left side of a piano), the lower the sound. In this section we will name some of the pitches, locate their positions on the piano keyboard, and learn to read the notation for pitch.

Score notation is the visual representation of music. It appears on a set of five long horizontal lines called a **staff**. Each oval **notehead** (or **note**) positioned on a **line** or in the **space** between two lines corresponds to an individual pitch. Example 1-1 shows noteheads in the first space (counting from the bottom up), on the third line, and on the fifth line.

pitches

score notation
staff
notehead
note
line
space

Example 1-1

Five is an ideal number of lines. It is always easy to see at a glance exactly where a notehead is positioned. That task would be more difficult if there were, say, eight lines. But observe that the nine positions on the staff (five lines and four spaces) are far fewer than the number of keys on the keyboard. What to do? One way to include more information within the visual field of the staff is to extend it upwards or downwards temporarily using **ledger lines**. As you see in Example 1-2, these short

ledger lines

horizontal lines are spaced the same width apart as the five lines of the staff. If a note-head fills a space, a ledger line will appear on its interior side only.

Example 1-2

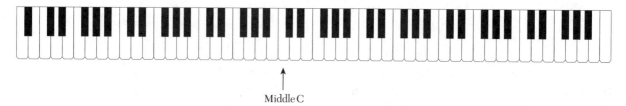

High noteheads
using ledger lines

Low noteheads
using ledger lines

Incorrect use
of ledger lines

clef

Another way to compress more information into staff notation is to use the same notehead to represent different pitches. A symbol called a **clef**, placed at the left edge of the staff, indicates which choice in pitch is intended. Several hundred years ago, there were numerous clefs in general use. Now most musicians read only two clefs fluently. In this chapter we will employ the **treble clef** (𝄞) for the pitches played by the right hand on the piano, or for the same pitches played on another instrument or sung in that range. For the lower pitches, another clef will be introduced in Chapter 3. That clef will give a different meaning to the same noteheads that we learn to read in the context of the treble clef in this chapter.

treble clef

Middle C

To find our way around the piano keyboard, we will use a specific key called **Middle C** as our point of reference. Its position is displayed in Example 1-3. If you sit centered at the keyboard, Middle C will be under your left eye. You can play it easily with your thumb when your right hand is centered in front of you.

Example 1-3

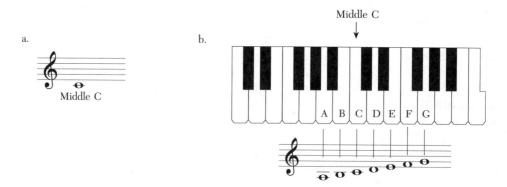

Middle C

Using the treble clef, we define the notehead shown in Example 1-4a as Middle C. Then, for each space or line lower or higher than Middle C that a notehead on the staff is positioned, we move one *white* key to the left or right on the keyboard. To the left of Middle C, we find a B and then an A. To the right, we find D, E, F, and G. These noteheads are displayed in Example 1-4b.

Example 1-4

Middle C

a.   b.

Middle C

A B C D E F G

Continuing upwards (*higher* on the staff, *to the right* on the keyboard), the A-to-G pattern recurs several times, as shown in Example 1-5. Observe that the pattern of white and black keys on the piano keyboard repeats after every seven white keys. That is why there are seven pitch names: A through G. Study the layout of the keyboard carefully, so that you know instantly that the pitch named C is just to the left of the two closely aligned black keys, that the pitch named F is just to the left of the three closely aligned black keys, and so on. If we did not mind having many ledger lines to read, we could continue downwards from the pitches of Example 1-4b as well. But, as mentioned previously, another clef will provide a more convenient means of representing those pitches in notation.

Example 1-5

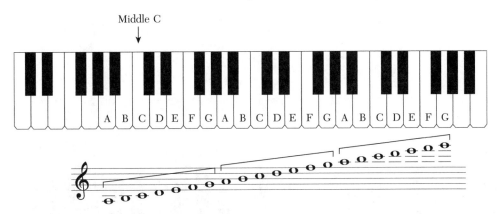

When playing the piano, be especially careful to distinguish among the various keys that have the same name. Three different noteheads in Example 1-5 correspond to pitches named C, but each C is activated by a different key on the keyboard: Middle C and two other keys some distance to the right of Middle C. It is a common mistake among beginners to play the wrong one. Always sit centered at the keyboard. Move your arm—not your posterior—to reach each key.

Practice Exercises 1-1

Practice creating music notation by drawing each symbol below twice to the right of its model.

a.

b.

c.

d.

e.

The note names for the four spaces of the treble-clef staff spell a word: F A C E. The five lines correspond to the note names E G B D F. Since this is not a word, create short sentences using words beginning with these letters as a memory aid. Compare your sentences with those of your classmates.

f. E _____ G _____ B _____ D _____ F _____

g. E _____ G _____ B _____ D _____ F _____

Name each pitch, using the letter names from A through G.

h. _____   i. _____   j. _____   k. _____   l. _____   m. _____   n. _____   o. _____

Draw arrows connecting each notehead to the appropriate key on the keyboard.

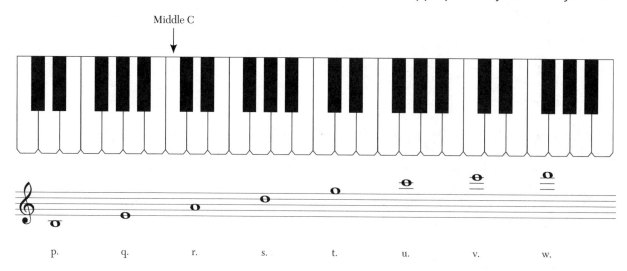

p.   q.   r.   s.   t.   u.   v.   w.

Now check your answers against the "Solutions to Practice Exercises" found at the back of your textbook (beginning on page 317).

Intervals

Though an individual pitch may have a beautiful sound, on its own it could hardly be called music. It is only when we combine pitches that something meaningful results. Two pitches that sound either together or one after the other establish a relationship called an **interval**. Do the two pitches that form an interval blend well? Or do they clash with one another? How far apart are the two pitches? Are they presented melodically (one pitch after the other) or harmonically (at the same time)? If melodically, do they form an ascending or a descending line? Such questions enter the domain of musical meaning: an interval may provide a sense of comfort and repose (playing, for example, Middle C and the G to the right simultaneously), or a sense of urgency and instability instead (playing Middle C and the B to the left simultaneously).

   Every interval has a unique name consisting of two components: a **quality** and a **size**. For example, when you played C–G, as suggested above, you were forming a

interval

quality
size

perfect fifth

perfect fifth: an interval whose quality is perfect and whose size is five. If you know before you perform it that an interval is a perfect fifth, then you can anticipate that the sound will be reposeful, which might affect *how* you perform it.

We calculate an interval's size by counting the number of lines and spaces spanned by its two noteheads. As Example 1-6 reveals, every line and space—including those on which *both* noteheads reside—is counted. Thus, the intervals presented in Example 1-6 are an ascending sixth and a descending fifth. Alternatively, you could perform this calculation by counting the letters between the two note names: G̲ A B C D E̲ = 6; G̲ F E D C̲ = 5.

Example 1-6

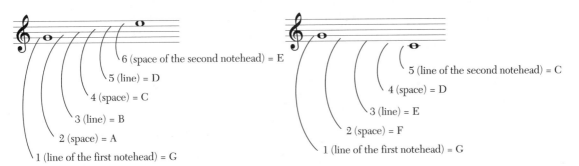

If the two pitches of an interval are to be performed melodically, they will appear one after the other (read from left to right) on the staff, with some space between them. If the two pitches are to be performed harmonically (for example, by two singers or by pressing two piano keys at the same time), their noteheads will appear either in vertical alignment or, when that is not possible, side by side and touching. Example 1-7 samples both possibilities.

Example 1-7

Melodic   Harmonic

For now, we will consider only the intervals with sizes ranging from one to eight. Samples of each are displayed in Example 1-8. Two of these intervals are constructed using pitches with the same letter name: the **perfect unison** and the **perfect octave**. By listening carefully to the perfect octave, you will come to understand that the naming of pitches is not arbitrary. Two pitches that are a perfect octave apart sound so similar that it is common for men and women singing together (for example, "Happy Birthday" at a party) to sing not at the perfect unison (which would be impossible, given the different ranges characteristic of men's and women's voices), but instead at the perfect octave. This strategy is successful because the vibrations of the two pitches that form a perfect octave blend together exceptionally well. For every vibration of a perfect octave's lower pitch, there are two vibrations of its upper pitch (that is, the ratio is 2 to 1). No other interval except the perfect unison (whose ratio is 1 to 1) is characterized by such a simple ratio. Though the unison and octave are of perfect quality, most of the remaining intervals in Example 1-8 have other qualities, which we will explore in the next few chapters.

perfect unison

perfect octave

Example 1-8

Unison Second Third Fourth Fifth Sixth Seventh Octave

Interval sizes are not additive. If you ascend a third and, from there, ascend another third, you might expect to have ascended a sixth. No! By studying Example 1-9, you will understand that you have ascended only a fifth.

Example 1-9

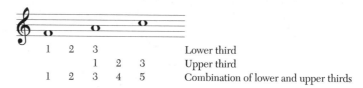

1	2	3			Lower third
		1	2	3	Upper third
1	2	3	4	5	Combination of lower and upper thirds

Practice Exercises 1-2

Name the two pitches of each interval, using the letter names from A through G. Then indicate the interval's size, using numbers from 1 through 8.

To the right of each notehead, add the notehead that forms the interval requested. Then name both pitches, using the letter names from A through G.

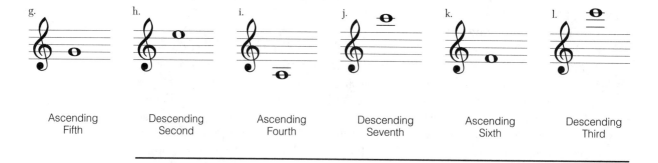

| g. | h. | i. | j. | k. | l. |
| Ascending Fifth | Descending Second | Ascending Fourth | Descending Seventh | Ascending Sixth | Descending Third |

The C Major Scale

tonal centers

tonics

modes

The program of a classical music concert may announce a Symphony in A Major, or a Sonata in D Major. "A" and "D" are among twelve possible **tonal centers**, or **tonics**, for a composition, along with B, C, E, F, and G, as well as the pitches that correspond to the five black keys. "Major" is one of two commonly employed **modes** (along with "minor," which we will explore in Chapter 4). The mode indicates which pitches are used along with the tonic pitch. When C is tonic and the mode is major, those other pitches are D, E, F, G, A, and B.

When we arrange these pitches in order and include the tonic pitch at both ends, we form a **scale.** The eight noteheads in Example 1-10 form an ascending C Major scale. The word "scale" comes from a root that means "ladder" or "stairs." Though the noteheads on the staff resemble a set of stairs, observe that not all of the steps are of the same height. The keyboard diagram reveals that some of the steps are twice as large as others. When a black key comes between two adjacent white keys (as in C–D or F–G), the white keys form a **whole step** (W). When no black key intervenes (as in E–F or B–C), the white keys form a **half step** (H). The pattern of steps characteristic of the ascending C Major scale is Whole-Whole-Half-Whole-Whole-Whole-Half.

scale

whole step
half step

Example 1-10

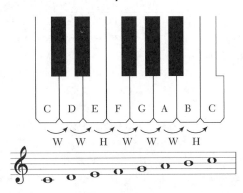

The tonal center and the mode together constitute the **key** of a composition: the key of C Major, for example. The seven pitches employed (selected from the twelve within an octave) are the **diatonic** pitches of the key. C Major is the only major key that does not employ any of the black keys.

key

diatonic

We will often use numbers called **scale degrees** to label the notes of a scale. These numbers, displayed in Example 1-11, will always be capped by a circumflex (^) to distinguish them from other numbers used in music, such as keyboard fingerings. In C Major, the pitch D is $\hat{2}$ (scale degree 2). D is $\hat{2}$ even when the scale descends, in which case the numbers read $\hat{8}$–$\hat{7}$–$\hat{6}$–$\hat{5}$–$\hat{4}$–$\hat{3}$–$\hat{2}$–$\hat{1}$. And if we write the scale in a higher range, the higher D would be labeled $\hat{2}$ as well.

scale degrees

Example 1-11

a. $\hat{1}$ $\hat{2}$ $\hat{3}$ $\hat{4}$ $\hat{5}$ $\hat{6}$ $\hat{7}$ $\hat{8}$　　b. $\hat{8}$ $\hat{7}$ $\hat{6}$ $\hat{5}$ $\hat{4}$ $\hat{3}$ $\hat{2}$ $\hat{1}$　　c. $\hat{1}$ $\hat{2}$ $\hat{3}$ $\hat{4}$ $\hat{5}$ $\hat{6}$ $\hat{7}$ $\hat{8}$

Practice Exercises 1-3

Use scale degree numbers ($\hat{2}$, $\hat{5}$, $\hat{7}$, etc.) to label the position of each pitch below in the key of C Major. Because the pitch C both begins and ends the scale, it may be labeled either $\hat{1}$ or $\hat{8}$.

a.　　b.　　c.　　d.　　e.　　f.

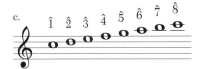

Tips for Success

✔ It is *very important* that you quickly gain fluency in reading music notation using treble clef. When you see a note, you should know its name (A through G) *instantly*, and also know exactly where to find it on a keyboard. Study the diagrams on the previous page and the fold-out diagram that accompanies this textbook, use the CD-ROM tutorial on the treble clef, and practice reading notation in the Activities section of this chapter. Don't put yourself at a disadvantage when new topics are introduced in the next few chapters by neglecting this essential skill. Put in some effort every day for the next week, and you should master the topic.

✔ Intervals are everywhere in music, and thus pervasive in this textbook. Practice until you can calculate an interval's size quickly and accurately. Remember that the first pitch of an interval is counted as 1: for example, the ascending interval from C to G is 5 (C–D–E–F–G), not 4 (D–E–F–G).

✔ Musicians use numbers in a variety of ways. Interval names are based on numbers, positions within the scale are specified using scale-degree numbers—capped by a circumflex (ˆ)— and, as you will learn in this chapter's Laboratory section, piano fingerings make use of numbers. In later chapters we will employ Roman numerals as well, for yet another purpose.

✔ Learn the Whole-Whole-Half-Whole-Whole-Whole-Half succession of the major scale by visualizing (or by playing) a keyboard: starting at C and proceeding to the right, say "Whole" when a black key appears between adjacent white keys and "Half" when no black key is present. Also practice the descending succession: Half-Whole-Whole-Whole-Half-Whole-Whole.

✔ When you write on the staff, look at the models of music notation supplied when each symbol was introduced. Be careful that the distance between ledger lines is the same as that between lines of the staff, and that each ledger line is not much wider than a notehead. Make each notehead correspond to the width between two lines of the staff, whether it falls on a line or in a space.

✔ Acquaint yourself with the Appendix at the back of this textbook. It contains information on a variety of topics that, though auxiliary to the basic thrust of the text, may be of interest to you. At this point, you are ready to read about Precise Pitch Designations for pitches in treble clef.

Quarter Notes and Half Notes in $\frac{4}{4}$ Meter

Music notation conveys not only what pitches to perform, but also when to perform them. In this chapter we explore meter, the grid of pulses that forms the foundation for rhythmic notation. In the context of $\frac{4}{4}$ meter, we will learn to read two common notational symbols—the quarter note and the half note. These symbols indicate the starting point and duration of a pitch.

Rhythm

To study **rhythm** is to explore how musical sounds unfold over time. The symbols on the staff reveal not only what pitches to perform, but also when to perform them. Without notation for the relative durations of musical sounds, composers could not convey their intentions. Performance by an ensemble of musicians would be next to impossible. Though rhythmic notation need not be obeyed slavishly—a performer may "bend" the rhythm for interpretive reasons, for example—the arithmetical integrity of the system ensures that each performer understands the symbols in the same way.

rhythm

Meter

Rhythmic notation depends upon a continuous flow of **pulses**, or **beats**. Such pulses follow one another at a uniform rate, as in the ticking of a clock or the beating of the heart. Like heartbeats, the beats of music may go slower or faster depending on the sentiment conveyed by the music and the energy of the performers. The bass drum is used in marching bands to reinforce the beats, so that everyone marches at the same pace and performs the music together.

pulses

beats

Music's pulses are grouped into **measures**—combinations of two, three, or four beats. Some of the beats within a measure are emphasized ("strong beats"), while others are not ("weak beats"). When there are four beats per measure, for example, the first beat is the strongest and the third is the next strongest, while the second and fourth beats are weak. By grouping pulses into measures and by organizing the pulses within each measure into strong and weak beats, we create **meter**.

measures

To get a sense of how meter shapes beats into measures containing strong and weak beats, recite the two lines in Example 1-12 at the rate of one number per second. Use greater emphasis the larger the number appears. When performing the rhythmic exercises in the Laboratory segments of this text, you should say the metrical counting numbers out loud.

meter

Example 1-12

Without meter: 1 1 1 1   1 1 1 1   1 1 1 1   1 1 1 1

With meter: 1 2 3 4   1 2 3 4   1 2 3 4   1 2 3 4

Quarter Notes and Half Notes in $\frac{4}{4}$ Meter

time signature

The symbol $\frac{4}{4}$, which appears near the left edge of the staff in Example 1-13, is a *time signature*. It designates which of the many meters employed in music applies to the melody written on that staff.

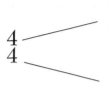

The upper 4 of the time signature indicates that four beats fill a measure.

quarter note

The lower 4 of the time signature indicates that the *quarter note* represents the beat.

stem

bar lines

double bar

A quarter note is formed by filling in the interior of a notehead and adding a vertical line called a *stem* to one side: up from the right side if the notehead is placed below the center line on the staff, or down from the left side if the notehead is placed on or above the center line on the staff. The melody shown in Example 1-13 contains sixteen quarter notes, which fill four measures. Vertical lines called *bar lines* extend from the first to the fifth line of the staff to show the boundaries between measures. Observe that instead of a bar line, the time signature appears at the beginning of a melody, and that instead of a single bar line, a *double bar* (two vertical lines, the second thicker than the first) appears at the end of a melody.

Example 1-13

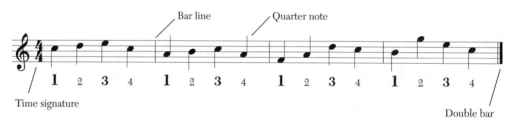

half note

common time

Just as a quarter note fills one-fourth of a measure in $\frac{4}{4}$ meter, a *half note*, which is formed by adding a stem to an open notehead, fills one-half of a measure. Both quarter notes and half notes are employed in Example 1-14. This example also employs the symbol **c**, which stands for *common time*. It is another way to indicate the $\frac{4}{4}$ meter.

Example 1-14

Note: When a melody extends to two or more lines of staff, the clef is written again on each staff, but the time signature is not.

Practice Exercises 1-4

Practice creating music notation by drawing each symbol below twice to the right of its model.

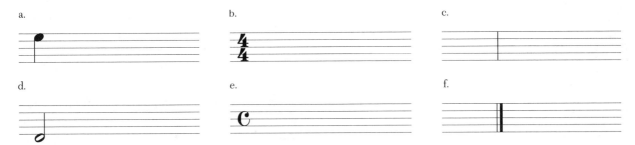

a.

b.

c.

d.

e.

f.

Add a quarter note or a half note to each measure below, so that it is filled by a total of four beats. Use a variety of noteheads: some high, some low, some with ledger lines. Make sure that the stems of your high notes hang down from the left side of the notehead, that the stems of your low notes point up from the right side of the notehead, that all stems are vertical, and that each stem is the length of three to four spaces.

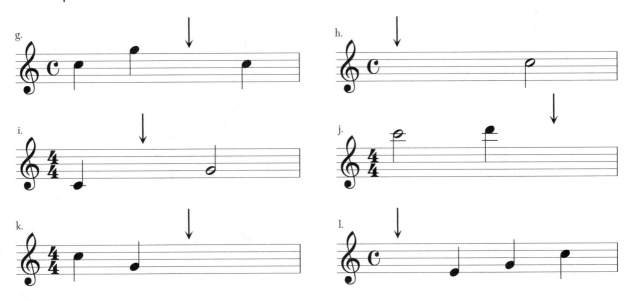

g.

h.

i.

j.

k.

l.

Tips for Success

✔ Count the meter out loud when performing rhythms. Emphasize beat 1, and to a lesser extent beat 3, in your counting.

✔ Develop good habits in writing music notation. Follow the notation of the typeset examples closely. Do not let bar lines extend beyond the top or bottom of the staff, fill the noteheads of quarter notes completely, and position stems carefully.

✔ One way to get a good feel for meter is to move your right hand the way an orchestral or choral conductor would. You can learn the standard conducting pattern for ¼ meter in the Conducting Patterns section of the Appendix.

Laboratory

L1-1. Play and Sing

a. Sit at the keyboard, positioning yourself so that you are exactly centered. You should be able to reach any key on the keyboard comfortably from this position. There should never be a need to move your posterior to the right or the left on the bench. Keep your feet flat on the floor—not on the pedals located directly in front of your feet.

If you have centered yourself correctly, the two white keys directly below your nose will be an E and an F. Middle C is the second white key to the left of this E. Always take the time to orient yourself by finding Middle C. The two keys that students most commonly mistake for Middle C are the F a fourth to the right of Middle C, and the C an octave to the right of Middle C. Compare their positions with that of Middle C.

Curving your fingers, place your right thumb above Middle C. Touch the key, but do not press it. Then place the remaining fingers above D, E, F, and G. You will not be able to do this if your fingers are straight. Curved fingers can easily cover five adjacent white keys. Long fingernails and good hand position are incompatible! Make contact with the keys using the left side of your thumb and the tips of your remaining fingers.

Push your thumb down to play Middle C. After a second, release. Then play D, E, F, and G in turn, using your remaining four fingers. You are now ready to begin making music notated in treble clef.

Use your right hand to play each of the intervals below. To accomplish this, you may have to move your hand to the left or right, and you may have to spread your fingers wider apart. Suggested fingerings are provided (1 = thumb, 2 = index finger, 3 = middle finger, 4 = ring finger, 5 = little finger). After you play each interval, name its size (unison, second, third, etc.).

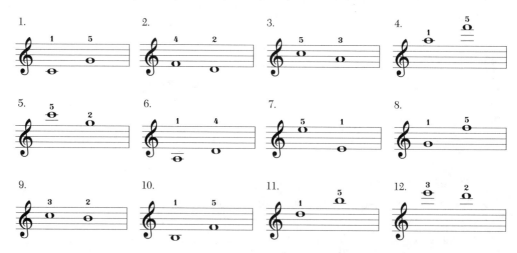

b. Now place the little finger of your *left* hand above Middle C and the next three fingers above D, E, and F. Place the second finger of your right hand above the adjacent G and the next three fingers above A, B, and C. (Let your thumbs dangle back a bit.) Now play each of these keys in succession from left to right, forming a C Major scale ascending from $\hat{1}$ to $\hat{8}$. Then play the scale descending from $\hat{8}$ to $\hat{1}$.

c. Play the ascending and descending scales again, but this time pause after each pitch and sing it. That is, play C, then sing C; play D, then sing D; and so on. You may sing on the neutral syllable "la," sing the pitch names ("C," "D," "E," etc.), or sing the scale degree numbers ("$\hat{1}$," "$\hat{2}$," "$\hat{3}$," etc.). Men and low-voiced women may need to sing these pitches in a more comfortable range, an octave lower.

L1-2. Listening

Team up with another student, work with your instructor in class, or make use of the CD-ROM that accompanies this textbook to practice these exercises.

a. *Performer:* Place three fingers on any three keys of the keyboard and play each once, in any order.

   Listener: Indicate whether the highest pitch sounded first, second, or third. Alternatively, indicate whether the lowest pitch sounded first, second, or third. Or, indicate whether the middle pitch sounded first, second, or third.

b. *Performer:* Place eight fingers above the eight keys corresponding to the C Major scale (as in L1-1b). Then either perform this scale (ascending or descending), or play the scale with one "wrong" pitch (using an adjacent black key in place of one of the white keys).

   Listener: Indicate "Yes," this is a C Major scale; or "No," this is not a C Major scale.

L1-3. Keyboard Album

Perform each of the following melodies at the keyboard using your right hand. Recommended fingerings are provided. You may wish to work first on the rhythm alone (counting out loud) and then the pitch alone before attempting to perform each melody as written.

Westminster Chimes

Schumann: *Album for the Young,* Op. 68, "Humming Song"

L1-4. Song Book

Sing each of the following melodies. You may

- play along at the keyboard,
- be accompanied by your instructor in class, or
- be accompanied by your CD-ROM at the computer.

You may sing the melodies on "la," use the note names ("C," "D," "E," etc.), or use the appropriate scale degree numbers ("1̂," "2̂," "3̂," etc.). Your instructor will probably indicate a preference. If you use the scale degree numbers, sing "7̂" as "sev" (a single syllable) rather than as "seven."

Men and low-voiced women should sing these melodies an octave lower than they are written.

L1-5. Rhythm

Perform exercises a. through c. by clapping or by playing the pitch F with the index finger of your right hand at the keyboard. Write in the counting numbers (that is, "1 2 3 4 1 2 3 4 . . .") in the appropriate positions below the staff notation, and pronounce them out loud as you perform the rhythm. Before you begin, count one measure out loud (1 2 3 4) at the rate of one number per second. Do not speed up or slow down during performance.

Once you are successful in these exercises, attempt exercises d. and e. by clapping one part while a classmate claps the other, by performing the upper part with the index finger of your right hand and the lower part with the index finger of your left hand at the keyboard, or by dividing the entire class into two groups. Observe that when two parts share the same staff, the stems of the upper part always point upward, while the stems of the lower part always point downward.

d.

e.

L1-6. Improvisation

At a keyboard, place eight fingers above the keys for the C Major scale (as in L1-1b). Now create your own melodies, using the following guidelines.

a. Play a total of four quarter notes. Make the first note C ($\hat{1}$) and the last note either C ($\hat{1}$), E ($\hat{3}$), G ($\hat{5}$), or C ($\hat{8}$).
b. Play a total of eight quarter notes. Make the first and last notes C (either $\hat{1}$ or $\hat{8}$).
c. Play a total of sixteen quarter notes, in which the pitches C ($\hat{1}$), E ($\hat{3}$), G ($\hat{5}$), and C ($\hat{8}$) predominate.

L1-7. Score Study

Listen to Selections 1 and 2 in the Scores for Music Analysis section at the back of the textbook. Then answer the questions under the "Chapter 1" headings that accompany these selections.

Name: _____

Instructor: _____

Date: _____

Pitch Exercises

Throughout the text, asterisks denote exercises for which solutions are provided on the text's website, http://music.wadsworth.com/damschroder_3e. Always check your solutions against these answers both to confirm that you understand what the problem asks you to do and that you have solved the marked problems correctly.

P1-1. Draw a line connecting each notehead with the appropriate white key. Note carefully the location of Middle C.

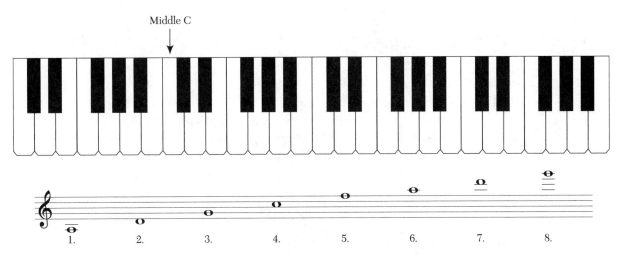

P1-2. On the staff, draw the noteheads that correspond to the given white keys. Note carefully the location of Middle C.

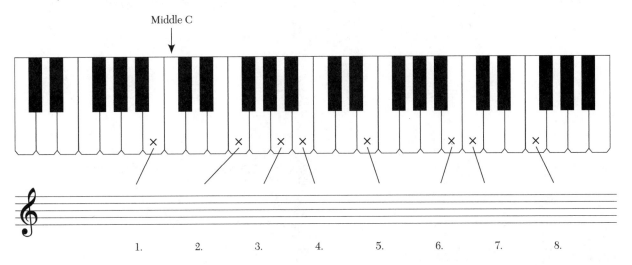

P1-3. 1. For each interval shown below, place a horizontal line above the staff if the two notes are to be performed melodically. Place a vertical line to the right of the staff if the two notes are to be performed harmonically.
2. Below the staff, indicate the name of each notehead (A, B, C, etc.).
3. Below the note names, indicate the interval's size (1, 2, 3, etc.).

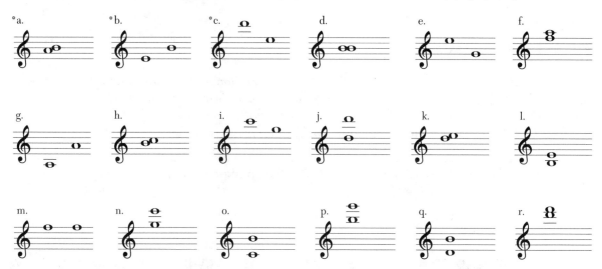

P1-4. 1. On the right half of each staff, supply the notehead that forms the requested melodic interval with the given notehead. You may wish to confirm your answers by numbering the lines and spaces enclosed by the two noteheads.
2. Below the staff, indicate the name of each notehead (A, B, C, etc.).

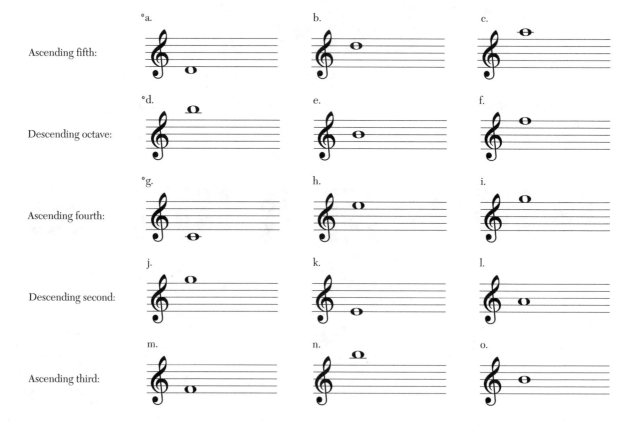

Name: _____

Instructor: _____

Date: _____

Descending sixth:

p.   q. 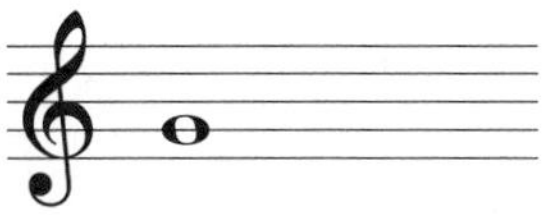   r.

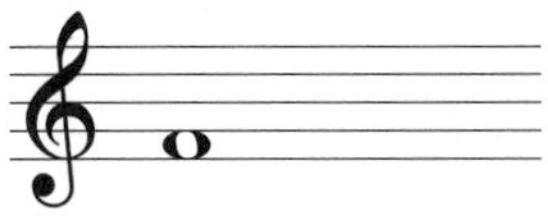

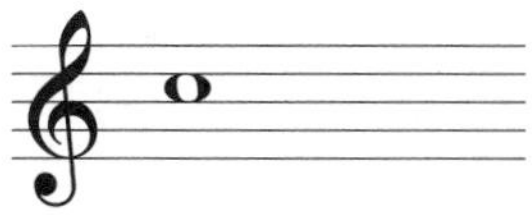

Ascending seventh:

s.   t. 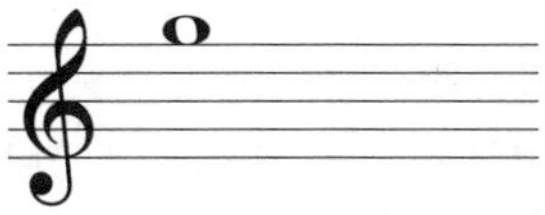   u.

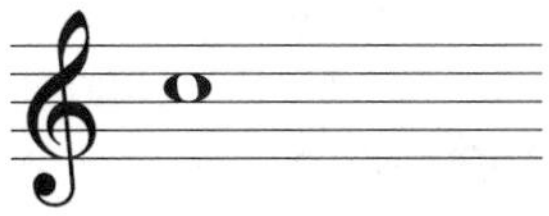

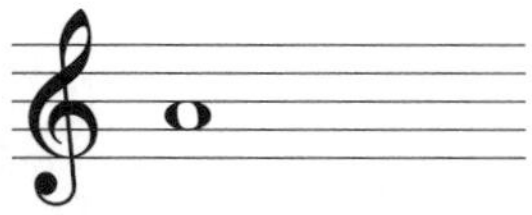

P1-5. In the work area provided, select any convenient notehead as a starting point and form the two intervals requested, one after the other. Then measure the interval formed by the first and third noteheads. For example, for an ascending third followed by an ascending third (such as C–E followed by E–G), your solution would be "ascending fifth."

*a. A descending second followed by a descending third
     Solution:

*b. An ascending third followed by an ascending fifth
     Solution:

c. A descending fourth followed by an ascending seventh
     Solution:

d. An ascending fifth followed by a descending octave
     Solution:

e. A descending sixth followed by a descending second
     Solution:

f. An ascending seventh followed by a descending sixth
     Solution:

g. A descending octave followed by an ascending fourth
     Solution:

h. An ascending second followed by a descending second
     Solution:

Work area:

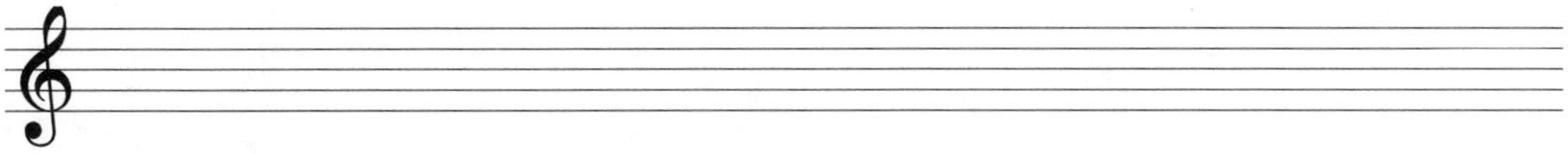

Work area:

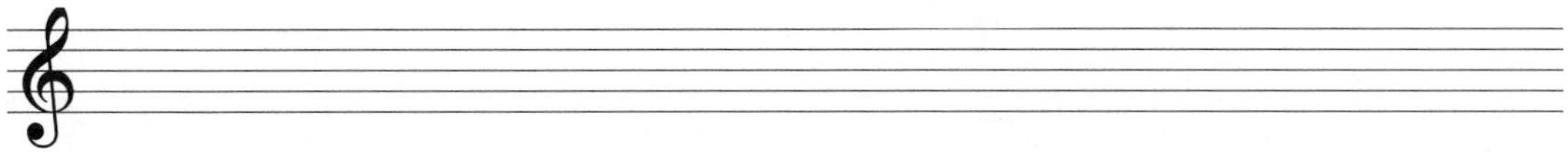

P1-6. Name each pitch, using the letter names A through G. Then indicate its scale degree number in the context of C Major, using the symbols 1̂ through 8̂.

Letter name: ____ ____ ____ ____ ____ ____ ____ ____ ____ ____

Scale degree: ____ ____ ____ ____ ____ ____ ____ ____ ____ ____

°a. °b. c. d. e. f. g. h. i. j.

P1-7. For each of the following patterns of ascending or descending whole and half steps, indicate the major-key scale degrees where the succession occurs. In some cases, several answers must be supplied; in others, there may be no succession of scale degrees that fits the pattern. Remember that since it takes two pitches to form a whole or a half step, patterns of two intervals (such as Whole-Half) require three consecutive scale degrees, patterns of three intervals (such as Whole-Whole-Half) require four consecutive scale degrees, and so on.

1̂	2̂	3̂	4̂	5̂	6̂	7̂	8̂
	Whole	Whole	Half	Whole	Whole	Whole	Half

°a. Whole-Half (Ascending)

f. Whole-Whole-Whole (Descending)

°b. Half-Whole (Descending)

g. Half-Whole-Half (Ascending)

c. Whole-Whole-Half (Ascending)

h. Half-Whole-Whole-Half (Descending)

d. Whole-Half-Whole (Descending)

i. Whole-Half-Whole-Whole (Ascending)

e. Half-Whole-Whole (Ascending)

j. Whole-Whole-Whole-Half (Descending)

Rhythm Exercises

R1-1. Convert each notehead below into a quarter note, making all necessary changes. Be careful to use the correct stem direction and to make your stems vertical (not slanted!). Assuming that the melody begins on the first beat of a measure, add bar lines and a double bar at appropriate spots.

Name: _____

Instructor: _____

Date: _____

R1-2. Convert each notehead below into a half note, making all necessary changes. Be careful to use the correct stem direction (inward!) and to make your stems vertical (not slanted!). Assuming that the melody begins on the first beat of a measure, add bar lines and a double bar at appropriate spots.

R1-3. Form a melody using the fragments provided. Only one ordering of these fragments will result in measures that contain the correct number of beats.

Audio Exercises

A1-1. Three pitches are performed.

a. Indicate which of the three pitches is the *highest*.

   *1.   First   Second   Third

   *2.   First   Second   Third

   3.   First   Second   Third

   4.   First   Second   Third

   5.   First   Second   Third

b. Indicate which of the three pitches is the *lowest*.

°1.　First　Second　Third

°2.　First　Second　Third

3.　First　Second　Third

4.　First　Second　Third

5.　First　Second　Third

c. Indicate which of the three pitches is in the *middle*.

°1.　First　Second　Third

°2.　First　Second　Third

3.　First　Second　Third

4.　First　Second　Third

5.　First　Second　Third

A1-2. Eight pitches starting on C are performed in either ascending or descending order. Circle "Yes" if they form a C Major scale, or "No" if they do not.

°a.　Yes　No　　　　f.　Yes　No

°b.　Yes　No　　　　g.　Yes　No

c.　Yes　No　　　　h.　Yes　No

d.　Yes　No　　　　i.　Yes　No

e.　Yes　No　　　　j.　Yes　No

A1-3. Circle the music notation that corresponds to the rhythm performed.

°a.

b.

Name: _____

Instructor: _____

Date: _____

c.

d.

CHAPTER 2

Intervals and Triads in C Major

PITCH

To become better acquainted with how a major key is structured, we now focus on some of the intervals that can be formed by the diatonic pitches of the major scale. In this chapter we build all the intervals that employ the tonic pitch (Î or 8̂). We also assess which of these intervals are stable, and which are unstable. Then we turn our attention to triads—combinations of three notes.

Intervals that Employ Î

One of the characteristic features of a major key is the set of intervals formed using Î as a component pitch. We have already named several of these intervals: the perfect unison (Î–Î), the perfect fifth (Î–5̂), and the perfect octave (Î–8̂). These and five other intervals—the **major second** (Î–2̂), **major third** (Î–3̂), **perfect fourth** (Î–4̂), **major sixth** (Î–6̂), and **major seventh** (Î–7̂)—appear in Example 2-1. Standard abbreviations—capital M for major and capital P for perfect—are employed for the interval qualities.

major second

major third

perfect fourth

major sixth

major seventh

Example 2-1

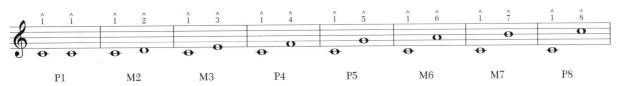

Some intervals are stable. The perfect fifth, for example, has a solidity that we will appreciate when constructing combinations of three pitches. Such stability is called **consonance.** The perfect unison, major third, perfect fifth, major sixth, and perfect octave are classified as consonances. The other intervals of Example 2-1 are unstable. Because we like to feel that there is a forward momentum in music—sounds leading to other sounds—instability, called **dissonance**, is often desirable. Example 2-2 shows these three dissonant intervals—the major second, perfect fourth, and major seventh—along with characteristic ways in which the tensions that they create are resolved.

consonance

dissonance

Example 2-2

Practice Exercises 2-1

Interpret each interval below in the key of C Major. Above each pitch, indicate its scale-degree number (1̂ through 8̂). Below each interval, indicate its quality and size (M3, P5, M7, etc.). If the interval is dissonant, circle it.

a.   b.   c.   d.   e.   f.

Intervals that Employ 8̂

When the tonic pitch is an interval's upper note—that is, when 8̂ is a component pitch instead of 1̂—a different set of intervals results. However, these two sets of intervals are closely related. Imagine forming a major third: 1̂ to 3̂. What is "left over" within the scale is 3̂ to 8̂. These intervals are shown in Example 2-3.

Example 2-3

Major third   Minor sixth

inversion

Even though one of these intervals is a third and the other is a sixth, and even though one is of major quality and the other is of minor quality, these two intervals make a similar impression. Listen to them! They complement one another. They are built using pitches with the same names. We call this relationship ***inversion***, a term that reflects the fact that the two pitch names exchange positions when the inversion is formed. First C is below E, and then E is below C.

Why is the quality of the E–C sixth minor? Consulting a keyboard diagram (Example 2-4), observe that C–A (1̂–6̂), which we named above as a major sixth, spans four whole steps and one half step. E–C (3̂–8̂) spans three whole steps and two half steps. Thus it is one half step smaller than the major sixth. An interval of minor quality is always one half step smaller than the major interval of the same size.

Example 2-4

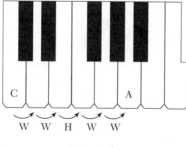

Major sixth

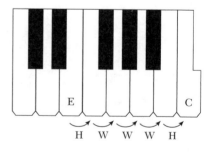

Minor sixth

Following this procedure, we can create and name the inversions of all the intervals listed in Example 2-1. Example 2-5 displays the results. (Small m, the abbreviation for minor, is employed in this example.) It doesn't matter whether an interval—such as the minor seventh formed by $\hat{2}$ and $\hat{8}$—is ascending ($\hat{2}$–$\hat{8}$), descending ($\hat{8}$–$\hat{2}$), or harmonic $\begin{smallmatrix}\hat{8}\\\hat{2}\end{smallmatrix}$). The size and quality depend on the distance between the two notes involved, not on which sounds first.

Example 2-5

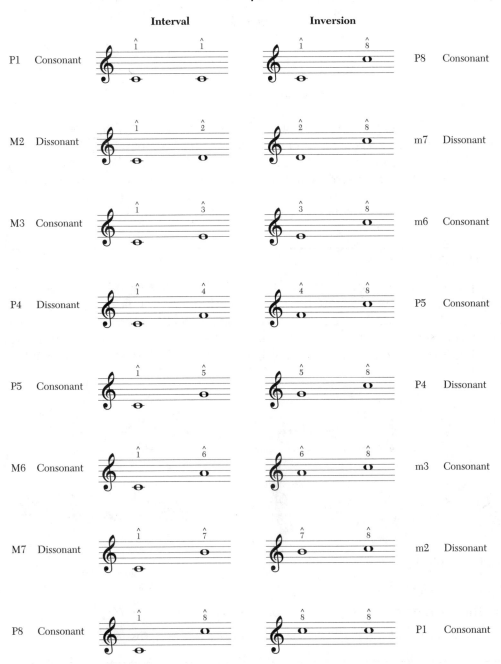

A few general principles are apparent from the information in Example 2-5:

- The sum of the sizes of two intervals that are inversions of one another is always 9 (for example, 1 + 8, 2 + 7, 3 + 6).
- The inversion of a perfect interval is always of perfect quality.
- The inversion of a major interval is always of minor quality.
- The inversion of a minor interval is always of major quality.

Among intervals formed from the diatonic pitches of major keys, if 1̂ is employed (that is, if tonic is the *lower* pitch of the interval), the interval quality will be major or perfect; if 8̂ is employed (that is, if tonic is the *higher* pitch of the interval), the interval quality will be minor or perfect. As Example 2-6 demonstrates, the same tonic pitch may sometimes be labeled 1̂, and at other times 8̂, depending on whether the other pitch of the interval is higher (as in C up to F) or lower (as in C down to F).

Example 2-6

Only one inversional pair—the perfect fourth and the perfect fifth—does not share the same consonance–dissonance status. This is a rather complicated subject that we will address again later when we use the perfect fourth in constructing combinations of four pitches. (When the fourth sounds with several other pitches, it often has a stable context.) When only two pitches sound, the perfect fourth will most often resolve in the manner shown in Example 2-2. Thus, it is appropriate to classify it as a dissonance.

Practice Exercises 2-2

Interpret each interval below in the key of C Major. Above each pitch, indicate its scale-degree number (1̂ through 8̂). Below each interval, indicate its quality and size (m3, P5, m7, etc.). If the interval is dissonant, circle it. Caution: since both 1̂ and 8̂ correspond to the pitch C, you must be careful in deciding which number to use. If C is the *lower* note of the interval, it is 1̂. If C is the *higher* note of the interval, it is 8̂.

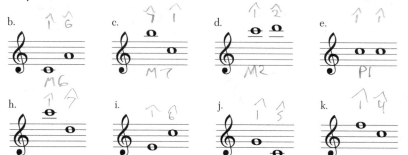

Fill in the blanks.

m. The inversion of m2 is M7 .

n. The inversion of P5 is P4 .

o. The inversion of M2 is m7 .

p. The inversion of M3 is m6 .

q. The inversion of m6 is M3 .

r. The inversion of m7 is M2 .

Triads

Perhaps as a child you sat at a keyboard and, impressed by the possibilities offered by the many keys in front of you, took command of the situation by confidently playing several keys at once. Chances are, your random selection of pitches didn't sound very good (at least to anyone else in the room). By the time you finish this text, you will be able to create a wide assortment of good-sounding pitch combinations, called **chords.**

chords

The essence of chord-creation is straightforward: choose any white key and, along with it, play the white keys a third and a fifth higher (to the right) to form a **triad.** Almost all chords used in music are based on triads. How to expand and modify triads to form chords will be one of our central concerns in future chapters.

triad

If we employ the white keys characteristic of C Major, there are seven triads, each of which occurs at various locations on the keyboard. A sample of each is displayed in Example 2-7.

Example 2-7

C–E–G   D–F–A   E–G–B   F–A–C   G–B–D   A–C–E   B–D–F

We name a triad according to its lowest pitch, or **root.** For example, the first triad of Example 2-7 is a "C triad." A triad's other pitches are its **third** and its **fifth,** terms that correspond to the sizes of the intervals these pitches form with the root. Like intervals, triads have qualities: the C triad of Example 2-7 is in fact a C **major** triad. Since these qualities depend on the qualities of the intervals used in building a triad, we should take a closer look at those intervals.

root

third

fifth

major

Staff notation does not reveal an interval's quality. We need to consult a keyboard diagram to see exactly how each of the triads of Example 2-7 is constructed. Example 2-8 displays the roots and fifths of these seven triads on keyboard diagrams. Six of these intervals contain, in some order, three whole steps and one half step, which form a perfect fifth. B–F differs from the others in that it contains two whole steps and two half steps. Because it is smaller than the perfect fifth by a half step, it is called a **diminished fifth** (abbreviated d5). Be careful! The B–F fifth in the last triad of Example 2-7 displays no visual clue that it is different from any of the other fifths in the example, and yet it is. By consulting a keyboard diagram, you will see that it is smaller; by comparing its sound with that of the other fifths, you will hear that it is different.

diminished fifth

Example 2-8

Example 2-9 displays the roots and thirds of the seven triads from Example 2-7.

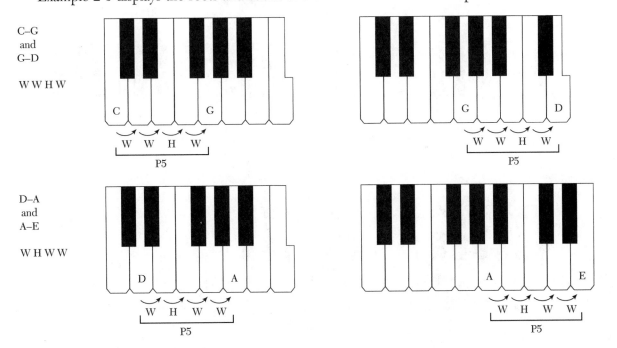

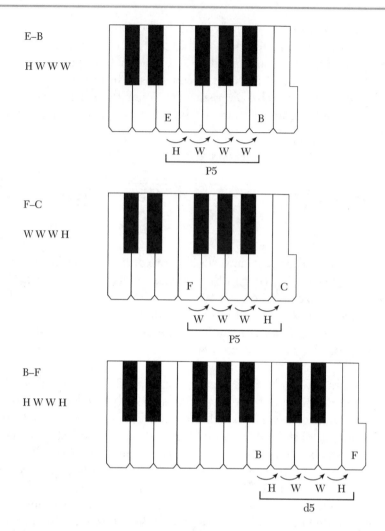

Three of these intervals contain two whole steps, which form a major third. Four of them contain, in some order, a whole step and a half step, which form a minor third.

Example 2-9

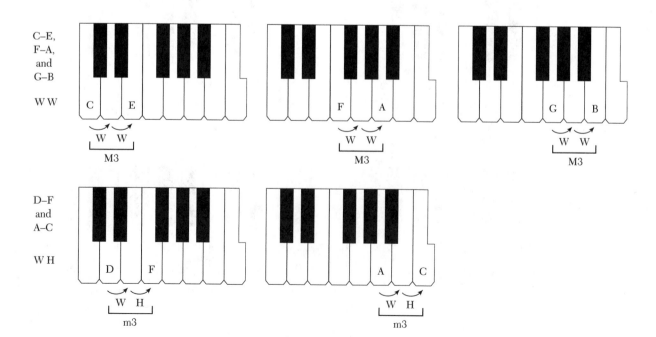

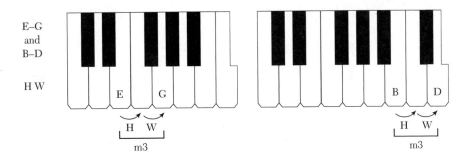

Any triad built using a major third and a perfect fifth is a ***major triad***. If, instead, the third is minor, then a ***minor triad*** results. If a triad is built using a minor third and a diminished fifth, it is a ***diminished triad***. Example 2-10 presents the triads of Example 2-7 arranged in these categories. Play these triads! You should hear that all three major triads have a similar character. The same should be true for the three minor triads, whose character differs from that of the major triads. The diminished triad offers yet another character.

| major triad |
| minor triad |
| diminished triad |

The distinctions among these qualities are not apparent from the score notation! Only with the aid of a keyboard diagram, or by carefully comparing the triads by ear, do we understand that the C, F, and G triads are major, the D, E, and A triads are minor, and the B triad is diminished.

Example 2-10

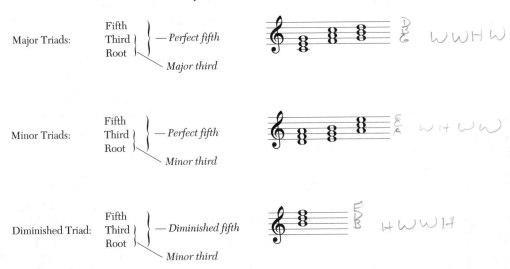

Practice Exercises 2-3

Draw arrows connecting each term to the appropriate notehead or interval. Some terms will not be employed.

Indicate the quality of each triad: major (M), minor (m), or diminished (d).

c.

Em

d.   e.   f.   g.   h.

Tips for Success

✔ The content of Example 2-5 will be used frequently throughout this text, so memorize this material without delay. Learn the intervals in terms of scale degree numbers: $\hat{1}$ to $\hat{3}$ is a major third, etc. C to E is one example of that, but $\hat{1}$–$\hat{3}$ is the relationship that will recur in every major key. Observe that the intervals of size 1, 4, 5, and 8 are always perfect. The remaining intervals (2, 3, 6, and 7) are major when $\hat{1}$ is one of the interval's pitches, and minor when $\hat{8}$ is one of the interval's pitches. A similar, but different, chart will be introduced when we encounter minor keys. To avoid confusion then, build a solid foundation for major-key intervals now.

✔ Memorize the four principles of inversion on page 29.

✔ Know exactly where to find major, minor, and diminished triads in C Major. Memorize that the triads rooted on C, F, and G are major and the triad rooted on B is diminished. All the others (with roots D, E, and A) are minor.

RHYTHM

$\frac{2}{4}$ and $\frac{3}{4}$ Meters

As does $\frac{4}{4}$, the $\frac{2}{4}$ and $\frac{3}{4}$ meters employ the quarter note as the basic time unit. They differ from $\frac{4}{4}$ in that their measures contain two and three beats, respectively. To fill measures in these various meters, we employ four different note symbols in this chapter—those that have a time value of one, two, three, and four beats.

$\frac{2}{4}$ and $\frac{3}{4}$ Meters

The $\frac{2}{4}$ and $\frac{3}{4}$ meters share with $\frac{4}{4}$ the time unit of the quarter note. Their measures contain two and three beats, respectively. As in $\frac{4}{4}$, the first beats of $\frac{2}{4}$ or $\frac{3}{4}$ measures are strong. The second beat in $\frac{2}{4}$ and the second and third beats in $\frac{3}{4}$ are weak. The melodies of Example 2-11 demonstrate these meters.

Example 2-11

a.

1 2 1 2 1 2 1 2 1 2 1 2 1 2 1 2

b.

Three-Beat and Four-Beat Notes

Just as the half note combines the value of two quarter notes, the **whole note** combines the value of four quarter notes. It is represented in notation by an open notehead, without a stem. It may be used only in $\frac{4}{4}$ meter, since the measures of $\frac{2}{4}$ and $\frac{3}{4}$ meters cannot accommodate a four-beat note. Both $\frac{3}{4}$ and $\frac{4}{4}$ meters can, however, accommodate a note that lasts for three beats. For this purpose, we place a dot to the right of the half-note symbol to form a **dotted half note.** The dot, called an **augmentation dot,** increases the time value of the half note by one-half. When the notehead is on a line or ledger line, the dot is placed in the middle of the space above the line, rather than on the line itself. Observe how dotted half notes and whole notes are used in Example 2-12.

whole note

dotted half note
augmentation dot

Example 2-12

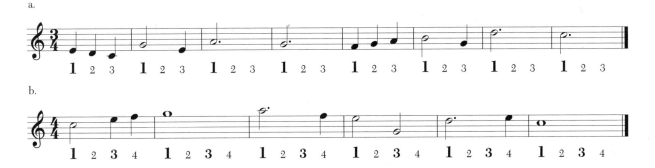

Tempo

The melodies presented above are accompanied by counting numbers, which must flow evenly and without interruption. As mentioned in Chapter 1, you should count out loud when practicing. Do not speed up or slow down depending on how easy or hard the music is. And do not pause at each bar line.

The **tempo** is the speed at which beats follow one another. A suitable tempo for your practice might be about one beat per second. If you cannot maintain that tempo, choose a slower tempo and, through practice, eventually work up to one beat per second. *Choose a tempo that you can maintain even in difficult passages.*

tempo

In some published music, a suggested tempo is indicated numerically. A moderate tempo, such as one beat per second, would be indicated as ♩ = 60 (60 quarter notes per minute). On the other hand, the composer might simply write *"Moderato"* and expect you to decide the precise tempo yourself. A slow tempo might be indicated as ♩ = 46 (46 quarter notes per minute), or by a term such as *"Adagio"* or *"Lento."* Or a composer might choose a number such as 80 or 132 for a fast tempo, or indicate *"Allegro"* or *"Presto."* A mechanical device called a **metronome,** which can be adjusted to tick from 40 to over 200 times per minute, is a common tool in the performer's practice room. Even without a metronome to reinforce your counting, try to maintain the tempo you establish at the beginning of an exercise.

metronome

Practice Exercises 2-4

Practice creating music notation by drawing each symbol below twice to the right of its model.

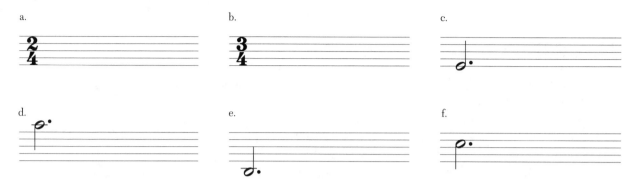

Add a quarter note, a half note, a dotted half note, or a whole note to each measure below, so that it is filled by the number of beats indicated by the time signature. Use a variety of noteheads: some high, some low, some with ledger lines. Be especially careful in the placement of the augmentation dot, if required. (Study the models in Example 2-12.)

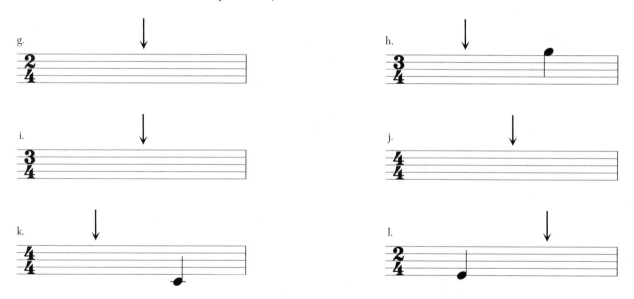

Tips for Success

✔ Always read the time signature before performing a melody.

✔ Do not exaggerate the size of an augmentation dot. It should not look like a notehead.

✔ If you intend a lifetime of activity in music, consider acquiring a dictionary of musical terms, which will list and define hundreds of terms that you may encounter in a musical score. For several centuries, Italian was the favored language for such terms, because many Italian musicians were active in musical centers throughout Europe.

✔ See the Conducting Patterns section of the Appendix for advice on conducting in the $\frac{2}{4}$ and $\frac{3}{4}$ meters.

Laboratory

L2-1. Play and Sing

Note: Men and low-voiced women may prefer to play these exercises one octave lower. If so, place your right, *rather than your left, little finger on Middle C.*

a. First review Example 2-5, and then sit at the keyboard, placing eight fingers (all except your thumbs) above the keys corresponding to the C Major scale, with your left little finger above Middle C and your right little finger above the C an octave higher. Now press a C (either of your little fingers) and one other key at the same time. Then press these two keys in ascending order, singing each pitch in turn. Sing the scale degree numbers ("$\hat{1}$," "$\hat{2}$," "$\hat{3}$," etc.). Then name the interval you have just performed (perfect fifth, minor third, etc.). Continue until you have performed and identified all thirteen combinations.

b. Now play one of the interior pitches of the scale (D through B) followed by either of your little-finger Cs. Then play the interval again, this time singing each pitch after you play it, using scale degree numbers. Name the interval. Then play and sing this interval's inversion and name it. (For example, if you first play and sing A down to C, now play and sing A up to C.) Continue until you have performed and identified all the inversional pairs.

c. First review Example 2-10. Then, using your right hand, play a white-key triad in the vicinity of Middle C. (For example, play D–F–A.) Indicate the triad's quality (major, minor, or diminished). Then play these three pitches in ascending order, singing each pitch after you play it. Sing the syllables "Root," "Third," and "Fifth." Then play and sing the triad in descending order, singing "Fifth," "Third," and "Root." Repeat for other triads within your vocal range.

   If you find this exercise easy, play only the triad's root. (For example, play E alone and then sing E–G–B.) Then play the triad to confirm that you have sung the correct pitches.

L2-2. Listening

Team up with another student, work with your instructor in class, or make use of the CD-ROM that accompanies this textbook to practice these exercises.

a. *Performer:* Play Middle C and then either the E or the G to the right.
   Listener: Sing Middle C (singing "$\hat{1}$"), then continue by step up the C Major scale ("$\hat{2}$"–"$\hat{3}$" or "$\hat{2}$"–"$\hat{3}$"–"$\hat{4}$"–"$\hat{5}$") until you reach the other pitch performed. Then identify the interval as a major third or a perfect fifth.

b. *Performer:* Play the three pitches of any white-key triad in ascending order (for example, D, then F, then A). Then play two of these pitches again, in ascending order (for example, D, then A).
   Listener: Indicate which two triad components were performed: Root-Third, Root-Fifth, or Third-Fifth.

L2-3. Keyboard Album

L2-4. Song Book

EC sing

EC play

L2-5. Rhythm

L2-6. Improvisation

Place your right thumb above Middle C and let the remaining right-hand fingers touch D, E, F, and G. Keep this hand close to the edge of the keyboard. Now place your left little finger above B, just to the left of Middle C, and let the remaining left-hand fingers touch C, D, E, and F. This hand will be forward of your right hand.

a. Play a total of thirteen notes: four quarter notes with your right hand, then four quarter notes with your left hand, then four quarter notes with your right hand, and finally a whole note on Middle C.

       Sample: C E G E | F D C B | C E G E | C

b. With the same hand position, play for four measures using your right hand, then for two measures using your left hand, and finally for two measures using your right hand. Employ quarter notes, half notes, dotted half notes, and/or whole notes.

c. Now move your left hand to the right, to cover the notes F–G–A–B–C. Repeat exercises a and b with this hand configuration.

If you create a melody that especially pleases you, write it down. Perhaps at your next class your instructor will put it on the board for the entire class to sing.

L2-7. Score Study

Listen to Selections 2 and 5 in the Scores for Music Analysis section at the back of the textbook. Then answer the questions under the "Chapter 2" headings that accompany these selections.

Name: _____

Instructor: _____

Date: _____

Pitch Exercises

P2-1. Intervals of C Major are presented in staff notation. Above each pitch, indicate the scale degree number (1̂ through 8̂). Below, indicate the interval quality and size (M3, P5, etc.). Remember that if C is the *lower pitch* of the interval, it is 1̂; and if it is the *higher pitch*, it is 8̂.

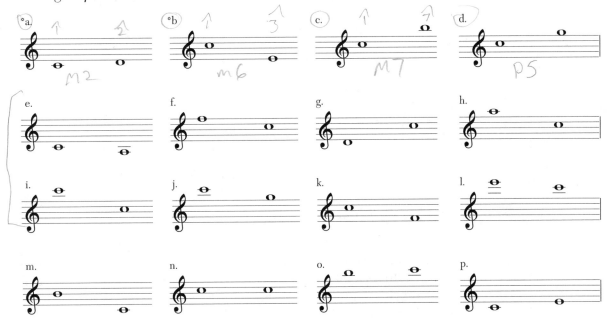

P2-2. Circle each interval of Exercise 2-1 that is classified as a dissonance.

P2-3. Fill in the blanks.

* a. The inversion of a perfect fourth is a _____.

* b. The inversion of a major sixth is a _____.

  c. The inversion of a minor seventh is a _____.

  d. The inversion of a perfect fifth is a _____.

  e. The inversion of a minor second is a _____.

  f. The inversion of a major second is a _____.

  g. The inversion of a minor sixth is a _____.

  h. The inversion of a major third is a _____.

  i. The inversion of a minor third is a _____.

  j. The inversion of a major seventh is a _____.

P2-4. Name the root of each triad (C through B). Then indicate its quality: major (M), minor (m), or diminished (d).

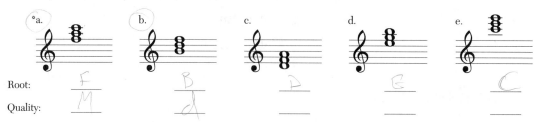

Root: F   B   D   E   C

Quality: M   d

P2-5. Build the triads requested. Choose a variety of ranges: some near Middle C, some higher (using ledger lines).

°a. Major triad with root F   b. Minor triad with root D   c. Diminished triad with root B   d. Minor triad with root E

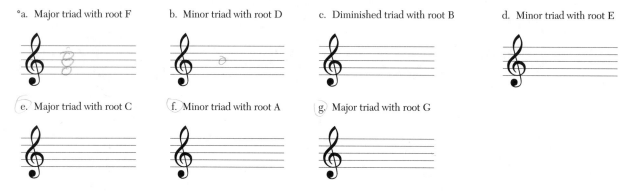

e. Major triad with root C   f. Minor triad with root A   g. Major triad with root G

Rhythm Exercises

R2-1. Convert each notehead on the staff below into a dotted half note, making all necessary changes. Be careful to use the correct stem direction. Remember that when the notehead is on a line or ledger line, the dot is placed in the middle of the space above the line. Add bar lines and a double bar.

R2-2. Use the model rhythm of the first two measures to form identical patterns in measures 3–4, 5–6, and 7–8 of the following melodies. For example, if the first two measures go "half, quarter | dotted half," then measure 3 will go "half, quarter," measure 4 will go "dotted half," measure 5 will go "half quarter," and so on. Add bar lines at appropriate spots.

°a.

b.

Name: _____

Instructor: _____

Date: _____

c.

R2-3. Modify the noteheads indicated by arrows to form measures containing the appropriate number of beats. You may find it helpful to write in the counting numbers below the staff.

R2-4. Create the melodies indicated by the positioning of the pitch names in relation to the counting numbers. Each pitch name represents a note that continues until the next pitch name appears. For example, the letter "G" above the numbers "1 2 3 4" would be drawn as a whole note, and the letter "F" above the numbers "1 2" would be drawn as a half note. From one note to the next, use only a unison, second, third, or fourth as a melodic interval. For example, from A to G, descend a second rather than ascending a seventh. Add bar lines and a double bar at appropriate spots.

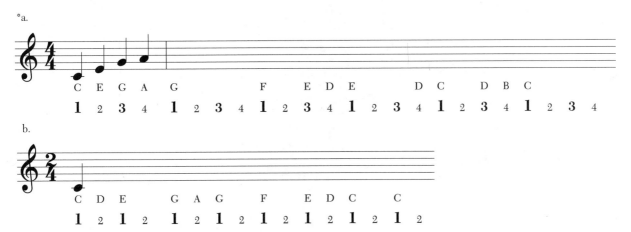

c.

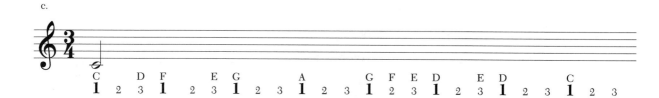

C D F E G A G F E E D C
1 2 3 1 2 3 1 2 3 1 2 3 1 2 3 1 2 3 1 2 3 1 2 3

Audio Exercises

A2-1. $\hat{1}$–$\hat{3}$ or $\hat{1}$–$\hat{5}$ in the key of C Major is performed. Identify the interval performed.

    *a. M3 P5   f. M3 P5

    *b. M3 P5   g. M3 P5

    c. M3 P5   h. M3 P5

    d. M3 P5   i. M3 P5

    e. M3 P5   j. M3 P5

A2-2. The three pitches of a white-key triad are performed in ascending order. Two of these three pitches are then performed a second time. Indicate which two.

    *a. Root-Third   Root-Fifth   Third-Fifth

    *b. Root-Third   Root-Fifth   Third-Fifth

    c. Root-Third   Root-Fifth   Third-Fifth

    d. Root-Third   Root-Fifth   Third-Fifth

    e. Root-Third   Root-Fifth   Third-Fifth

    f. Root-Third   Root-Fifth   Third-Fifth

    g. Root-Third   Root-Fifth   Third-Fifth

    h. Root-Third   Root-Fifth   Third-Fifth

    i. Root-Third   Root-Fifth   Third-Fifth

    j. Root-Third   Root-Fifth   Third-Fifth

A2-3. Circle the music notation that corresponds to the pitches performed.

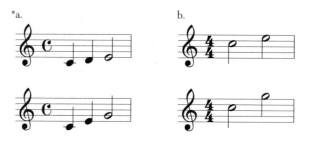

Name: _____

Instructor: _____

Date: _____

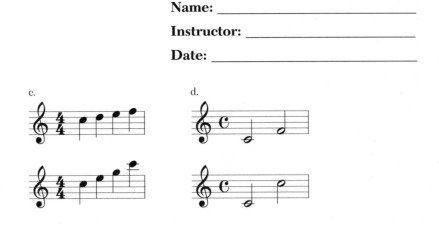

A2-4. Circle the music notation that corresponds to the rhythm performed.

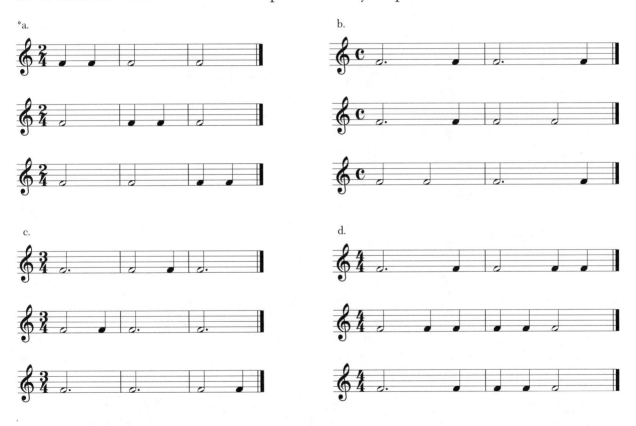

CHAPTER 3

The Keys of F Major and G Major

In getting to know the key of C Major, we explored how its scale is constructed, formed the intervals that employ 1̂ or 8̂, and built triads on each scale degree. Now, as we begin to learn about other major keys, we will continue to emphasize scales, intervals, and triads. Because F Major and G Major are major keys, all of the characteristics of C Major will be retained, but at new pitch levels. In order for this to happen, we utilize both white and black keys on the keyboard. In this chapter we also introduce the bass clef, used for the notation of music's lower pitches.

F Major and G Major

Three scales containing only white keys appear in Example 3-1. The C Major scale is in the middle. Though the other scales are similar, there are points of difference. In the F scale, the span between A and C does not match the corresponding positions of the C scale: it ascends Whole-Half instead of Half-Whole. And in the G scale, the span between E and G does not match the corresponding positions of the C scale: it ascends Half-Whole instead of Whole-Half. Consult a keyboard diagram to *see* these differences. Play and sing these scales to *hear* these differences.

Example 3-1

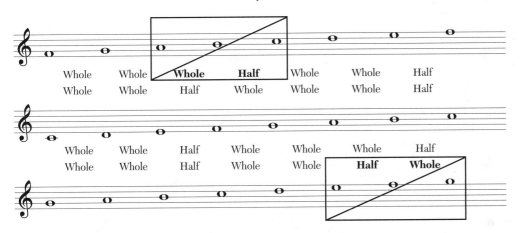

Music students 400 years ago would have learned each of these scales. The one on C was named Ionian; the one on F, Lydian; and the one on G, Mixolydian. Around the year 1600 things started to change. Now, when F is tonic, B is replaced by the pitch of the black key to the left of B, named B-*flat* (B♭). As a result, the relationship among pitches exactly matches the whole- and half-step succession of the C Major scale. Likewise, when G is tonic, F is replaced by the pitch of the black key to the right of F, named F-*sharp* (F♯). Thus, instead of three different "modes" of ascent from tonic, the mode that corresponds to the white keys between two Cs is used in all three cases.

F Major and G Major scales are displayed in Example 3-2, along with keyboard diagrams that confirm the Whole-Whole-Half-Whole-Whole-Whole-Half pattern.

flat

sharp

Observe that a whole step occurs not only when two white keys are separated by a black key (white-black-white), but also in the contexts of B♭ to C (black-white-white) and E to F♯ (white-white-black). In all cases, a whole step is the second key from the starting key. Similarly, a half step occurs from A to B♭ (white-black) and from F♯ to G (black-white).

Example 3-2

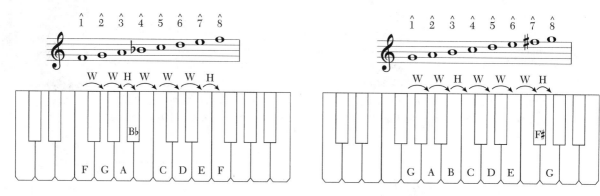

accidentals

By employing *accidentals* (symbols such as the sharp and the flat) to form the appropriate succession of whole and half steps, any pitch can be a major-key tonic: not only C, but also F, G, or any other pitch. J. S. Bach, who lived from 1685 to 1750, used all twelve major keys in his famous keyboard work *The Well-Tempered Clavier.*

Practice Exercises 3-1

Draw the notation for B♭ and for F♯ three times after the models provided. Make sure that the accidental is *beside* the notehead, not higher or lower.

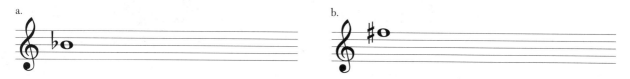

Indicate the scale degree of each pitch in the key indicated.

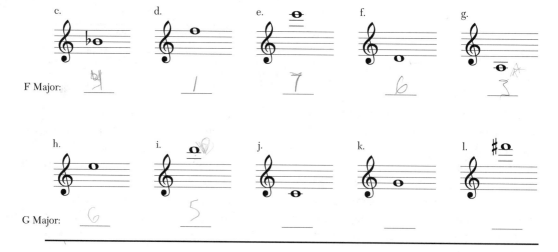

F Major:

G Major:

Key Signatures

The label "key of C Major" implies two things: first, that the pitch C serves as tonic; second, that the other diatonic pitches are in the relationship of Whole-Whole-Half-Whole-Whole-Whole-Half above C. The key of F Major shares with C Major the Whole-Whole-Half-Whole-Whole-Whole-Half pattern, but in this case starting from tonic F rather than tonic C. Ascending C Major and F Major scales are displayed in Example 3-3.

Example 3-3

Because B♭ will occur consistently in compositions written in F Major, we may employ a ***key signature***, a shorthand method for indicating the required flat. The third-line flat just to the right of the treble clef in Example 3-4 is the key signature for F Major. It instructs performers to read *every* B notehead written on the staff as B♭. This also includes any B noteheads written using ledger lines above or below the staff. In all cases, the B notehead means B♭.

key signature

Example 3-4

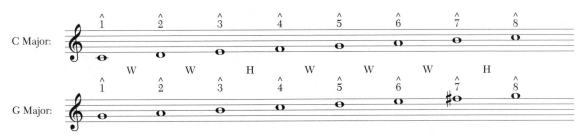

Similarly, the key of G Major shares with C Major the Whole-Whole-Half-Whole-Whole-Whole-Half pattern, but in this case starts from tonic G rather than tonic C. Ascending scales in C Major and G Major are displayed in Example 3-5. To preserve the pattern of the C scale, one sharp (F♯) is required for the G scale.

Example 3-5

Because F♯ will occur consistently in compositions written in G Major, G Major's key signature (employed in Example 3-6) consists of one sharp. It instructs us to read *every* F notehead written on the staff as F♯. Though the key signature's sharp is always placed on the fifth line, it affects noteheads written in the first space or using ledger lines as well.

Example 3-6

F♯   F♯

The remaining major keys require key signatures with anywhere from two to seven sharps or flats. We will continue our exploration of these keys in Chapter 5.

Practice Exercises 3-2

a. Employing a key signature, create an ascending G Major scale. Add scale degree numbers (1̂ through 8̂).

b. Employing a key signature, create a descending F Major scale. Add scale degree numbers (8̂ through 1̂).

Intervals in F Major and G Major

All of the intervals we formed in the key of C Major occur in every major key. Though Example 2-5 was presented in the context of C Major, the information about interval quality that it provides is valid for all major keys. It is important to keep an awareness of the scale degree of each pitch, because the same two scale degrees will always form the same interval in *any* major key. For example, the interval formed by F and A in Example 3-7a is a major third, because these pitches are 1̂ and 3̂ in the key of F Major; and the interval formed by A and G in Example 3-7b is a minor seventh, because these pitches are 2̂ and 8̂ in the key of G Major.

Example 3-7

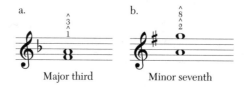

a.   b.

Major third   Minor seventh

Practice Exercises 3-3

Name the key in which each interval is to be interpreted (F Major or G Major), by viewing the key signature. Above each pitch indicate its scale degree in the context of that key. (Use 1̂ for the tonic pitch when it is *lower* than the interval's other pitch, and $\hat{8}$ when it is *higher*.) Then name the interval formed by the two pitches (M3, m6, etc.).

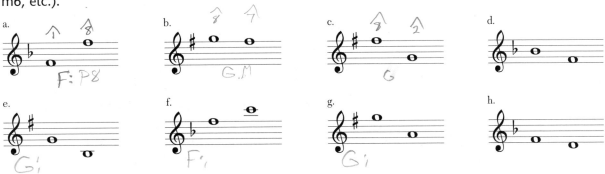

Labeling the Triads in Major Keys

When building triads using the white keys, we observed that those on C, F, and G are of major quality; those on D, E, and A are of minor quality; and that on B is of diminished quality. These triad qualities are characteristic features of the key of C Major. To say the same thing in a way that pertains to *all* major keys, we may instead convey this information using **Roman numerals**. Each Roman numeral indicates both the triad's root (the Roman numeral corresponds to the scale degree of the triad's root) and its quality (following the convention of using a capital Roman numeral if the triad's quality is major, a small numeral if the triad's quality is minor, and a small numeral followed by a degree circle if the triad's quality is diminished). Thus, the seven triads of *any* major key may be labeled as follows:

Roman numerals

I   ii   iii   IV   V   vi   vii°

Example 3-8 displays a sample of each triad in C Major, F Major, and G Major. Remember that triads may occur in various positions on the staff—sometimes higher, sometimes lower.

Example 3-8

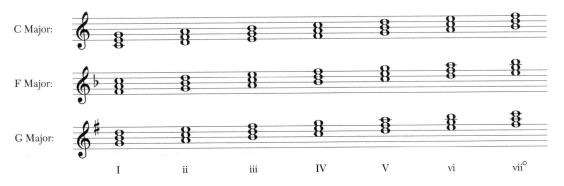

As Example 3-9 displays, a scale degree number always corresponds to a single pitch, while a Roman numeral always corresponds to several pitches—a triad or a chord whose *root* is the scale degree that corresponds to the Roman numeral. The scale degree number is generally placed above a note, while the Roman numeral is generally placed below a triad or chord. The symbol "VIII" is never employed. When the tonic pitch is the root, the Roman numeral is always I.

Example 3-9

F Major   G Major

A triad's quality may be affected by a flat or sharp in the key signature. For example, the G triad in C Major (Example 3-10a) is of major quality (G–B major third and G–D perfect fifth), whereas the same noteheads in the context of F Major's key signature produce a minor triad (G–B♭ minor third and G–D perfect fifth). Likewise, the B triad in C Major (Example 3-10b) is of diminished quality (B–D minor third and B–F diminished fifth), whereas the same noteheads in the context of G Major's key signature produce a minor triad (B–D minor third and B–F♯ perfect fifth) and in the context of F Major's key signature produce a major triad (B♭–D major third and B♭–F perfect fifth).

Example 3-10

C Major: V   F Major: ii   C Major: vii°   G Major: iii   F Major: IV

Practice Exercises 3-4

Name the key indicated by the key signature (C Major, F Major, or G Major). Then place the appropriate Roman numeral (I through vii°) below each triad.

F Major: vi   G Major: V   F Major: vii°   G Major: iii   F Major: IV   G Major: ii

First draw in a treble clef and the correct key signature. Then create the triad requested.

g.   h.   i.   j.   k.   l.

F Major: vi   G Major: V   F Major: vii°   G Major: iii   F Major: IV   G Major: ii

The Bass Clef

bass clef

Music for low instruments or voices will generally be written using the ***bass clef*** (𝄢). Use your left hand to play these notes at the keyboard. In the context of bass clef, Middle C is positioned above the staff, as shown in Example 3-11a. To the right of

Middle C on the keyboard, we find a D, E, F, and G (the same pitches we have encountered often in treble clef). To the left of Middle C, we find a B and an A. Continuing downwards (*lower* on the staff, *to the left* on the keyboard), the A-to-G pattern recurs several times. Example 3-11b displays these pitches.

Example 3-11

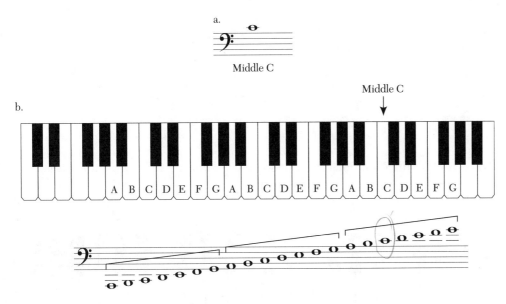

Though key signatures perform the same function in bass clef as in treble clef, the positioning of their accidentals will be different, since the lines and spaces have different meanings in the two clefs. Example 3-12 shows the correct notation for key signatures in F Major and G Major.

Example 3-12

Practice Exercises 3-5

a. Practice creating music notation by drawing the bass clef twice to the right of its model.

The five lines in bass clef correspond to the note names G B D F A. Create short sentences using words beginning with these letters as a memory aid. Compare your sentences with those of your classmates.

b. G_____ B_____ D_____ F_____ A_____

c. G_____ B_____ D_____ F_____ A_____

The four spaces in bass clef correspond to the note names A C E G. Create short sentences using words beginning with these letters as a memory aid. Compare your sentences with those of your classmates.

d. A_____ C_____ E_____ G_____

e. A_____ C_____ E_____ G_____

Name each pitch, using the letter names from A through G.

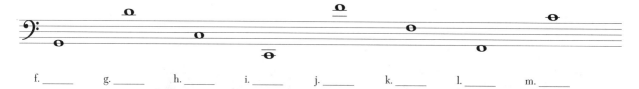

f. _____   g. _____   h. _____   i. _____   j. _____   k. _____   l. _____   m. _____

Draw arrows connecting each notehead to the appropriate key on the keyboard.

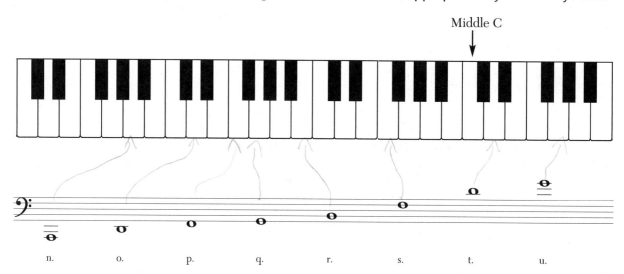

n.   o.   p.   q.   r.   s.   t.   u.

Tips for Success

✔ Having learned to read music notation in treble clef, you understand how important that is to all of our endeavors in this text. The same is true of reading bass clef. Study the diagrams above and the fold-out diagram that accompanies this textbook, use the CD-ROM tutorial on the bass clef, and practice reading notation in the Activities section of this chapter. Failure to do so will put you at a disadvantage when new topics are introduced in the next few chapters, so put in some effort every day for the next week, and you should master the topic.

✔ When an F notehead appears in the context of a G Major key signature, it should always be named as "F-sharp," not as "F." When an B notehead appears in the context of an F Major key signature, it should always be named as "B-flat," not as "B."

✔ Know exactly where the major, minor, and diminished triads reside in major keys. Memorize that I, IV, and V are major and vii° is diminished. All the others (ii, iii, and vi) are minor.

✔ When talking, convert the abbreviation P5 into "perfect fifth" and the Roman numeral V into "five" or "major five." Never use "fifth" for V. Follow this practice for the other intervals and Roman numerals as well.

✔ Precise Pitch Designations for bass-clef pitches are presented in the Appendix. You might also want to study the Clefs segment of the Appendix to learn about other clefs used in music notation.

RHYTHM

Rests

Because music contains both sound and the absence of sound, symbols for silence (called rests) are a vital part of music notation. In this chapter we explore the notation for silence.

Rests in $\frac{4}{4}$ Meter

Suppose that a measure of music in $\frac{4}{4}$ meter contains two quarter-note pitches, with silence during the remaining beats. Would Example 3-13 adequately instruct performers what to do? Where do these two quarter notes fall? Clearly, this notation is ambiguous. Different performers might interpret it in different ways, compromising the composer's intentions.

Example 3-13

A **quarter rest** instructs performers to remain silent for one beat. Its shape, a somewhat bizarre combination of curved lines, is one of the harder symbols of music notation to draw. Example 3-14 shows several ways in which two quarter notes and two quarter rests may fill a measure.

quarter rest

Example 3-14

A **half rest**, which corresponds to two quarter rests, is used when the first half (beats 1 and 2) or the second half (beats 3 and 4) of a $\frac{4}{4}$ measure contains no pitches. It should not be employed to fill beats 2 and 3, since these two beats straddle the first and second halves of a measure. A **whole rest** is used when there are no pitches for an entire measure. The half rest appears as a filled-in rectangle placed on top of the third line, while the whole rest appears as a filled-in rectangle that hangs from the fourth line. These rests are employed in Example 3-15. Observe that for three consecutive beats of rest within a measure, the combination of a half and a quarter rest is used, arranged so that the half rest fills beats 1 and 2 (as in measure 8) or beats 3 and 4 (as in measure 4).

half rest

whole rest

Example 3-15

Rests in $\frac{2}{4}$ and $\frac{3}{4}$ Meters

Only two of the rests introduced above are employed in $\frac{2}{4}$ meter: the quarter rest, when either beat 1 or beat 2 contains no pitch; and the whole rest, when there are no pitches for an entire measure. Example 3-16 displays these possibilities. Note the irregularity: the half rest, which in $\frac{4}{4}$ meter represents two beats, is *not* employed for two beats in $\frac{2}{4}$ meter.

Example 3-16

Similarly, the half rest is not employed in $\frac{3}{4}$ meter. Use a quarter rest, when either beat 1, beat 2, or beat 3 contains no pitch; two quarter rests, when two consecutive beats contain no pitch; and the whole rest, when there are no pitches for an entire measure. Example 3-17 displays these possibilities.

Example 3-17

None of the rest notation in Example 3-18 is correct. Make sure that you understand, from the discussion above, what should appear instead in each case.

Example 3-18

Practice Exercises 3-6

Practice creating music notation by drawing each symbol below twice to the right of its model.

Each of the following measures contains an *incorrect* usage of rest. On the staves to the right, reconstruct each measure using correct rest notation.

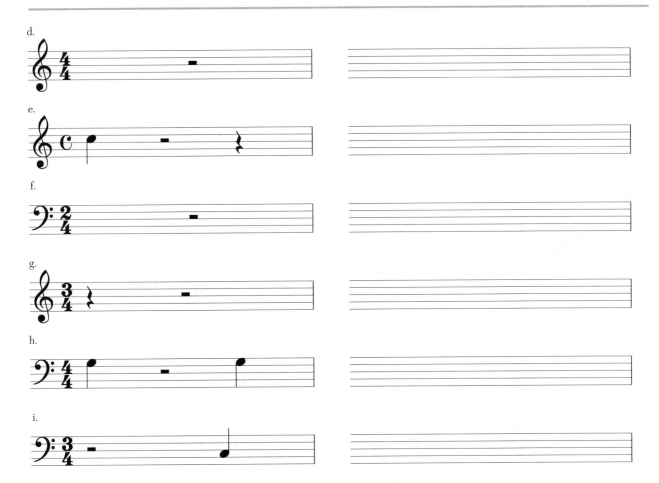

Tips for Success

✔ Rest notation has its quirks. Though it might seem that a half rest and two quarter rests would always be interchangeable, they are not. And a whole rest may be required for a measure of two or three beats.

✔ Do not confuse the notation for half and whole rests. Think "above/below: half/whole." (Above the third line, and below the fourth line, that is.)

Laboratory

L3-1. Play and Sing

Note: Depending on your vocal range, you may prefer to perform these exercises in the region of the keyboard above Middle C, or instead below Middle C—maybe even more than an octave below Middle C. Experiment until you find a comfortable region. However, not all voices have a wide enough range to accommodate all major scales. If this is a problem for you, start on the lowest F or G in your vocal range, sing the pitches within your range, and imagine singing pitches that are too high.

a. Place the little finger of your left hand above F (either above or below Middle C, depending on your vocal range) and the next three fingers above G, A, and B♭. Place the second finger of your right hand above the adjacent C and the next three fingers above D, E, and F. (Let your thumbs dangle back a bit.) Now play each of these keys in succession from left to right, forming an F Major scale ascending from $\hat{1}$ to $\hat{8}$. Then play the scale descending from $\hat{8}$ to $\hat{1}$.

b. Play the ascending and descending F Major scales again, but this time, pause after each pitch and sing it. That is, play F, then sing F; play G, then sing G; and so on. You may sing on the neutral syllable "la"; sing the pitch names ("F," "G," "A," etc., singing B♭ as "flat"); or sing the scale degree numbers ("$\hat{1}$," "$\hat{2}$," "$\hat{3}$," etc.).

c. Repeat exercises a and b for the G Major scale, remembering that $\hat{7}$ is F♯ (sung as "sharp" if you are using pitch names).

d. First review Example 2-5, and then sit at the keyboard, placing eight fingers (all except your thumbs) above the keys corresponding to the F Major scale. Now press an F (either of your little fingers) and one other key at the same time. Then press these two keys in ascending order, singing each pitch in turn. Sing the scale degree numbers ("$\hat{1}$," "$\hat{2}$," "$\hat{3}$," etc.). Then name the interval you have just performed (perfect fifth, minor third, etc.). Continue until you have performed and identified all thirteen combinations.

e. Now play one of the interior pitches of the scale (G through E) followed by either of your little-finger Fs. Then play the interval again, this time singing each pitch after you play it, using scale degree numbers. Name the interval. Then play and sing this interval's inversion and name it. (For example, if you first play and sing B♭ down to F, now play and sing B♭ up to F.)

f. Repeat exercises d and e for the G Major scale, remembering that $\hat{7}$ is F♯.

g. Pick a Roman numeral (I through vii°). Play that triad in C Major. Then play these three pitches in ascending order, singing each pitch after you play it. Sing the syllables "Root," "Third," and "Fifth." Then play and sing the triad in descending order, singing "Fifth," "Third," and "Root." Then play a triad with the same Roman numeral in F Major and sing it, ascending and descending. Then play a triad with the same Roman numeral in G Major and sing it, ascending and descending.

> SAMPLE: For ii, play and sing D–F–A (ascending and descending), then G–B♭–D, then A–C–E.

L3-2. Listening

Team up with another student, work with your instructor in class, or make use of the CD-ROM that accompanies this textbook to practice these exercises.

a. *Performer:* Play the three pitches of any white-key triad in descending order (for example, A, then F, then D). Then play two of these pitches again, in descending order (for example, A, then F).

Listener: Indicate which two triad components were performed: Fifth-Root; Fifth-Third; or Third-Root.

b. *Performer:* Play a major triad. Then play another triad. Then repeat both.
Listener: Given that the first triad is of major quality, indicate whether the second triad is also of major quality.

L3-3. Keyboard Album
For melodies written in treble clef, use your right hand. For melodies written in bass clef, use your left hand. The thumb is 1 and the little finger is 5 on both hands.

L3-4. Song Book
Sing these melodies in the range appropriate for your voice. You may need to move a bass-clef melody up an octave or two, and a treble-clef melody down an octave or two. If you sing using letter names, sing "flat" for B♭ and "sharp" for F♯. If you sing using scale degrees, there are no changes: B♭ in F Major is 4̂ and F♯ in G Major is 7̂.

L3-5. Rhythm

L3-6. Improvisation

a. Place your right thumb above F and let the remaining right-hand fingers touch G, A, Bb, and C. Keep this hand close to the edge of the keyboard. Now place your left little finger above E, just to the left of F, and let the remaining left-hand fingers touch F, G, A, and Bb. This hand will be forward of your right hand. Create an eight-measure melody, with a varied rhythm, according to the following plan:

measures 1 and 2:	right hand
measures 3 and 4:	left hand
measures 5 and 6:	right hand
measure 7:	left hand
measure 8:	right hand, ending on F

b. Place your right thumb above G and let the remaining right-hand fingers touch A, B, C, and D. Keep this hand close to the edge of the keyboard. Now place your left little finger above F♯, just to the left of G, and let the remaining left-hand fingers touch G, A, B, and C. This hand will be forward of your right hand. Create an eight-measure melody, with a varied rhythm, according to the following plan:

measure 1:	right hand
measure 2:	left hand
measures 3 and 4:	right hand
measures 5 and 6:	left hand
measures 7 and 8:	right hand, ending on G

If you create a melody that especially pleases you, write it down. Perhaps at your next class your instructor will put it on the board for the entire class to sing.

L3-7. Score Study

Listen to Selections 1, 2, and 5 in the Scores for Music Analysis section at the back of the textbook. Then answer the questions under the "Chapter 3" headings that accompany these selections.

Name: _____

Instructor: _____

Date: _____

Pitch Exercises

P3-1. Draw a line connecting each notehead with the appropriate white key. Note carefully the location of Middle C.

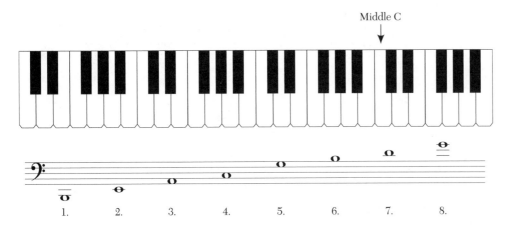

P3-2. On the staff, draw the noteheads that correspond to the given white keys. Note carefully the location of Middle C.

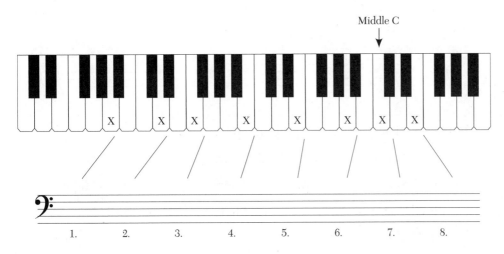

P3-3. A notehead and the scale degree number indicating its position within some major scale appear on an empty staff. After determining the appropriate major key (C Major, F Major, or G Major):

- add the key signature, if required;
- write in the remaining noteheads of the scale; and
- label each notehead with its scale degree number.

Remember that descending scales begin on $\hat{8}$.

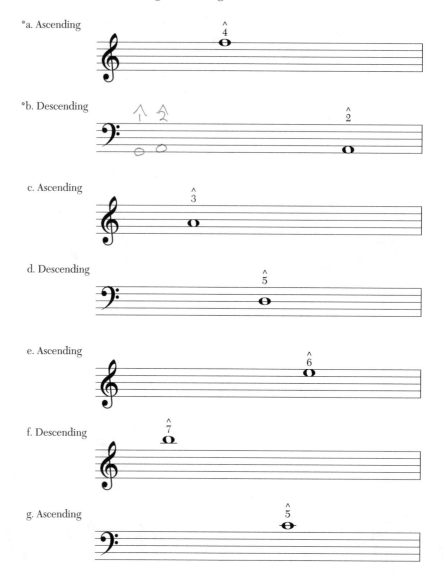

P3-4. Fill in the blanks with the appropriate pitch names.

°a. $\hat{6}$ in G Major: _____   g. $\hat{3}$ in G Major: _____   m. $\hat{4}$ in F Major: _____

°b. $\hat{3}$ in C Major: _____   h. $\hat{7}$ in C Major: _____   n. $\hat{2}$ in G Major: _____

c. $\hat{7}$ in F Major: _____   i. $\hat{3}$ in F Major: _____   o. $\hat{6}$ in C Major: _____

d. $\hat{4}$ in G Major: _____   j. $\hat{2}$ in F Major: _____   p. $\hat{6}$ in F Major: _____

e. $\hat{2}$ in C Major: _____   k. $\hat{5}$ in G Major: _____   q. $\hat{7}$ in G Major: _____

f. $\hat{5}$ in F Major: _____   l. $\hat{4}$ in C Major: _____   r. $\hat{5}$ in C Major: _____

P3-5. If the given pitch is diatonic in C Major, indicate its scale degree number in the first row. If it is diatonic in F Major, indicate its scale degree number in the second row. If it is diatonic in G Major, indicate its scale degree number in the third row. Some pitches are diatonic in all three keys, while others are diatonic in only one or two of these keys.

Name: _____

Instructor: _____

Date: _____

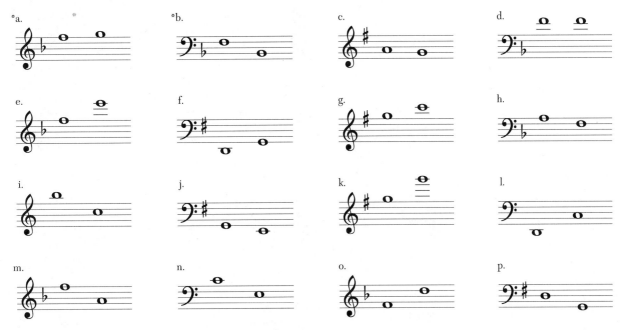

C Major: ___   ___   ___   ___   ___   ___   ___   ___   ___   ___

F Major: ___   ___   ___   ___   ___   ___   ___   ___   ___   ___

G Major: ___   ___   ___   ___   ___   ___   ___   ___   ___   ___

P3-6. Intervals in the keys of C Major, F Major, and G Major are presented in staff notation. Below the key signature, indicate the key (C Major, F Major, or G Major). Above each pitch, indicate the scale degree number ($\hat{1}$ through $\hat{8}$). Below, indicate the interval quality and size (M3, P5, etc.).

P3-7. Place a circle around each interval of Exercise P3-6 that is classified as a dissonance.

P3-8. Create the intervals requested by treating the given pitch as $\hat{1}$ (for ascending intervals) or as $\hat{8}$ (for descending intervals). Draw the appropriate key signature on the staff. Then ascend or descend the major scale until you arrive at the desired pitch. (For example, to create an ascending perfect fifth from F, draw the F Major key signature of one flat on the staff and then ascend F–G–A–Bb–C. Your answer is C.)

°a.   M6 above C is _____

°b.   m3 below F is _____

c.   P4 below G is _____

d.   P5 above G is _____

e.   m6 below F is _____

f.   M7 above G is _____

g.   M6 above F is _____

h.   P5 below F is _____

i.   P4 above F is _____

j.   m7 below F is _____

Name: _____

Instructor: _____

Date: _____

k. M3 above C is _____

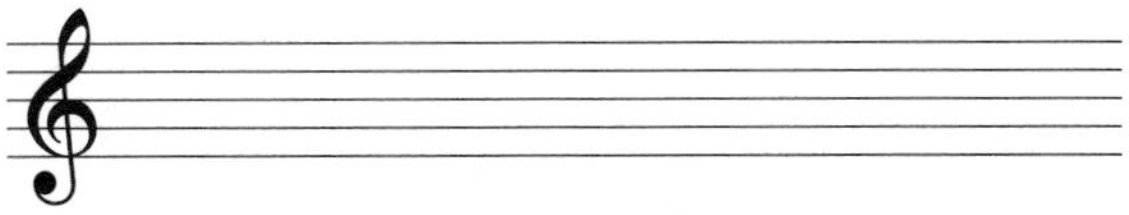

l. m7 below G is _____

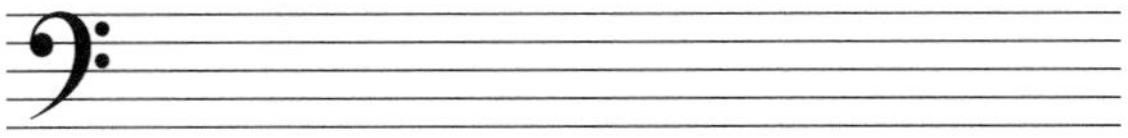

m. M3 above F is _____

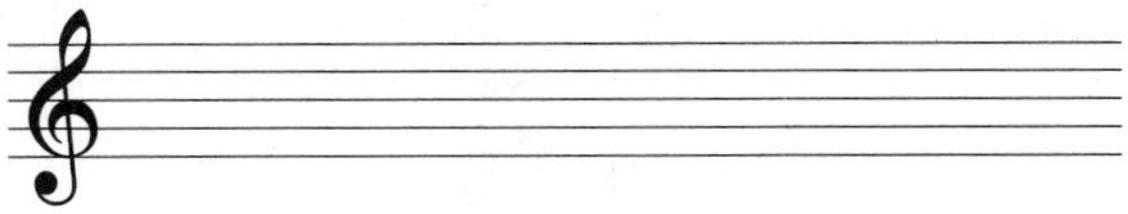

n. m2 below G is _____

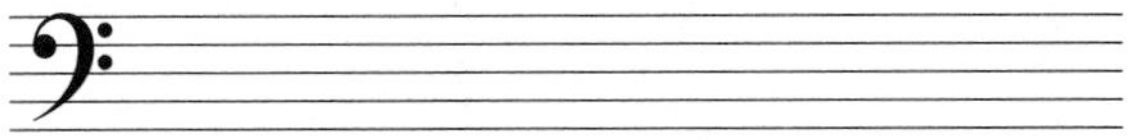

P3-9. Build the triads requested. If appropriate, add a key signature. Then add the three notes of the triad.

°a.

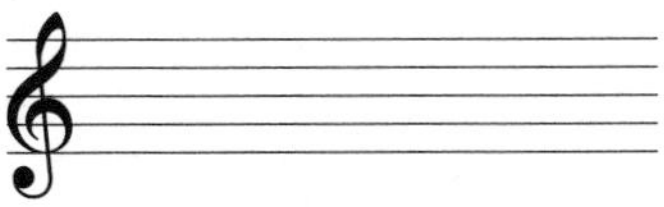

F Major: ii

°b.

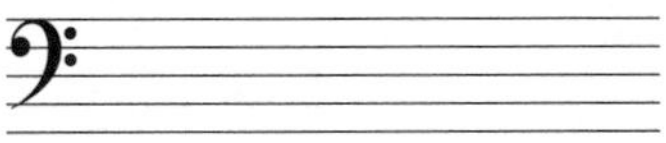

G Major: V

c.

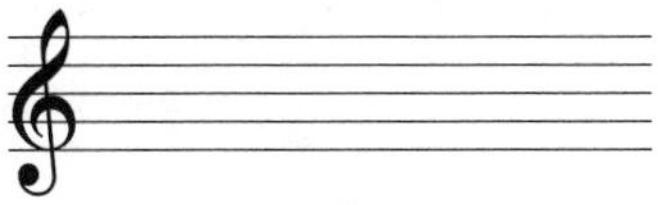

C Major: iii

d.

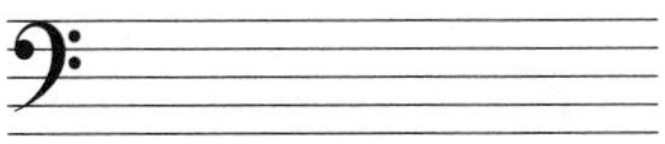

G Major: ii

e.

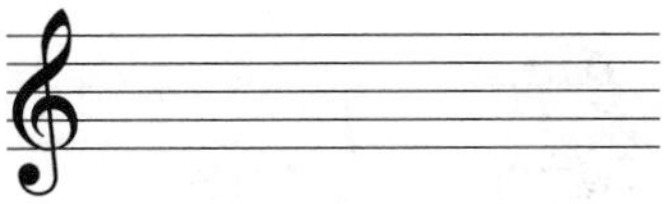

C Major: vi

f.

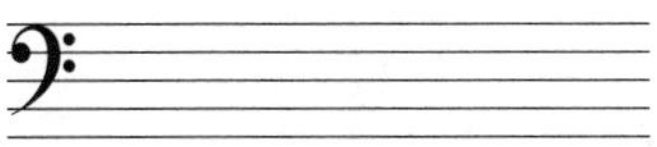

F Major: I

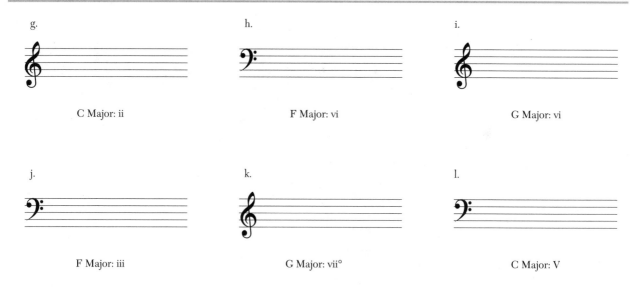

g.

C Major: ii

h.

F Major: vi

i.

G Major: vi

j.

F Major: iii

k.

G Major: vii°

l.

C Major: V

P3-10. For each triad, name the major key indicated by the key signature and supply the appropriate Roman numeral. Remember to distinguish the triad quality by the way you write the numeral (capital for major, small for minor, and small followed by a degree circle for diminished).

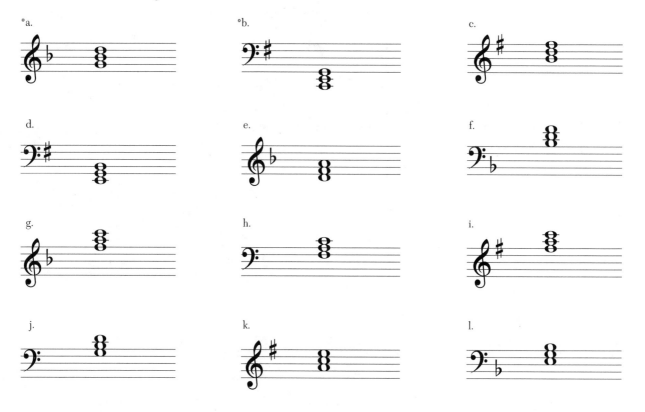

°a.

°b.

c.

d.

e.

f.

g.

h.

i.

j.

k.

l.

Name: _____

Instructor: _____

Date: _____

Rhythm Exercises

R3-1. Add the appropriate rests at the points marked by arrows.

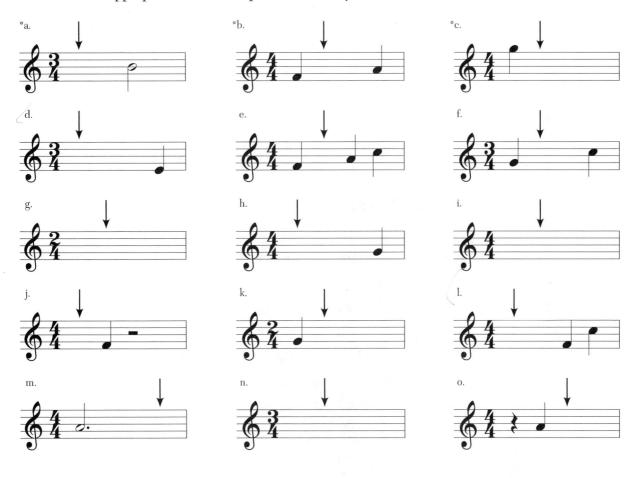

R3-2. Create the melodies indicated by the positioning of the pitch names in relation to the counting numbers. From one note to the next, use only a unison, second, third, or fourth as a melodic interval. Do not add rests.

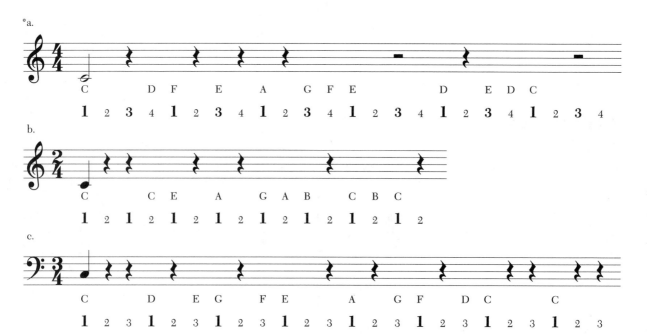

Audio Exercises

A3-1. The three pitches of a white-key triad are performed in descending order. Two of these three pitches are then performed a second time. Indicate which two.

°a.	Fifth-Third	Fifth-Root	Third-Root
°b.	Fifth-Third	Fifth-Root	Third-Root
c.	Fifth-Third	Fifth-Root	Third-Root
d.	Fifth-Third	Fifth-Root	Third-Root
e.	Fifth-Third	Fifth-Root	Third-Root
f.	Fifth-Third	Fifth-Root	Third-Root
g.	Fifth-Third	Fifth-Root	Third-Root
h.	Fifth-Third	Fifth-Root	Third-Root
i.	Fifth-Third	Fifth-Root	Third-Root
j.	Fifth-Third	Fifth-Root	Third-Root

A3-2. Two triads are performed. The first triad is a major triad. Is the second triad a major triad also?

°a.	Yes	No	f.	Yes	No
°b.	Yes	No	g.	Yes	No
c.	Yes	No	h.	Yes	No
d.	Yes	No	i.	Yes	No
e.	Yes	No	j.	Yes	No

Name: _____

Instructor: _____

Date: _____

A3-3. Circle the music notation that corresponds to the pitches performed.

A3-4. Circle the music notation that corresponds to the rhythm performed.

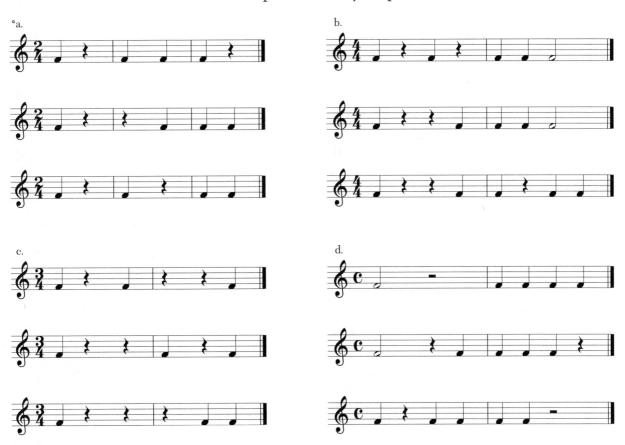

CHAPTER 4

Three Minor Keys

Not all music is written in a major key. By choosing a different set of diatonic pitches for a given tonic, a minor key results. Because minor intervals are more prominently positioned when the mode is minor, minor keys are particularly effective when a somber mood is desired.

Major versus Minor

In drama, plays fall into two basic categories: comedies and tragedies. That is not to say that even in a tragedy as blood-filled as Shakespeare's *Hamlet* there are not light-hearted moments, or that a comedy is full of laughs from start to finish. But there is a prevailing mood, which the playwright contemplates before the first word is written. Likewise in music, there are two basic categories, called *modes*. The major mode, with its abundance of major and perfect intervals ascending from tonic, is generally regarded as cheerful. The **minor mode**, in which three of the intervals ascending from tonic are of minor quality, is appropriate for more somber sentiments. Or, as Roger North wrote three hundred years ago, the major mode is characterized by "triumph, mirth and felicity," while the minor mode corresponds to "querulousness, sorrow and dejection." Wagner's Wedding March and Chopin's Funeral March (Example 4-1) demonstrate the characteristics of the major and minor modes, respectively.

minor mode

Example 4-1

Wagner: *Lohengrin,* Wedding March
(Transposed; Rhythmic notation simplified)

a.

Chopin: Piano Sonata No. 2, Funeral March
(Transposed; Rhythmic notation simplified)

b.

We explored major keys by analyzing how their scales are formed, by constructing the intervals that employ the tonic pitch ($\hat{1}$ or $\hat{8}$), and by building triads on each scale degree. We will follow the same path now for minor keys. Before proceeding, however, one special note: composers rarely persist with a minor key's set of diatonic pitches for very long without intermingling some elements of the major mode. Most instances of a minor key are one of two versions of combined minor/major that we will explore in Chapter 10 under the names *harmonic minor* and *melodic minor*. To distinguish these hybrid modes from a minor key in its pure state, we will call that pure state ***natural minor***. The key signatures that we introduce in this chapter will always pertain to the natural minor mode. The alternative pitches used in harmonic and melodic minor will be indicated by placing accidentals beside individual noteheads, and not by means of a key signature.

| natural minor |

The Natural Minor Scale

The eight noteheads in Example 4-2 form an ascending A Natural Minor scale. The pattern of steps characteristic of this scale is Whole-Half-Whole-Whole-Half-Whole-Whole. Play the A Natural Minor scale. It should sound different from the major scales we have explored.

Example 4-2

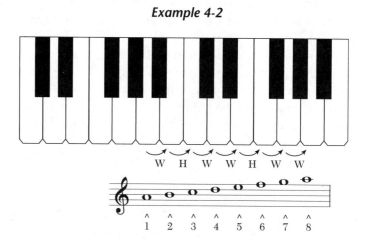

Three scales containing only white keys appear in Example 4-3. The A Natural Minor scale is in the middle. Though the other scales are similar, there are points of difference. In the D scale, the span between A and C does not match the corresponding positions of the A scale: it ascends Whole-Half instead of Half-Whole. And in the E scale, the span between E and G does not match the corresponding positions of the A scale: it ascends Half-Whole instead of Whole-Half. Consult a keyboard diagram to *see* these differences. Play and sing these scales to *hear* these differences.

Example 4-3

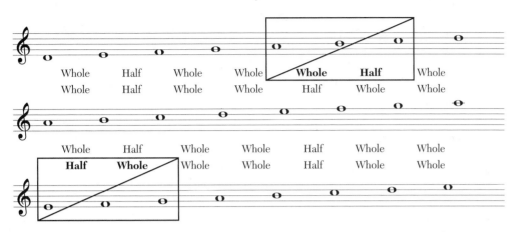

Whole	Half	Whole	Whole	**Whole**	**Half**	Whole
Whole	Half	Whole	Whole	Half	Whole	Whole

Whole	Half	Whole	Whole	Half	Whole	Whole
Half	**Whole**	Whole	Whole	Half	Whole	Whole

Music students 400 years ago would have learned each of these scales. The one on A was named Aeolian; the one on D, Dorian; and the one on E, Phrygian. Around the year 1600, things started to change. Now, when D is tonic, B is lowered to B♭. As a result, the relationship among pitches exactly matches the whole- and half-step succession of the A Natural Minor scale. Likewise, when E is tonic, F♯ replaces F. Thus, instead of three different "modes" of ascent from tonic, that which corresponds to the white keys between two A's is used in all three cases. D Natural Minor and E Natural Minor scales are displayed in Example 4-4, along with keyboard diagrams that confirm the Whole-Half-Whole-Whole-Half-Whole-Whole pattern.

Example 4-4

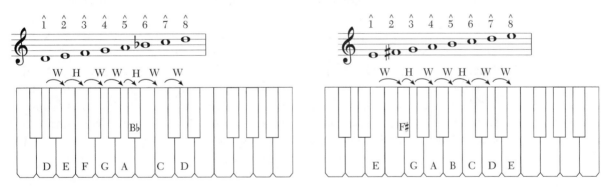

By employing accidentals to form the appropriate succession of whole and half steps, any pitch can be a minor-key tonic: not only A, but also D, E, or any other pitch. J. S. Bach used all twelve minor keys in his *Well-Tempered Clavier.*

Practice Exercises 4-1

Indicate the scale degree of each pitch in the key indicated.

A Natural Minor: _____   _____   _____   _____   _____

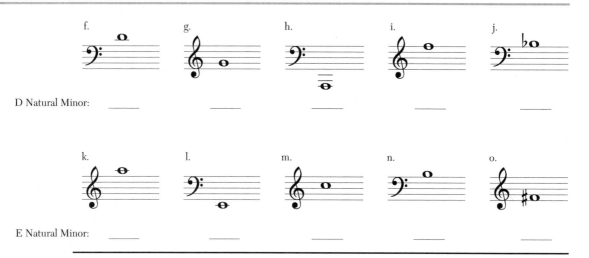

D Natural Minor: _____   _____   _____   _____   _____

E Natural Minor: _____   _____   _____   _____   _____

Relative Keys and Their Key Signatures

Though A Natural Minor and C Major have distinctly different characters, they do share one important feature: the same set of diatonic pitches (corresponding to the white keys). The choice of tonic (A or C) affects the configuration of whole and half steps in the scale, the qualities of the intervals that employ the tonic pitch, and the qualities of the key's triads. Two keys that share the same diatonic pitches are called **relative keys** *relative keys*. Because the pitch content is the same, we use the same key signature for both. (For A Natural Minor and C Major, the key signature contains no sharps or flats.) C Major is the "relative major" of A Natural Minor, and A Natural Minor is the "relative minor" of C Major.

Just as A Natural Minor and C Major are relative keys, so, too, are D Natural Minor and F Major (which share the one-flat key signature), and so, too, are E Natural Minor and G Major (which share the one-sharp key signature). As Example 4-5 displays, the tonic of a major key's relative minor is found by descending the major scale to its sixth scale degree, while the tonic of a minor key's relative major is found by ascending the minor scale to its third scale degree. The interval of a minor third (Half-Whole or Whole-Half) separates the two tonics.

Example 4-5

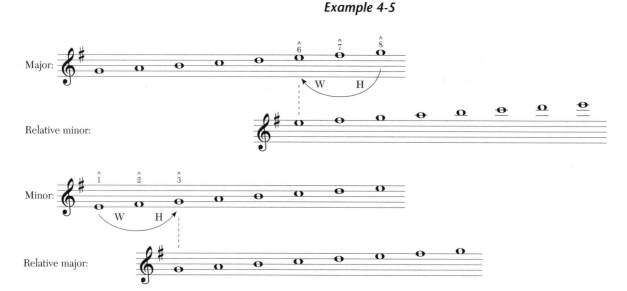

Practice Exercises 4-2

a. Employing a key signature, create an ascending D Natural Minor scale. Add scale degree numbers (1̂ through 8̂).

b. Employing a key signature, create a descending E Natural Minor scale. Add scale degree numbers (8̂ through 1̂).

Ascending from 1̂ or Descending from 8̂

In major keys, all the intervals made by ascending from tonic (1̂) are of major or perfect quality. In minor keys, minor intervals replace three of the ascending major intervals: the minor third, minor sixth, and minor seventh. These intervals are displayed in Example 4-6. All the other intervals that employ 1̂ are the same as in major (that is, the perfect unison, major second, perfect fourth, perfect fifth, and perfect octave).

Example 4-6

If 1̂–3̂ forms a minor third, then its inversion, 3̂–8̂, will form a major sixth. Likewise 6̂–8̂, the inversion of the 1̂–6̂ minor sixth, forms a major third; and 7̂–8̂, the inversion of the 1̂–7̂ minor seventh, forms a major second. All of the diatonic intervals that employ the tonic pitch in natural minor are displayed in Example 4-7, in the context of A Natural Minor. The differences from major-mode intervals are indicated in bold print.

Example 4-7

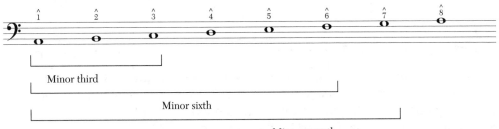

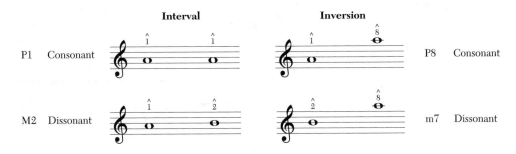

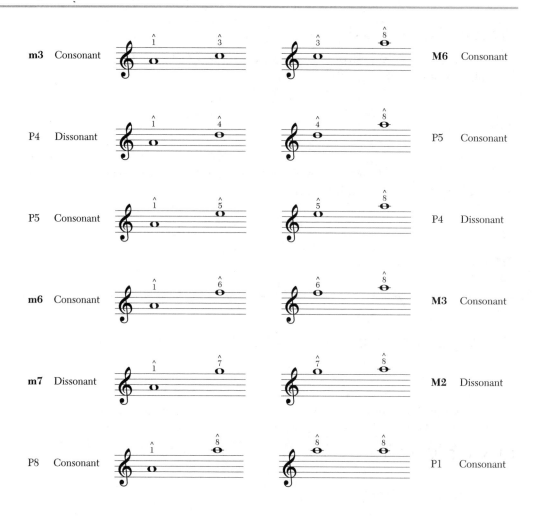

m3	Consonant		**M6**	Consonant
P4	Dissonant		P5	Consonant
P5	Consonant		P4	Dissonant
m6	Consonant		**M3**	Consonant
m7	Dissonant		**M2**	Dissonant
P8	Consonant		P1	Consonant

Practice Exercises 4-3

Name the minor key in which each interval is to be interpreted (A Natural Minor, D Natural Minor, or E Natural Minor), by viewing the key signature. Then indicate the scale degree of both pitches that form the interval, in the context of that key. Finally, name the interval formed by the two pitches (M3, m6, etc.).

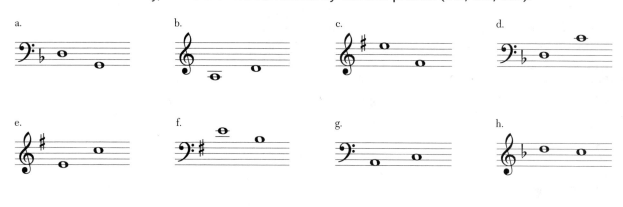

a.   b.   c.   d.

e.   f.   g.   h.

Labeling the Triads in Minor Keys

Whether in the context of a major key or its relative minor key, the diatonic pitches produce three major triads, three minor triads, and one diminished triad. Where these triads reside within the key depends on which pitch serves as tonic. For example, in C Major the tonic triad is major (C E G), but in A Natural Minor the tonic triad is minor (A C E).

In minor keys, the i, iv, and v triads are of minor quality; the III, VI, and VII triads are of major quality; and the ii° triad is of diminished quality. Example 4-8 compares the triad labels of major and minor keys. Observe that the triads on each scale degree differ in quality in the two modes. This is one of the principal reasons why major and minor keys have such contrasting characters.

Example 4-8

Root:	$\hat{1}$	$\hat{2}$	$\hat{3}$	$\hat{4}$	$\hat{5}$	$\hat{6}$	$\hat{7}$
Major keys:	I	ii	iii	IV	V	vi	vii°
Minor keys:	i	ii°	III	iv	v	VI	VII

Practice Exercises 4-4

Name the minor key indicated by the key signature (A Natural Minor, D Natural Minor, or E Natural Minor). Then place the appropriate Roman numeral (i through VII) below each triad.

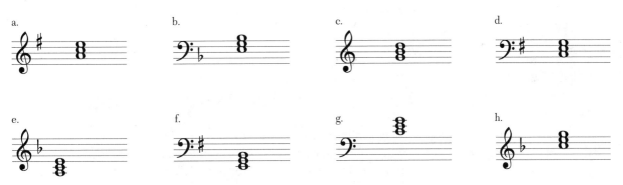

First draw in the correct key signature. Then create the triad requested.

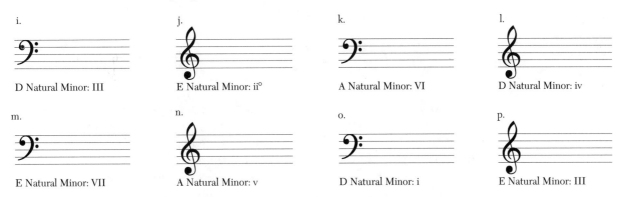

i. D Natural Minor: III

j. E Natural Minor: ii°

k. A Natural Minor: VI

l. D Natural Minor: iv

m. E Natural Minor: VII

n. A Natural Minor: v

o. D Natural Minor: i

p. E Natural Minor: III

Tips for Success

✔ Each of the key signatures introduced thus far corresponds to one major key and one minor key. Make sure you know exactly how to draw these signatures in both treble clef and bass clef, as shown in Example 3-12. (The signature for C Major or A Natural Minor requires no effort!) In Chapter 5, six new signatures await, so do not delay in learning those introduced thus far.

✔ If you see a key signature and then an interval or a triad, there is no way to know from context whether the mode should be regarded as major or as minor. For example, if you see a one-sharp signature and then the triad A C E, you cannot tell whether this triad is G Major: ii or E Minor: iv. For practice purposes, you will be told whether to think in the context of a major or a minor key. In this chapter we deal exclusively with minor keys.

✔ Note that in *both* major and minor keys, the interval from $\hat{1}$ to $\hat{2}$ is a *major* second. Only three of the four major intervals ascending from $\hat{1}$ in major keys become minor in quality in minor keys: $\hat{1}$–$\hat{3}$, $\hat{1}$–$\hat{6}$, and $\hat{1}$–$\hat{7}$.

✔ Know exactly where to find major, minor, and diminished triads in minor keys. Memorize that i, iv, and v are minor and that ii° is diminished. All the others (III, VI, and VII) are major.

RHYTHM

Eighth Notes and Eighth Rests

The notes and rests we have explored thus far all equal or exceed the value of the beat. In this chapter we begin to explore symbols whose values are less than a beat. For example, an eighth note fills half a beat in $\frac{4}{4}$ meter.

Subdivisions of the Quarter-Note Beat

eighth notes

beam

Quarter-note beats combine to form half notes, dotted half notes, and whole notes. **Eighth notes**, on the other hand, result from the subdivision of the beat. Two eighth notes fill the same musical time as one quarter note. They are written by connecting the stems of filled-in noteheads with a solid horizontal or diagonal line called a **beam**. Example 4-9 shows that four, six, and eight eighth notes fill measures in $\frac{2}{4}$, $\frac{3}{4}$, and $\frac{4}{4}$ meters, respectively.

Example 4-9

In $\frac{2}{4}$ and $\frac{3}{4}$ meters, each beat may be beamed separately; however, if consecutive beats contain nothing but eighth notes, a single beam may connect them all. In $\frac{4}{4}$ meter, a beam should not cross the midpoint of the measure. (That is, beats one and two, or beats three and four, may be beamed together, but not beats two and three.) The stem direction appropriate for the note farthest from the center line of the staff governs the direction of all stems joined by a beam, as shown in Examples 4-9 and

4-10. Observe that the conventional direction of an individual note's stem may be altered when it is attached to a beam.

Example 4-10

Counting the Beats and Their Eighth-Note Subdivisions

You should count the eighth-note subdivisions of the beat whenever eighth notes play an important role in a melody. The syllable "and" (written as "+") marks the moment in time when the second half of a beat begins. By pronouncing the syllables for the beats and their subdivisions at a uniform rate, your performance should be more successful. Example 4-11 shows how to count in $\frac{2}{4}$, $\frac{3}{4}$, and $\frac{4}{4}$ meters.

Example 4-11

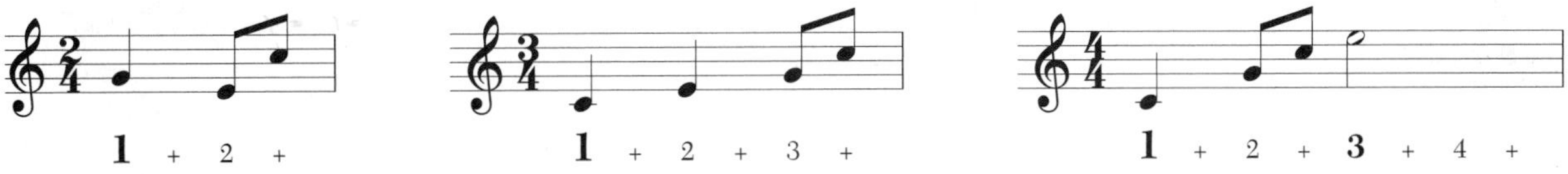

Individual Eighth Notes and Rests

Remember that the dotted half note's augmentation dot increases the time value of the half note by one-half (three beats instead of two). Similarly, by adding an augmentation dot to a quarter note to form a ***dotted quarter note*** (♩.), the quarter note's value is increased by one-half to a total of one and one-half beats. The second beat will be completed using either an ***eighth rest*** (𝄾) or a single eighth note (♪) Example 4-12 displays both possibilities. Observe that the horizontal portion of an eighth rest falls in the third space on the staff. The ***flag*** that forms a part of the single eighth note's symbol is placed to the right of the stem both when the stem ascends and when it descends.

dotted quarter note

eighth rest

flag

Example 4-12

Example 4-13 shows all of our new symbols employed in a melody. Observe that an eighth note and an eighth rest may together fill a beat (measure 3). Also observe that beam notation is employed when eighth notes share the same beat (measures 2

and 4), but that flag notation is employed when two consecutive eighth notes fall within different beats (measure 3).

Example 4-13

Practice Exercises 4-5

Practice creating music notation by drawing each symbol below twice to the right of its model.

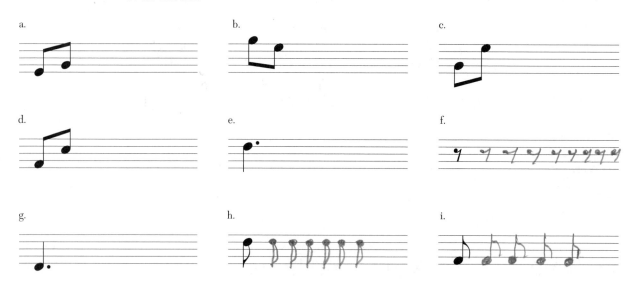

Each of the following measures contains an error. On the staves to the right, reconstruct each measure using correct notation.

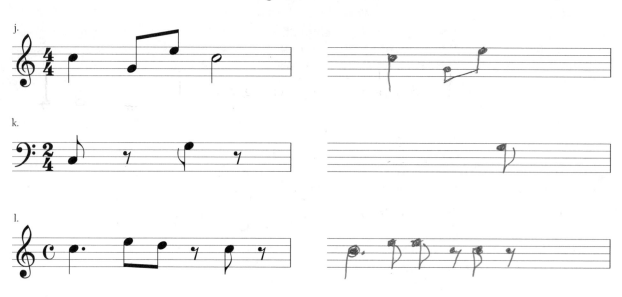

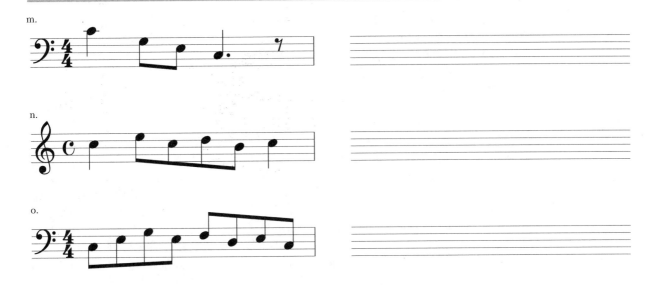

Tips for Success

✔ Writing in the counting syllables (1 + 2 + . . .) beneath a melody you intend to perform is a good way to make sure you understand the rhythmic notation. Each measure needs to "add up" correctly. If you have made a mistake, then you may find at the end of the measure that you either have a leftover syllable or not enough syllables. Time to erase!

✔ Be very careful concerning stem direction when multiple notes are connected to the same beam. One note (the farthest from center) determines the direction for all the notes attached to the same beam.

Laboratory

L4-1. Play and Sing

a. Place the little finger of your left hand above A (either a third below Middle C or an octave lower, depending on your vocal range) and the next three fingers above B, C, and D. Place the second finger of your right hand above the adjacent E and the next three fingers above F, G, and A. (Let your thumbs dangle back a bit.) Now play each of these keys in succession from left to right, forming an A Natural Minor scale ascending from $\hat{1}$ to $\hat{8}$. Then play the scale descending from $\hat{8}$ to $\hat{1}$.

b. Play the ascending and descending A Natural Minor scales again, but this time pause after each pitch and sing it. That is, play A, then sing A; play B, then sing B; and so on. You may sing on the neutral syllable "la," sing the pitch names ("A," "B," "C," etc.), or sing the scale degree numbers ("$\hat{1}$," "$\hat{2}$," "$\hat{3}$," etc.).

c. Repeat exercises a and b for the D Natural Minor scale, remembering that $\hat{6}$ is B♭ (sung as "flat" if you are using pitch names) and for the E Natural Minor scale, remembering that $\hat{2}$ is F♯ (sung as "sharp" if you are using pitch names).

d. First review Example 4-7, and then sit at the keyboard, placing eight fingers (all except your thumbs) above the keys corresponding to the A Natural Minor scale. Now press an A (either of your little fingers) and one other key at the same time. Then press these two keys in ascending order, singing each pitch in turn. Sing the scale degree numbers ("$\hat{1}$," "$\hat{2}$," "$\hat{3}$," etc.). Then name the interval you have just performed (perfect fifth, minor third, etc.). Continue until you have performed and identified all thirteen combinations.

e. Now play one of the interior pitches of the scale (B through G) followed by either of your little-finger A's. Then play the interval again, this time singing each pitch after you play it, using scale-degree numbers. Name the interval. Then play and sing this interval's inversion and name it. (For example, if you first play and sing C down to A, now play and sing C up to A.)

f. Repeat exercises d and e for the D Natural Minor scale (remembering that $\hat{6}$ is B♭) and E Natural Minor scale (remembering that $\hat{2}$ is F♯).

g. Pick a minor-key Roman numeral (i through VII). Play that triad in A Natural Minor. Then play these three pitches in ascending order, singing each pitch after you play it. Sing the syllables "Root," "Third," and "Fifth." Then play and sing the triad in descending order, singing "Fifth," "Third," and "Root." Then play the triad with the same Roman numeral in D Natural Minor and sing it, ascending and descending. Then play the triad with the same Roman numeral in E Natural Minor and sing it, ascending and descending.

  SAMPLE: For v, play and sing E–G–B (ascending and descending), then A–C–E, then B–D–F♯.

h. Play each of the triads below. After you play it, name the natural minor key that corresponds to the given key signature and the Roman numeral that corresponds to the triad.

  SAMPLE: For 1, play the triad and then say "D Minor: iv (minor four)."

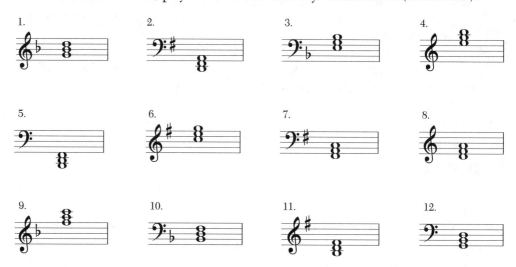

L4-2. Listening
Team up with another student, work with your instructor in class, or make use of the CD-ROM that accompanies this textbook to practice these exercises.

a. *Performer*: Place eight fingers above the eight keys corresponding to the A Natural Minor scale. Then either perform this scale (ascending or descending) or play the scale with one "wrong" pitch (using an adjacent black key in place of one of the white keys).
  Listener: Indicate "Yes," this is an A Natural Minor scale; or "No," this is not an A Natural Minor scale.

b. *Performer*: Play Middle C and then either the E♭ or the G to the right.
  Listener: Sing Middle C (singing "$\hat{1}$"), then continue by step up the C Natural Minor scale ("$\hat{2}$"–"$\hat{3}$" or "$\hat{2}$"–"$\hat{3}$"–"$\hat{4}$"–"$\hat{5}$") until you reach the other pitch performed. Then identify the interval as a minor third or a perfect fifth.

c. *Performer:* Play a minor triad. Then play another triad. Then repeat both.
   Listener: Given that the first triad is of minor quality, indicate whether the second
   triad is also of minor quality.

L4-3. Keyboard Album

L4-4. Song Book

d. Tchaikovsky: Symphony No. 4, Op. 36, Mvmt. 4

L4-5. Rhythm

a.

b.

c.

d.

e.

L4-6. Improvisation

a. Place your right thumb above A and let the remaining right-hand fingers touch B, C, D, and E. Keep this hand close to the edge of the keyboard. Now place your left little finger above G, just to the left of A, and let the remaining left-hand fingers touch A, B, C, and D. This hand will be forward of your right hand. Create an eight-measure melody, with a varied rhythm, according to the following plan:

measures 1 and 2:   right hand
measures 3 and 4:   left hand
measures 5 and 6:   right hand
measure 7:   left hand
measure 8:   right hand, ending on A

b. Place your right thumb above D and let the remaining right-hand fingers touch E, F, G, and A. Keep this hand close to the edge of the keyboard. Now place your left little finger above G, in the midst of your right-hand fingers, and let the remaining left-hand fingers touch A, B♭, C, and D. This hand will be forward of your right hand. Create an eight-measure melody, with a varied rhythm, according to the following plan:

measures 1 and 2:	right hand
measure 3:	left hand
measure 4:	right hand
measures 5 and 6:	left hand
measures 7 and 8:	right hand, ending on D

If you create a melody that especially pleases you, write it down. Perhaps at your next class your instructor will put it on the board for the entire class to sing.

L4-7. Score Study

Listen to Selections 1, 2, and 7 in the Scores for Music Analysis section at the back of the textbook. Then answer the questions under the "Chapter 4" headings that accompany these selections.

Name: _____

Instructor: _____

Date: _____

Pitch Exercises

P4-1. For each of the following patterns of ascending or descending whole and half steps, indicate the minor-key scale degrees where the succession occurs. In some cases, several answers must be supplied; whereas in others, there may be no succession of scale degrees that fits the pattern. Remember that since it takes two pitches to form a whole or a half step, patterns of two intervals (such as Whole-Half) require three consecutive scale degrees, patterns of three intervals (such as Whole-Whole-Half) require four consecutive scale degrees, and so on.

$\hat{1}$		$\hat{2}$		$\hat{3}$		$\hat{4}$		$\hat{5}$		$\hat{6}$		$\hat{7}$		$\hat{8}$
	Whole		Half		Whole		Whole		Half		Whole		Whole	

*a. Whole-Half (Descending)
　　　　　　　f. Whole-Whole-Whole (Ascending)

*b. Half-Whole (Ascending)
　　　　　　　g. Half-Whole-Half (Descending)

c. Whole-Whole-Half (Descending) h. Half-Whole-Whole-Half (Ascending)

d. Whole-Half-Whole (Ascending) 　i. Whole-Half-Whole-Whole (Descending)

e. Half-Whole-Whole (Descending) 　j. Whole-Half-Whole-Whole (Ascending)

P4-2. Fill in the blanks with the appropriate pitch names.

*a. $\hat{7}$ in A Natural Minor: _____ 　　j. $\hat{4}$ in D Natural Minor: _____

*b. $\hat{4}$ in A Natural Minor: _____ 　　k. $\hat{4}$ in E Natural Minor: _____

*c. $\hat{6}$ in D Natural Minor: _____ 　　l. $\hat{2}$ in A Natural Minor: _____

d. $\hat{7}$ in E Natural Minor: _____ 　　m. $\hat{7}$ in D Natural Minor: _____

e. $\hat{3}$ in A Natural Minor: _____ 　　n. $\hat{5}$ in A Natural Minor: _____

f. $\hat{2}$ in E Natural Minor: _____ 　　o. $\hat{2}$ in D Natural Minor: _____

g. $\hat{3}$ in E Natural Minor: _____ 　　p. $\hat{5}$ in D Natural Minor: _____

h. $\hat{3}$ in D Natural Minor: _____ 　　q. $\hat{6}$ in E Natural Minor: _____

i. $\hat{5}$ in E Natural Minor: _____ 　　r. $\hat{6}$ in A Natural Minor: _____

P4-3. If the given pitch is diatonic in A Natural Minor, indicate its scale degree number in the first row. If it is diatonic in D Natural Minor, indicate its scale degree number in the second row. If it is diatonic in E Natural Minor, indicate its scale degree number in the third row. Some pitches are diatonic in all three keys, while others are diatonic in only one or two of these keys.

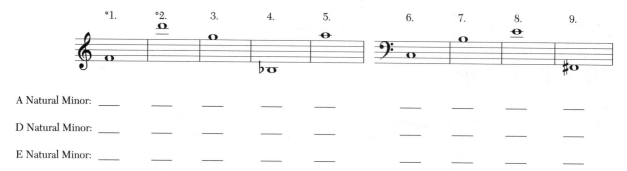

A Natural Minor: ____ ____ ____ ____ ____ ____ ____ ____ ____

D Natural Minor: ____ ____ ____ ____ ____ ____ ____ ____ ____

E Natural Minor: ____ ____ ____ ____ ____ ____ ____ ____ ____

P4-4. Intervals of A Natural Minor are presented in staff notation. Above each pitch, indicate its scale degree number ($\hat{1}$ through $\hat{8}$). Below, indicate the interval quality and size (m3, P5, etc.). Remember that if A is the *lower* pitch of the interval, it is $\hat{1}$; if it is the *higher* pitch, it is $\hat{8}$.

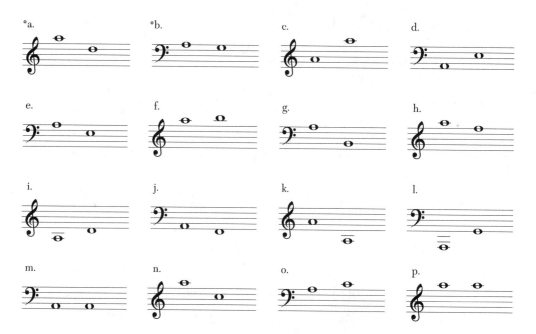

P4-5. Intervals in the keys of A Natural Minor, D Natural Minor, and E Natural Minor are presented in staff notation. Below the key signature, indicate the key (A Natural Minor, D Natural Minor, or E Natural Minor). Above each pitch, indicate its scale degree number ($\hat{1}$ through $\hat{8}$). Below, indicate the interval quality and size (m3, P5, etc.).

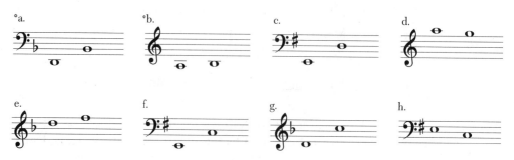

Name: _____

Instructor: _____

Date: _____

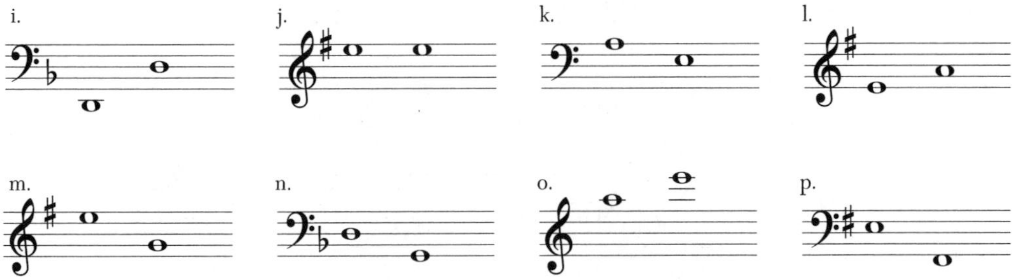

i.

j.

k.

l.

m.

n.

o.

p.

P4-6. Create the intervals requested by treating the given pitch as Î (for ascending intervals) or as 8̂ (for descending intervals) in a natural minor key. Draw the appropriate key signature on the staff. Then ascend or descend the natural minor scale until you arrive at the desired pitch. (For example, to create an ascending perfect fifth from E, draw the E Natural Minor key signature of one sharp on the staff, and then ascend E–F♯–G–A–B. Your answer will be B.)

°a. m7 above D is _____

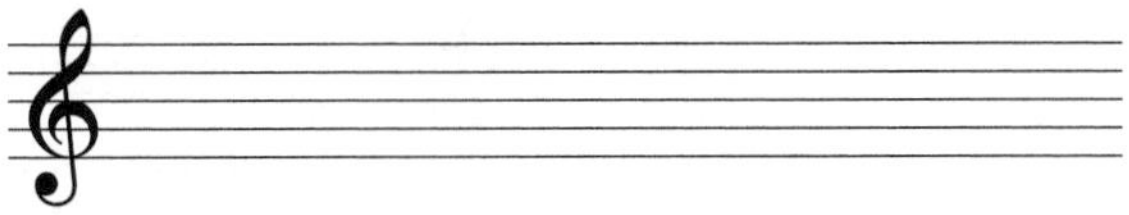

°b. P4 below A is _____

c. M3 below D is _____

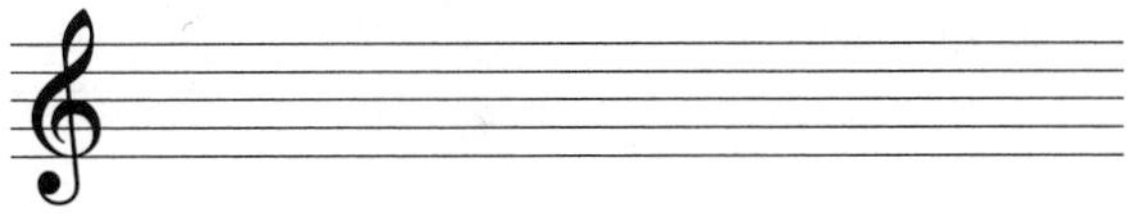

d. P5 above E is _____

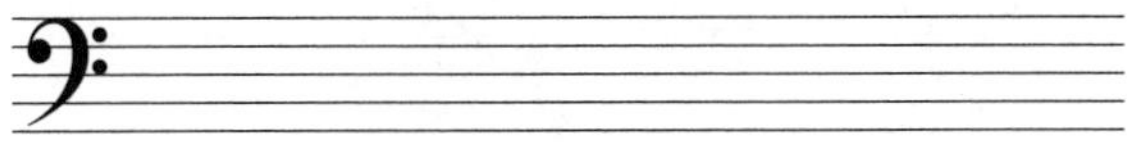

e. m7 below A is _____

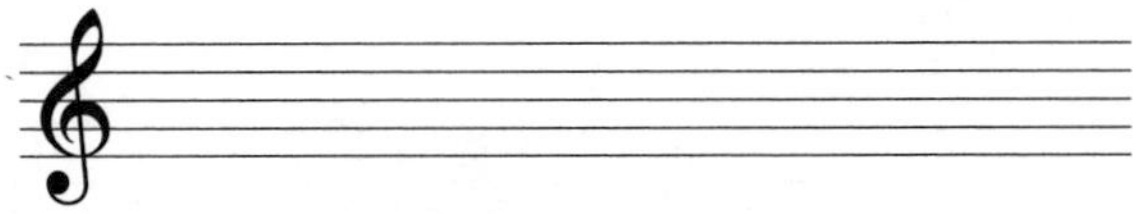

f. M2 above E is _____

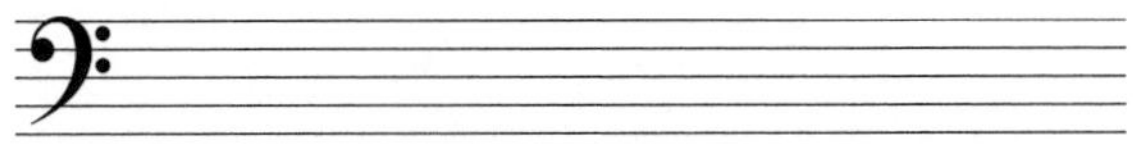

g.   m6 above D is _____

h.   m7 below E is _____

i.   P4 above A is _____

j.   P5 below E is _____

k.   m3 above A is _____

l.   M2 below D is _____

m.   m6 above E is _____

n.   M3 below E is _____

P4-7. Build the triads requested. First add a key signature, if appropriate. Then add the three notes of the triad.

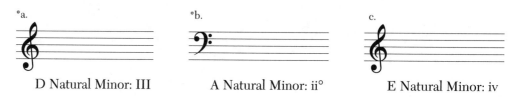

°a.   °b.   c.

D Natural Minor: III   A Natural Minor: ii°   E Natural Minor: iv

Name: _____

Instructor: _____

Date: _____

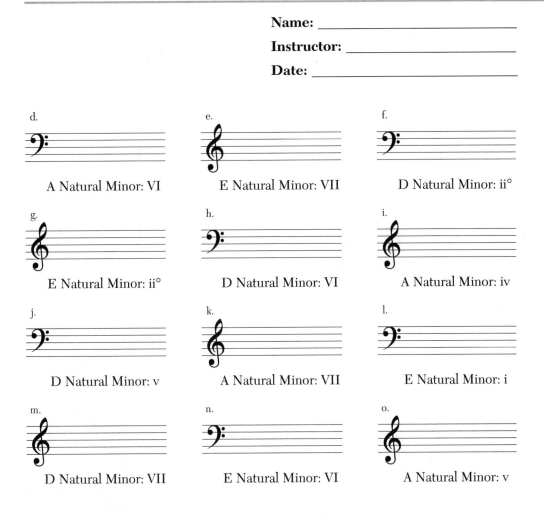

d.

A Natural Minor: VI

e.

E Natural Minor: VII

f.

D Natural Minor: ii°

g.

E Natural Minor: ii°

h.

D Natural Minor: VI

i.

A Natural Minor: iv

j.

D Natural Minor: v

k.

A Natural Minor: VII

l.

E Natural Minor: i

m.

D Natural Minor: VII

n.

E Natural Minor: VI

o.

A Natural Minor: v

P4-8. For each triad, name the natural minor key indicated by the key signature and supply the appropriate Roman numeral. Remember to distinguish the triad quality by the way you write the numeral (capital for major, small for minor, and small followed by a degree circle for diminished).

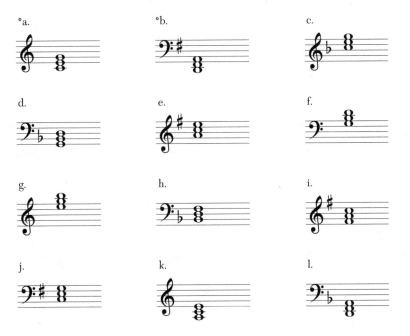

Rhythm Exercises

R4-1. Convert each notehead on the staff below into an eighth note, using beam notation. Be careful to use the correct stem direction. Add bar lines.

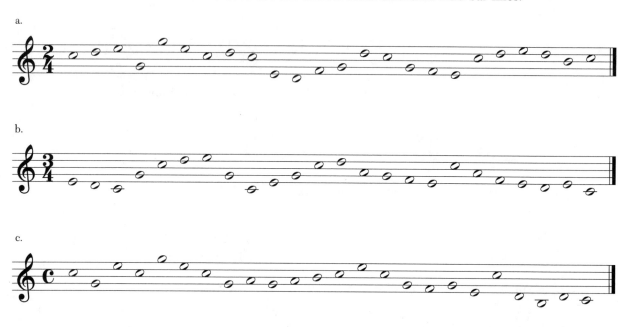

R4-2. Use the model rhythm of the first two measures to form identical patterns in measures 3–4, 5–6, and 7–8 of the following melodies. Add bar lines at appropriate spots.

Name: _____

Instructor: _____

Date: _____

R4-3. Modify the noteheads indicated by arrows to form measures containing the appropriate number of beats.

R4-4. Create the melodies indicated by the positioning of the pitch names in relation to the counting numbers. From one note to the next, use only a unison, second, third, or fourth as a melodic interval. Use beam notation when two eighth notes share a beat. Use flag notation when an eighth note shares a beat with an eighth rest, or comes after a dotted quarter note. Do not add rests.

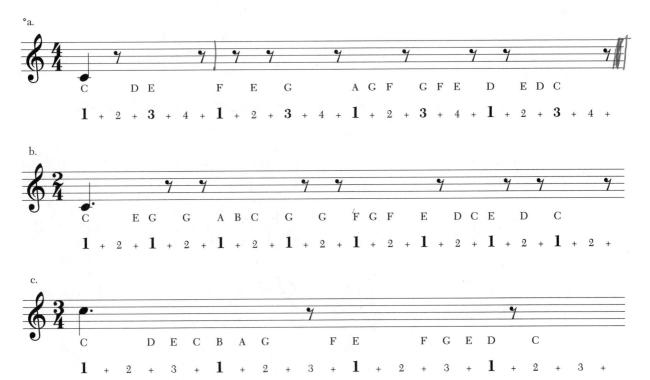

Audio Exercises

A4-1. Eight pitches starting on A are performed in either ascending or descending order. Circle "Yes" if they form an A Natural Minor scale or "No" if they do not.

°a. Yes No   f. Yes No

°b. Yes No   g. Yes No

c. Yes No   h. Yes No

d. Yes No   i. Yes No

e. Yes No   j. Yes No

A4-2. $\hat{1}$–$\hat{3}$ or $\hat{1}$–$\hat{5}$ in the key of A Natural Minor is performed. Identify the interval performed.

°a. m3 P5   f. m3 P5

°b. m3 P5   g. m3 P5

c. m3 P5   h. m3 P5

d. m3 P5   i. m3 P5

e. m3 P5   j. m3 P5

A4-3. Two triads are performed. The first triad is a minor triad. Is the second triad a minor triad also?

°a. Yes No   f. Yes No

°b. Yes No   g. Yes No

c. Yes No   h. Yes No

d. Yes No   i. Yes No

e. Yes No   j. Yes No

A4-4. Circle the music notation that corresponds to the pitches performed.

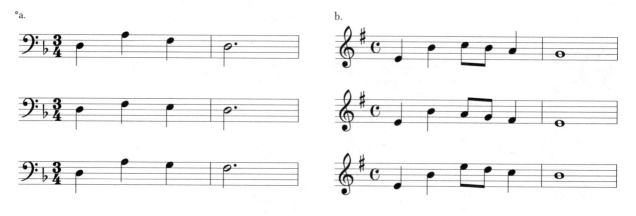

°a.   b.

Name: _____

Instructor: _____

Date: _____

c.

d.

A4-5. Circle the music notation that corresponds to the rhythm performed.

°a.

b.

c.

d.

CHAPTER 5

Keys with Two through Four Sharps or Flats

Any of the twelve pitches within an octave may serve as tonic for a major or natural minor key. However, some keys require more sharps or flats than others. In this chapter we explore those keys that utilize between two and four sharps or flats, adding twelve new keys to the six we have explored already.

Parallel Keys

So far we have employed six keys: C, F, and G have served as major-key tonics, while A, D, and E have served as minor-key tonics. Since composers do not restrict their works to these six keys, it is time to develop greater fluency by exploring the twelve keys whose signatures employ between two and four sharps or flats.

Remember that relative keys share the same key signature. For example, G Major and E Natural Minor share the key signature of one sharp. Their diatonic pitches are the same, but a different pitch serves as tonic in each. Another relationship is that of **parallel keys**, two keys that have differing sets of diatonic pitches (and thus different key signatures), but the same tonic pitch. For example, the diatonic pitches in C Major are C, D, E, F, G, A, and B. If we retain C as tonic, and choose the natural minor mode (whose scale ascends Whole-Half-Whole-Whole-Half-Whole-Whole), the diatonic pitches are C, D, Eb, F, G, Ab, and Bb. The C Major and C Natural Minor scales are compared in Example 5-1. Observe that three black keys are employed in C Natural Minor: Eb, Ab, and Bb. This example confirms that $\hat{1}$–$\hat{3}$, $\hat{1}$–$\hat{6}$, and $\hat{1}$–$\hat{7}$ are all major intervals in major keys, and minor intervals in minor keys.

	parallel keys

The relationship between C Major and C Natural Minor is matched in all other pairs of parallel keys. Exactly three pitches, corresponding to $\hat{3}$, $\hat{6}$, and $\hat{7}$, will be a half step lower in the parallel minor, compared with its parallel major. This will be clearly visible in the key signatures: C Major's signature has no sharps or flats, while C Natural Minor's signature has the three flats that convert C Major's third, sixth, and seventh from major to minor quality. Let's follow the same procedure for the two other major keys we learned in Chapter 3. Since F Major has a signature of one flat, then F Natural Minor will have a signature of four flats (three additional flats, lowering its third, sixth, and seventh scale degrees). For G Major, whose signature has one sharp, our first "flat" (or "lowering") is to remove that sharp, and then we add two additional flats, for a total of two flats in the key of G Natural Minor. These transformations are displayed in Example 5-2. (Note that one may abbreviate "Natural Minor" to "Minor" when the context is clear.)

Example 5-1

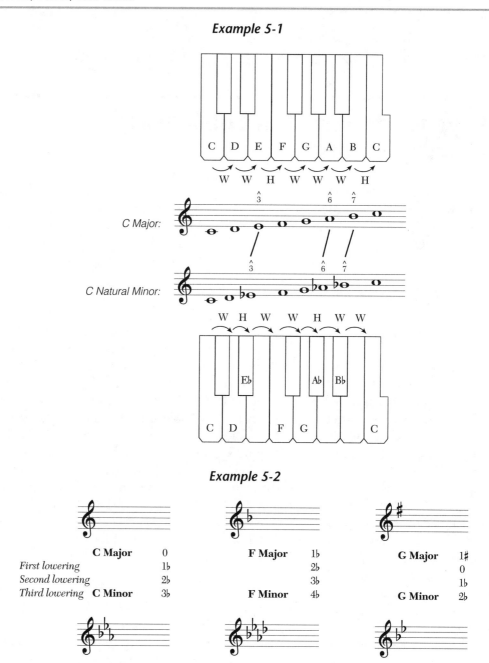

Example 5-2

	C Major	0		F Major	1♭		G Major	1♯
First lowering		1♭			2♭			0
Second lowering		2♭			3♭			1♭
Third lowering	**C Minor**	3♭		**F Minor**	4♭		**G Minor**	2♭

A similar procedure corresponds to the sharp direction: from C Natural Minor to C Major, three flats are removed (that is, three pitches become "sharper," namely those corresponding to the third, sixth, and seventh scale degrees). Let's follow the same procedure for the three minor keys we learned in Chapter 4. Since A Natural Minor's key signature has no sharps or flats, then A Major's key signature will have three sharps. Since E Natural Minor has a signature of one sharp, then E Major will have a signature of four sharps (three additional sharps). For D Natural Minor, whose signature has one flat, our first "sharp" (or "raising") is to remove that flat, and then we add two additional sharps, for a total of two sharps in the key of D Major. These transformations are displayed in Example 5-3.

Example 5-3

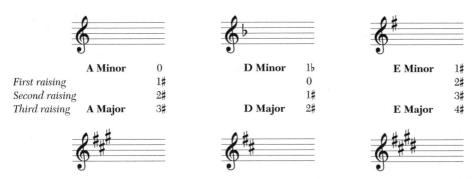

Example 5-4

| D Major | A Major | E Major | G Minor | C Minor | F Minor |

All six new key signatures are displayed in Example 5-4, in both treble and bass clefs. The signatures are always drawn exactly as shown in these models. For example, if an Eb is required in treble clef, it must be placed in the fourth space, never on the first line. And it must be the second flat in the signature.

Now that we are using more sharps and flats, you will observe that there is some redundancy built into the system of music notation. The C♯ of D Major is the same sound as the Db of F Minor. (Two notes that sound the same but are spelled differently are called ***enharmonic equivalents***.) But one would never construct a D Major scale as D E F♯ G A B **Db** D, or an F Minor scale as F G Ab Bb C **C♯** Eb F. Every scale contains *one* representative of each letter name—the one that is indicated by the key signature.

enharmonic equivalents

Practice Exercises 5-1

Study Example 5-4 carefully for several minutes. Then, without looking at that example, create the key signatures requested below. Finally, check your work against the example.

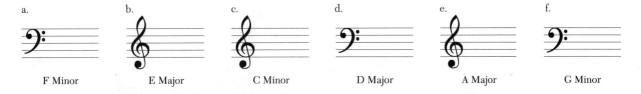

| a. | b. | c. | d. | e. | f. |
| F Minor | E Major | C Minor | D Major | A Major | G Minor |

Indicate the scale degree of each pitch in the keys indicated. Not every pitch belongs in every key: some blanks should remain empty. CAREFUL: C♯ is not the same pitch as Db, G♯ is not the same pitch as Ab, and D♯ is not the same pitch as Eb. Though these pairs *sound* the same, they are not used in place of one another.

g.　　h.　　i.　　j.　　　　　　　　　　k.　　l.　　m.　　n.

A Major: ＿＿＿　＿＿＿　＿＿＿＿　　　E Major: ＿＿＿　＿＿＿　＿＿＿　＿＿＿

F Minor: ＿＿＿　＿＿＿　＿＿＿＿　　　C Minor: ＿＿＿　＿＿＿　＿＿＿　＿＿＿

G Minor: ＿＿＿　＿＿＿　＿＿＿＿　　　D Major: ＿＿＿　＿＿＿　＿＿＿　＿＿＿

New Relative Keys

The six parallel relationships introduced above double the number of keys that we may use, from six to twelve. But there is more! Each of our six new keys employs a new key signature. As we know, every key signature pertains to two relative keys—one major, one minor. Thus, when learning D Major, A Major, and E Major, we should learn B Natural Minor, F♯ Natural Minor, and C♯ Natural Minor as well. And when learning G Natural Minor, C Natural Minor, and F Natural Minor, we should learn B♭ Major, E♭ Major, and A♭ Major as well. (Remember that the relative minor's tonic is determined by descending the major scale from $\hat{8}$ to $\hat{6}$, and that the relative major's tonic is determined by ascending the natural minor scale from $\hat{1}$ to $\hat{3}$.)

To assist you in coming to terms with this information, three separate diagrams are provided in Example 5-5. In all three, relative keys are positioned near one another. The major tonic is indicated using a capital letter, and the natural minor tonic is indicated using a small letter. In the first diagram, parallel keys are juxtaposed (indicated by the parallel vertical lines, contrasting the diagonal lines connecting relative keys). In the second, the keys are arranged in a circular array, with relative keys on opposite sides of each key signature. In the third, the keys are arranged from left to right, with separate rows for sharp keys and flat keys. This diagram also displays all the key signatures in both treble and bass clefs.

Example 5-5

a.

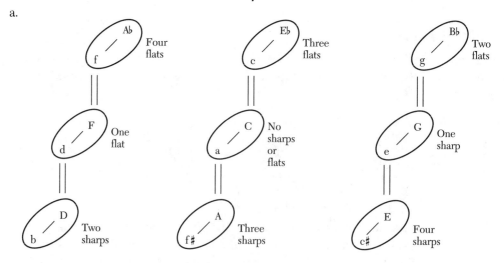

b.

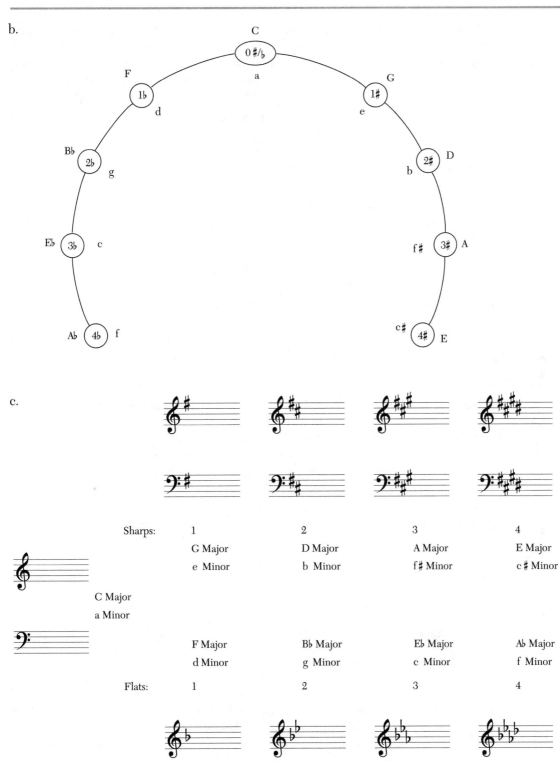

c.

	Sharps:	1	2	3	4
		G Major	D Major	A Major	E Major
		e Minor	b Minor	f♯ Minor	c♯ Minor

C Major

a Minor

		F Major	B♭ Major	E♭ Major	A♭ Major
		d Minor	g Minor	c Minor	f Minor
	Flats:	1	2	3	4

Observe that keys differing by exactly one sharp or flat have tonics that are a perfect fifth apart. In Example 5-5b, every clockwise motion corresponds to an ascending perfect fifth, and every counterclockwise motion corresponds to a descending perfect fifth. (Remember from Chapter 2 that B and F form a diminished fifth. The perfect fifth below F is B♭ and the perfect fifth above B is F♯.) Be careful! Sharps and flats are necessary components of some key names. The key of "A Major" and the key of "A♭ Major" are not the same!

Practice Exercises 5-2

Study Example 5-5 carefully, for several minutes. Then, without looking at that example, create the key signatures requested below. Finally, check your work against the example.

a.	b.	c.	d.	e.	f.
C♯ Minor	A♭ Major	F♯ Minor	B♭ Major	E♭ Major	B Minor

Recognizing a Key from Its Signature

There is an easy way to recognize a key by looking at its signature. For sharp keys, imagine a notehead in the line or space just above the last sharp in the signature. That will be the major tonic. As always, the relative minor tonic will be a third lower. Example 5-6a displays these noteheads. For flat keys, imagine a notehead in the line or space occupied by the next-to-last flat in the signature. That will be the major tonic. Again, the relative minor tonic will be a third lower. Example 5-6b displays these noteheads.

Example 5-6

Since a key signature corresponds to two different keys—one major, one minor—you must examine the composition more closely to see which of the two potential tonics is employed. The best place to look is at the end, where you will find the tonic chord. For a signature of four sharps, you would examine the last chord to determine whether it contains the pitches of the E major triad (E G♯ B), or the pitches of the C♯ minor triad (C♯ E G♯). Usually the first chord of a composition will be tonic as well, but not always. For an unaccompanied melody, you have less information to go by, but the last pitch will usually be tonic. The modifications of the minor mode that we will explore in Chapter 10 will further distinguish minor from major.

Practice Exercises 5-3

Name both the major key and the minor key that correspond to each key signature.

a.   b.   c.   d.   e.   f.

_____ Major   _____ Major   _____ Major   _____ Major   _____ Major   _____ Major

_____ Minor   _____ Minor   _____ Minor   _____ Minor   _____ Minor   _____ Minor

Triads in Eighteen Keys

Though we now have access to eighteen different keys, only two sets of characteristics may prevail: that of major keys, or that of minor keys. Thus it is not necessary to memorize eighteen separate sets of characteristics regarding scales, intervals, and triads. The key signature is a wonderful device that reliably selects the seven pitches per octave that will be the principal focus of musical activity in a key and that automatically generates the scale, intervals, and triads characteristic of that key. (In Chapters 6 and 10 we will explore ways in which the other five pitches may be employed as well.) Though it might seem daunting that each of eighteen keys possesses seven different triads, you should focus your attention on the fact that there are just seven possible triads in a major key, and seven in a minor key. (Of course, these triads may occur in higher or lower positions within music's range.) If you understand these fourteen triads (where they occur within a key, and the quality of each), you will be well equipped for the study of chord-building and harmony in future chapters.

To form a triad, proceed just as you have in preceding chapters, but now with more choices of key. Follow these steps (displayed for a iii triad in E♭ Major in Example 5-7):

- Draw the appropriate key signature on the staff. (For E♭ Major, this is the signature of three flats.)
- Ascend the scale until you reach the scale degree that corresponds to the Roman numeral. (For iii, we ascend to $\hat{3}$.)
- Add the triadic third and fifth to the root you just located.

Note that you do not need to worry about making a triad major, minor, or diminished. It is the key signature's task to determine what sharps or flats may be required so that the third and fifth sounded above the root result in a triad of the appropriate quality.

Example 5-7

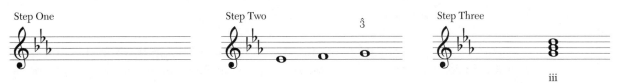

iii

To determine the appropriate Roman numeral for an existing triad, follow these steps (displayed in Example 5-8):

- Determine the key indicated by the key signature. Since every signature corresponds to two keys, you will be instructed whether to think in terms of major or minor; or, proceed in both keys.
- Measure the span between tonic and the triad's root, either by ascending from $\hat{1}$ or by descending from $\hat{8}$. You need to know the scale degree of the root.
- Convert the scale degree number into the appropriate Roman numeral, being careful when drawing the numeral to correctly indicate major, minor, or diminished quality. (Review Example 4-8.)

Example 5-8

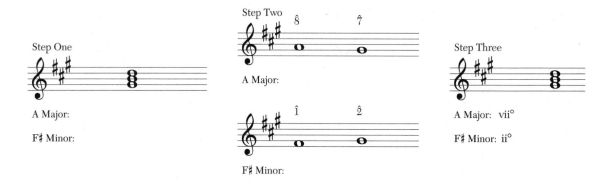

Though a key contains only seven triads, a far larger number of intervals can be formed. Some you know: $\hat{1}$ and $\hat{4}$ form a perfect fourth in both major and minor keys; $\hat{3}$ and $\hat{8}$ form a minor sixth in major keys and a major sixth in minor keys, for example. But what about $\hat{2}$ and $\hat{7}$? $\hat{4}$ and $\hat{6}$? Such questions will be addressed in Chapter 6.

Practice Exercises 5-4

Build the triads requested. Employ a key signature.

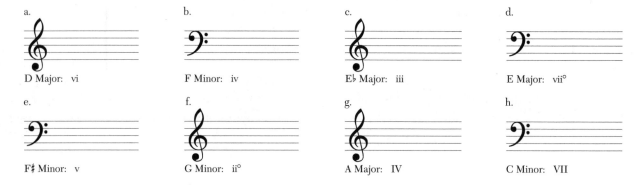

Indicate the appropriate Roman numeral for the following triads in the context of the major key indicated by the key signature. Remember that a capital Roman numeral is used for a major triad, a small numeral for a minor triad, and a small numeral followed by the degree symbol (°) for a diminished triad.

i.  j.  k.  l.

Indicate the appropriate Roman numeral for the following triads in the context of the minor key indicated by the key signature. Remember that a capital Roman numeral is used for a major triad, a small numeral for a minor triad, and a small numeral followed by the degree symbol (°) for a diminished triad.

m.  n.  o.  p.

Tips for Success

✔ Be careful to distinguish among keys with similar names. E Major is not the same as E Minor, or as E♭ Major. The first has four sharps in its signature, the second one sharp, and the third three flats.

✔ Devote some time each day to memorizing the key signatures introduced in this chapter, so that you have the ability to create a signature or name a key with no hesitation. A key-signature tutorial is provided on the CD-ROM.

✔ When you write a key signature on a staff, be very careful in the order and placement of the sharps or flats, and remember that the signatures in treble and bass clefs employ different lines and spaces.

✔ Thus far, we have explored nine of the twelve major keys, and nine of the twelve minor keys. The remaining keys are introduced in the Appendix entry "Keys with Five through Seven Sharps or Flats." Though your first priority needs to be mastering the twelve new keys introduced in this chapter, keep in mind that the remaining keys await you in the Appendix.

Upbeats and Repeats

RHYTHM

Not every melody begins on the first beat of a measure. In this chapter we encounter melodies that begin with an "upbeat"—that is, a note or notes that come before beat 1. We also introduce repeat signs, notation that tells performers to play a passage over again.

Downbeats and Upbeats

Melodies often begin on a ***downbeat***, the first beat of a measure. However, we are not restricted to this one choice. A melody may begin on any beat, or even between beats. Whatever precedes the first downbeat is called an ***upbeat***, or ***pickup***. Though

downbeat

upbeat

pickup

an upbeat often fills one beat, it may instead fill half a beat, two beats, or any other number of beats.

Compare the two numbering schemes provided for "She'll Be Comin' 'Round the Mountain" (Example 5-9). Which one seems to fit the melody better? Certainly the second one, which begins on "4." (Try them both: it will seem awkward to say "2" on the melody's strongest beats.)

Example 5-9

When an upbeat occurs, the label "measure 1" refers to the first complete measure of a melody, not to the upbeat. This convention is followed in Example 5-9. Observe that the last measure is shortened when there is an upbeat. As do measures 2 and 4 of Example 5-9, measure 8 employs a dotted half note, even though there would be room for a whole note in that case. Remember that this song has several verses. When you sing the second verse ("She'll be riding six white horses . . ."), you will again begin with an upbeat. It would make no sense to hold the last note of the verse for four beats preceding this upbeat. As a general rule, whatever time value serves as an upbeat before measure 1 is deleted from the final measure.

Repeats

repeat sign

It is very common for a segment of music—as little as a few measures, or as much as a hundred measures or more—to be repeated during performance. Though one could write all the notes out twice, it is more efficient to use a ***repeat sign***, which instructs performers to play a passage again. Three repeat signs are displayed in Example 5-10, along with an explanation of what they imply.

Example 5-10

‖: 　　Marks the starting point of a passage to be repeated. This symbol will generally be omitted if it would coincide with the opening of a composition.

:‖ 　　Marks the ending point of a passage to be repeated.

:‖: 　　Marks a point that is both the ending point of one passage to be repeated and the starting point of another passage to be repeated.

The waltz presented in Example 5-11 consists of two segments, both of which are to be repeated in performance. The first repeat sign, in the middle of measure 8, instructs the performer to go back *to the beginning* (since there is no other repeat sign instructing that a different point should begin the repeat), and to play the first eight measures a second time. The second repeat sign, at the end of the waltz, instructs the performer to go back to the middle of measure 8 and play the second half of the waltz again. Observe that since both segments of the waltz begin with an upbeat, the repeat signs occur after beat 2.

Example 5-11

Schubert: Waltz, Op. 77, No. 10 (D. 969)

Practice Exercises 5-5

a. The melody below employs repeat signs. Write the melody out in its full form on the staves provided.

Modify each last measure so that it contains the correct number of beats. Add counting syllables for both the upbeat measures and last measures.

Laboratory

L5-1. Play and Sing

a. Using four fingers of each hand, play ascending and descending scales in the following keys: C Natural Minor, C♯ Natural Minor, D Major, E♭ Major, E Major, F Natural Minor, F♯ Natural Minor, G Natural Minor, A♭ Major, A Major, B♭ Major, B Natural Minor.

b. Pick a major-key Roman numeral (I through vii°). Play that triad in C Major. Then play the triad with the same Roman numeral in D Major, E♭ Major, E Major, F Major, G Major, A♭ Major, A Major, and B♭ Major.

c. Pick a minor-key Roman numeral (i through VII). Play that triad in C Natural Minor. Then play the triad with the same Roman numeral in C♯ Natural Minor, D Natural Minor, E Natural Minor, F Natural Minor, F♯ Natural Minor, G Natural Minor, A Natural Minor, and B Natural Minor.

d. Pick a set of parallel keys: C Major/C Natural Minor; D Major/D Natural Minor; E Major/E Natural Minor; F Major/F Natural Minor; G Major/G Natural Minor; or A Major/A Natural Minor. Now play I in major and sing "Root-Third-Fifth," and then play i in minor and sing "Root-Third-Fifth." Next play and sing ii and ii°. Continue with iii and III, IV and iv, V and v, vi and VI, and vii° and VII. Remember that in three cases the root will not be the same for both triads. (For example, iii in C Major is E–G–B, whereas III in C Natural Minor is E♭–G–B♭.) Then repeat the exercise with other sets of parallel keys.

e. Play each of the triads below. After you play it, name the two keys that correspond to the given key signature and the Roman numeral that corresponds to the triad in each.

   SAMPLE: For 1, play the triad and then say "E♭ Major: IV (major four); C Minor: VI (major six)."

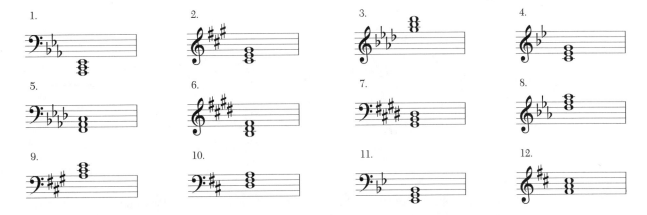

L5-2. Listening

Team up with another student, work with your instructor in class, or make use of the CD-ROM that accompanies this textbook to practice these exercises.

a. *Performer:* Place eight fingers above the eight keys corresponding to a major or a natural minor scale. Then play this scale, either ascending or descending.
   Listener: Indicate whether a major or a natural minor scale is performed.

b. *Performer:* Play a diminished triad. Then play another triad. Then repeat both.
   Listener: Given that the first triad is of diminished quality, indicate whether the second triad is also of diminished quality.

L5-3. Keyboard Album

a.

Schubert: Piano Sonata, D. 575, Op. post. 147, Mvmt. 3

b.

Mozart: *The Marriage of Figaro*, Act 1

c.

Mozart: Piano Sonata, K. 331, Mvmt. 3

d.

Schubert: Waltz, D. 146, Op. 127, No. 9, Trio

L5-4. Song Book

If you sing using letter names, it is now time to expand your vocabulary of singing syllables. Sing C♯ as "Cis," D♯ as "Dis," F♯ as "Fis," and G♯ as "Gis." Sing D♭ as "Des," E♭ as "Es," A♭ as "As," and B♭ as "Bes." For exercise c, sing "E | Gis Fis E | Dis Cis | B . . ." For exercise d, sing "Bes Bes Es Es | D C D . . ."

a.   Puccini: *Madama Butterfly*, Act 2

b.   The Ash Grove

The ash grove how grace - ful, how plain - ly 'tis speak - ing, The

harp thro' it play - ing has lan - guage for me.

c.   Schubert: Sonata for Violin and Piano, D. 574, Op. 162, Mvmt. 4

d.   Fauré: Requiem, Op. 48, Mvmt. 4

L5-5. Rhythm

a.

b.

c.

d.

e.

L5-6. Improvisation

a. In this improvisation, the hands alternate between two different configurations. In Configuration 1, the right hand covers the white-key notes from C to G, while the left hand covers the white-key notes from B to F. In Configuration 2, the relative minor is emphasized: the right hand covers the white-key notes from A to E, while the left hand covers the white-key notes from G to D. Create a melody, with a varied rhythm, according to the following plan:

Set hands in Configuration 1

measures 1 and 2:	right hand
measure 3:	left hand
measure 4:	right hand, ending on C
Repeat measures 1 through 4	

Switch hands to Configuration 2

measures 5 and 6:	right hand
measure 7:	left hand
measure 8:	right hand, ending on A
Repeat measures 5 through 8	

Switch hands to Configuration 1

measures 9 and 10:	right hand, the same as measures 1 and 2
measure 11:	left hand, the same as measure 3
measure 12:	right hand, C for the entire measure

b. Repeat exercise a for another pair of keys: F Major/D Natural Minor (with B♭) or G Major/E Natural Minor (with F♯).

   If you create a melody that especially pleases you, write it down, using repeat signs. Perhaps at your next class your instructor will put it on the board for the entire class to sing.

L5-7. Score Study

Listen to Selections 1, 3, 4, and 6 in the Scores for Music Analysis section at the back of the textbook. Then answer the questions under the "Chapter 5" headings that accompany these selections.

Name: _____

Instructor: _____

Date: _____

Pitch Exercises

P5-1. Fill in the blanks.

    °a. The key of D Natural Minor has a key signature of ____ flat(s), as does its relative major key, ____ Major. In contrast, its parallel major key, ____ Major, has a key signature of ____ sharp(s).

    b. The key of ____ Natural Minor has a key signature of 3 sharps, as does its relative major key, ____ Major.

    c. The key of C Natural Minor has a key signature of ____ flat(s), as does its relative major key, ____ Major. In contrast, its parallel major key, ____ Major, has a key signature of _____.

    d. The key of ____ Natural Minor has a key signature of ____ sharp(s), as does its relative major key, G Major. In contrast, its parallel major key, ____ Major, has a key signature of ____ sharp(s).

    e. The key of ____ Natural Minor has a key signature of no sharps or flats, as does its relative major key, ____ Major. In contrast, its parallel major key, ____ Major, has a key signature of ____ sharp(s).

    f. The key of ____ Natural Minor has a key signature of ____ flat(s), as does its relative major key, ____ Major. In contrast, its parallel major key, G Major, has a key signature of ____ sharp(s).

    g. The key of ____ Natural Minor has a key signature of ____ flat(s), as does its relative major key, ____ Major. In contrast, its parallel major key, ____ Major, has a key signature of 1 flat.

P5-2. If the given pitch is a scale degree in the key indicated, write down its scale degree number. Otherwise, leave that blank empty. Some pitches are diatonic in many of these keys, while others are diatonic in only a few of these keys.

	°1.	°2.	3.	4.	5.
D Major:	____	____	____	____	____
G Minor:	____	____	____	____	____
A Major:	____	____	____	____	____
C Minor:	____	____	____	____	____
E Major:	____	____	____	____	____
F Minor:	____	____	____	____	____

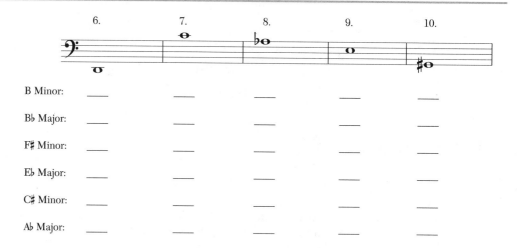

	6.	7.	8.	9.	10.
B Minor:	___	___	___	___	___
Bb Major:	___	___	___	___	___
F# Minor:	___	___	___	___	___
Eb Major:	___	___	___	___	___
C# Minor:	___	___	___	___	___
Ab Major:	___	___	___	___	___

P5-3. Build the triads requested. First add a key signature. Then add the three notes of the triad.

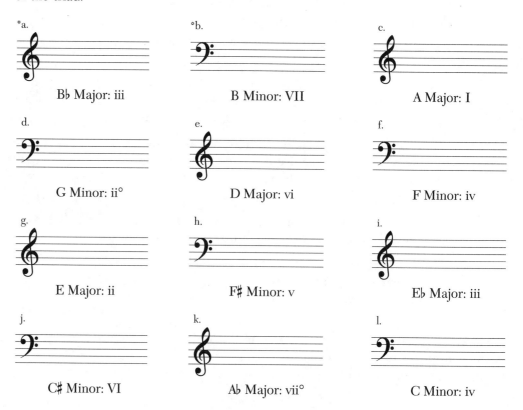

°a.

Bb Major: iii

°b.

B Minor: VII

c.

A Major: I

d.

G Minor: ii°

e.

D Major: vi

f.

F Minor: iv

g.

E Major: ii

h.

F# Minor: v

i.

Eb Major: iii

j.

C# Minor: VI

k.

Ab Major: vii°

l.

C Minor: iv

P5-4. For each triad, name the major key indicated by the key signature and supply the appropriate Roman numeral for that context. Then name the natural minor key indicated by the same key signature, and supply the appropriate Roman numeral for that context. Remember to distinguish the triad quality by the way you write the numeral (capital for major, small for minor, and small followed by a degree circle for diminished).

°a.

°b.

c.

Name: _____

Instructor: _____

Date: _____

Rhythm Exercises

R5-1. Modify the time value of the last notehead in each of the following rhythms so that it represents the correct number of beats. Keep in mind how an upbeat affects the last measure.

R5-2. Create the melodies indicated by the positioning of the pitch names in relation to the counting numbers. From one note to the next, use only a unison, second, third, or fourth as a melodic interval. Do not add rests.

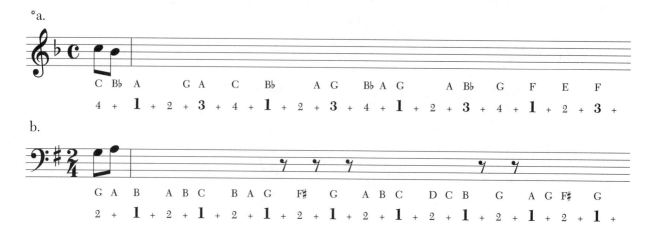

Audio Exercises

A5-1. A succession of eight pitches, ascending or descending, is performed. Identify it as a major or natural minor scale.

*a.	Major	Natural Minor	f.	Major	Natural Minor
*b.	Major	Natural Minor	g.	Major	Natural Minor
c.	Major	Natural Minor	h.	Major	Natural Minor
d.	Major	Natural Minor	i.	Major	Natural Minor
e.	Major	Natural Minor	j.	Major	Natural Minor

A5-2. Two triads are performed. The first triad is a diminished triad. Is the second triad a diminished triad also?

*a.	Yes	No	f.	Yes	No
*b.	Yes	No	g.	Yes	No
c.	Yes	No	h.	Yes	No
d.	Yes	No	i.	Yes	No
e.	Yes	No	j.	Yes	No

A5-3. Circle the music notation that corresponds to the pitches performed.

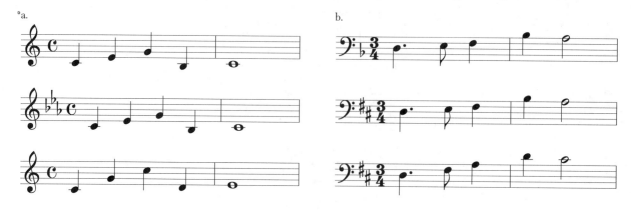

Name: _____

Instructor: _____

Date: _____

A5-4. Circle the music notation that corresponds to the rhythm performed.

CHAPTER 6

PITCH

Five Interval Qualities

An interval's size depends solely on the distance between its two noteheads. Placing an A above C forms a sixth no matter what accidentals modify these noteheads. To account for the subtle shifts created by accidentals, an interval's name includes a designation of quality. For example, A above C is a major sixth, whereas A♭ above C is a minor sixth. In this chapter we carefully consider the effect of five accidentals—sharp, flat, natural, double sharp, and double flat—on interval quality. Intervals may be major, minor, perfect, augmented, or diminished in quality. Some of these qualities result from employing a chromatic pitch, one not indicated in the key signature. For example, in C Major the pitch C♯ is a chromatic pitch.

Creating Intervals of Major, Minor, or Perfect Quality

Our study of intervals in recent chapters has focused on those that are formed using $\hat{1}$ or $\hat{8}$ in a major or minor key. These intervals are always of major, minor, or perfect quality, as Examples 2-5 and 4-7 reveal. In compact form, that information can be stated as follows:

$\hat{1}$–$\hat{1}$, $\hat{1}$–$\hat{4}$, $\hat{1}$–$\hat{5}$, and $\hat{1}$–$\hat{8}$ are of perfect quality in all keys.

$\hat{1}$–$\hat{2}$ is of major quality in all keys.

$\hat{1}$–$\hat{3}$, $\hat{1}$–$\hat{6}$, and $\hat{1}$–$\hat{7}$ are of major quality in major keys, and minor quality in minor keys.

$\hat{1}$–$\hat{8}$, $\hat{4}$–$\hat{8}$, $\hat{5}$–$\hat{8}$, and $\hat{8}$–$\hat{8}$ are of perfect quality in all keys.

$\hat{2}$–$\hat{8}$ is of minor quality in all keys.

$\hat{3}$–$\hat{8}$, $\hat{6}$–$\hat{8}$, and $\hat{7}$–$\hat{8}$ are of minor quality in major keys, and major quality in minor keys.

Now that we have learned eighteen keys, we know at least one key whose tonic corresponds to each of the twelve pitches within the octave: C Major, C Minor, C♯ Minor, D Major, D Minor, E♭ Major, etc. Their key signatures are potent tools that we can call upon when forming intervals. For example, suppose we want to create the interval of a minor sixth above F (Example 6-1a). By counting lines and spaces we find that the notehead used to form an interval of *size six* with F is D (Example 6-1b). Yet that is not sufficient. We know three pitches that employ that notehead: D♭, D, and D♯. Which of these pitches forms a sixth of *minor quality* above F? Thinking about $\hat{1}$–$\hat{6}$ in both major and minor keys, we realize that only in a minor key is the interval from $\hat{1}$ to $\hat{6}$ of minor quality. So we make F tonic in F Minor (employing its four-flat signature), ascend the scale to $\hat{6}$, and discover that the minor sixth above F is D♭ (Example 6-1c). Since the context of our original question did not include a key signature, we place a flat to the left of the D notehead for our answer (Example 6-1d).

Example 6-1

a. *Create a minor sixth above F* b. *The correct notehead is D* c. F Minor

$\hat{1}$–$\hat{6}$ in F Minor *forms a minor sixth*

d. *The minor sixth above F is D♭*

Now let's create the interval of a minor third below E (Example 6-2a). By counting lines and spaces we find that the notehead used to form an interval of *size three* with E is C (Example 6-2b). We know two pitches that employ that notehead: C and C♯. Which of these pitches forms a third of *minor quality* below E? Thinking about $\hat{8}$–$\hat{6}$ in both major and minor keys, we realize that only in a major key is the interval from $\hat{8}$ to $\hat{6}$ of minor quality. So we make E tonic in E Major (employing its four-sharp signature), descend the scale to $\hat{6}$, and discover that the minor third below E is C♯ (Example 6-2c). Since the context of our original question did not include a key signature, we place a sharp to the left of the C notehead for our answer (Example 6-2d).

Example 6-2

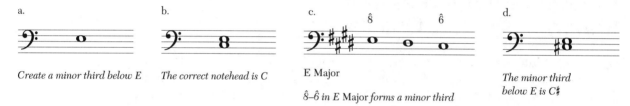

a. *Create a minor third below E* b. *The correct notehead is C* c. E Major

$\hat{8}$–$\hat{6}$ in E Major *forms a minor third*

d. *The minor third below E is C♯*

In some cases there are two ways to find an interval. For example, the perfect fourth below C is G whether one descends $\hat{8}$–$\hat{5}$ in C Major (C–B–A–G) or in C Minor (C–B♭–A♭–G). A few intervals cannot be created using this method, given the keys you have learned thus far. For example, finding the major third above B requires the key of B Major. You may either take the time now to learn those additional keys (presented in the Appendix) or you may find a closely related interval and modify it: for example, you know that the *minor* third above B is D (B Minor: $\hat{1}$–$\hat{3}$). Since a major interval is always one half step larger than a minor interval of the same size, the major third above B is D♯.

Practice Exercises 6-1

Create the intervals requested. A work area is provided to the right of each question. Use it to draw in a key signature and ascend the appropriate scale (major or natural minor), as in Example 6-1 above.

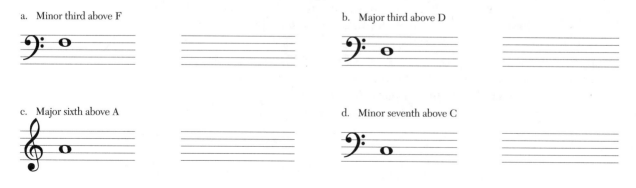

a. Minor third above F

b. Major third above D

c. Major sixth above A

d. Minor seventh above C

e. Major second above E

f. Perfect fifth above F♯

Create the intervals requested. A work area is provided to the right of each question. Use it to draw in a key signature and descend the appropriate scale (major or natural minor), as in Example 6-2 above.

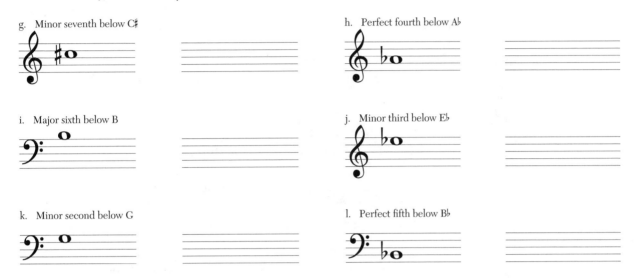

g. Minor seventh below C♯

h. Perfect fourth below A♭

i. Major sixth below B

j. Minor third below E♭

k. Minor second below G

l. Perfect fifth below B♭

Naming Intervals

In some music fundamentals textbooks, the precise naming of intervals is accomplished through a laborious and unmusical process of counting half steps. For example, the pitches E and C♯, shown in Example 6-3a, form a sixth. It is easy to see that the interval is a sixth, because six lines and spaces separate the noteheads. But is the sixth major or minor? One *could* answer that question by consulting a keyboard diagram and counting the nine half steps, characteristic of the major sixth, between E and C♯. But it is more musical, and in the long run simpler, to assess these pitches within the context of a key. Examples 6-3b and 6-3c display $\hat{1}$–$\hat{6}$ in E Major and in E Minor. Clearly, C♯ occurs in the context of E Major, not E Minor. Since $\hat{1}$–$\hat{6}$ forms a major sixth in any major key, the interval from E up to C♯ is a major sixth.

Example 6-3

E and C♯ may form an interval in other keys as well. For example, in D Major, E is $\hat{2}$ and C♯ is $\hat{7}$. Even in this context, the interval formed is a major sixth. Instead of memorizing the intervals of all possible combinations of scale degrees ($\hat{2}$–$\hat{3}$, $\hat{2}$–$\hat{4}$, $\hat{2}$–$\hat{5}$, etc.) characteristic of both major and natural minor keys, we can assess an interval's quality by following the procedure of Example 6-3. That is, think of one of the interval's pitches as if it were tonic (even if, in its context, it does not function as tonic) and use the information we already know about the intervals formed above $\hat{1}$ or below $\hat{8}$ in any major or natural minor key. With eighteen keys now at our disposal, this method is very powerful.

In practice, it is not even necessary to find an exact match when using this method for naming intervals. For example, to identify the interval formed by D and B♭ (Example 6-4a), we may compare this "unknown" with the "known" interval formed by $\hat{1}$ and $\hat{6}$ in D *Major* (Example 6-4b). Since the span between D and B♭ is one half step smaller than that between D and B, which we know forms a major sixth, D and B♭ form a minor sixth, because a minor interval is always one half step smaller than a major interval of the same size. Had we chosen D *Minor* for our "known," we would have gotten the answer more quickly, since $\hat{1}$ and $\hat{6}$ in D Minor are D and B♭. The point is, however, that one does not need to be careful in choosing between D Major and D Minor for the "known." One can attain the correct interval quality via either route.

Example 6-4

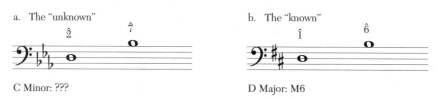

a. The "unknown"

C Minor: ???

b. The "known"

D Major: M6

Practice Exercises 6-2

Name each interval, including both quality and size. A work area is provided to the right of each question. Use it to draw in an interval that employs the same note-heads and whose quality and size you know. (Include an appropriate key signature.) Then compare the unknown with the known to determine the quality and size of the given interval, as in Example 6-4.

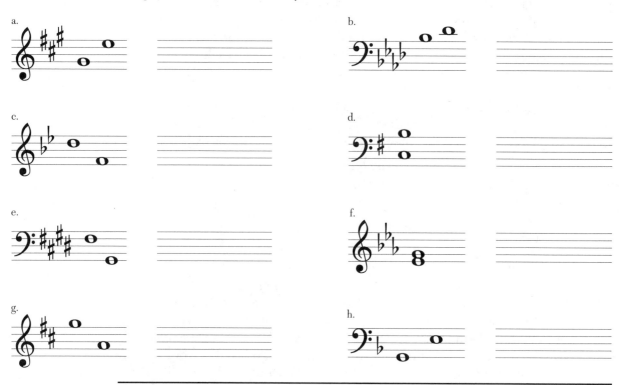

Chromatic Pitches

A whole step contains two half steps. Since there are five whole steps within any major or natural minor scale, composers have numerous opportunities to substitute two consecutive half-step motions for a single whole-step motion. These intervening pitches, the **chromatic** pitches, add an exotic flavor to a melody. Because a key signature generates only diatonic pitches, the staff notation and name of each chromatic pitch will include an accidental: a sharp (♯), a flat (♭), a *natural* (♮), a *double sharp* (𝄪), or a *double flat* (♭♭). The effect of each symbol is displayed in Example 6-5.

chromatic

natural

double sharp

double flat

Example 6-5

A sharp raises a white-key pitch by a half step:

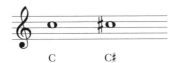

A flat lowers a white-key pitch by a half step:

A natural cancels the effect of a key signature's sharp or flat, *raising* a flat pitch or *lowering* a sharp pitch by a half step:

A double sharp *raises* a sharp pitch by a half-step:

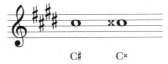

A double flat *lowers* a flat pitch by a half-step:

"While Strolling Through the Park One Day" (Example 6-6) is a fun melody in part because it contains numerous chromatic pitches. They are used both as **chromatic passing notes** (CP), connecting two consecutive diatonic pitches (such as B–B♯–C♯), and as **chromatic neighboring notes** (CN), embellishing a single diatonic pitch (such as B–A♯–B). Observe that notes with accidentals may correspond to white keys on the piano: B♯, one half step higher than B, is the same piano key as C; while C𝄪, one half step higher than C♯, is the same piano key as D. By convention, once an accidental appears, it holds force until the next bar line. If one wants the diatonic pitch later in the measure, the original key signature must be restored. (In measure 7, the ♮♯ symbol first cancels the double sharp and then restores the key signature's sharp.)

chromatic passing notes

chromatic neighboring notes

Example 6-6

"While Strolling Through the Park One Day"

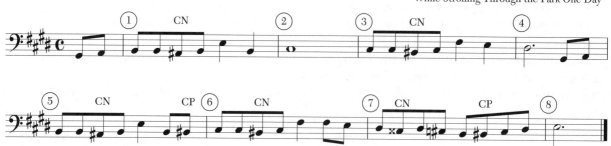

Practice Exercises 6-3

a. Every pitch used in music has multiple names, each of which is appropriate in certain contexts. For example, the A Major scale employs C♯ as 3̂, while the A♭ Major scale employs D♭ (which sounds the same as C♯) as 4̂. In the keyboard diagram below, the most common names for the white keys are written in. Inside the key one half step to the right of each of these starting keys, write in the names B♯, C♯, D♯, E♯, F♯, G♯, A♯, B♯, C♯, and D♯. (Most of these keys will be black, but some will be white.) Inside the key one half step to the left of each of these starting keys, write in the names B♭, C♭, D♭, E♭, F♭, G♭, A♭, B♭, C♭, and D♭. (Most of these keys will be black, but some will be white.) Carefully study what you have accomplished to this point. Then proceed one half step to the right and to the left of the keys you just labeled, using the names B𝄪, C𝄪, D𝄪, E𝄪, F𝄪, G𝄪, A𝄪, B𝄪, C𝄪, and D𝄪, and B♭♭, C♭♭, D♭♭, E♭♭, F♭♭, G♭♭, A♭♭, B♭♭, C♭♭, and D♭♭.

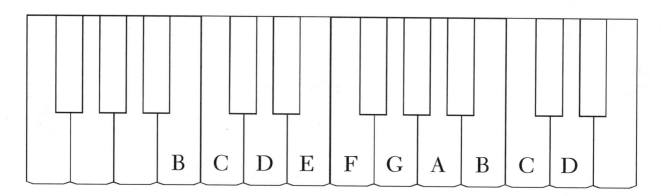

Place the appropriate accidental to the left of each notehead, so that it corresponds to the marked key on the keyboard.

b.

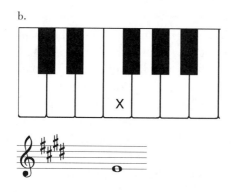

c.

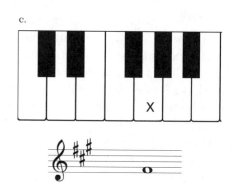

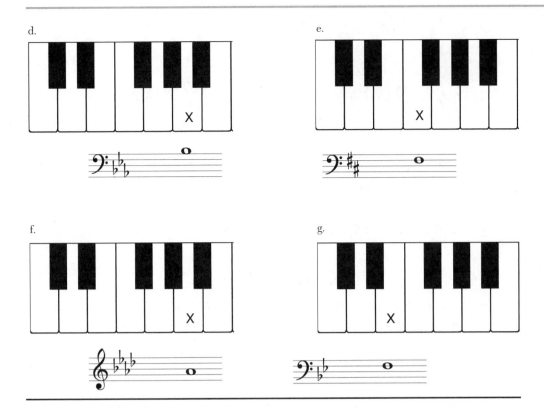

Chromatic Intervals

Chromaticism not only occurs in solo melodies, but may also arise when several pitches sound simultaneously, in which case an uncommon harmonic interval may be formed. In Example 6-7a, a chromatic passing note connects $\hat{2}$ and $\hat{3}$ in C Major. D forms a perfect fifth against the G below it. When D♯ arises, the interval with G becomes an ***augmented*** fifth. Any augmented interval is one half step larger than the perfect or major interval of the same size. In fact, since G, B, and D♯ sound simultaneously, the combination could be called an ***augmented triad.***

In Example 6-7b, a chromatic passing note connects $\hat{4}$ and $\hat{5}$, forming a diminished fifth with C. Though we have encountered this interval before (for example, in the vii° triad in major keys), it does not arise against the tonic pitch unless chromaticism is employed. Any diminished interval is one half step smaller than the perfect or minor interval of the same size. In this case, since the *lower* pitch of the interval is raised, the distance between the two pitches becomes smaller, and thus the interval's quality is diminished. All augmented and diminished intervals are classified as dissonant.

In Example 6-7c, two chromatic passing notes occur simultaneously: while F♯ connects $\hat{4}$ and $\hat{5}$ melodically, A♭ connects $\hat{6}$ and $\hat{5}$ melodically. The resulting harmonic interval is an augmented sixth. If an augmented interval is one half step larger than a major interval, then it is two half steps larger than a minor interval. Here, the minor sixth $\begin{smallmatrix}F\\A\end{smallmatrix}$ is transformed into the augmented sixth $\begin{smallmatrix}F♯\\A♭\end{smallmatrix}$.

augmented

augmented triad

Example 6-7

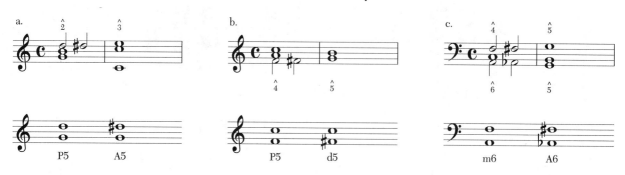

Example 6-8 displays the relationships among all the basic interval qualities.

Example 6-8

To identify or form intervals that contain chromatic pitches, first assess the interval without any chromatic accidentals (following the strategy presented earlier in this chapter). Then use the information of Example 6-8 to determine how any accidentals modify the situation. For example, to identify the interval in Example 6-9a, first think about the diatonic interval formed without any chromatic accidentals (Example 6-9b). That is a minor seventh. (Think about Î to 7̂ in C♯ Minor, as in Example 6-9c.) Since the B♭ of Example 6-9a makes the interval one half step smaller, the interval is a diminished seventh (Example 6-9d).

Example 6-9

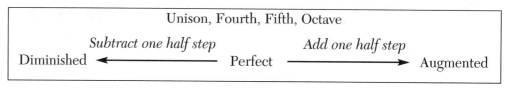

To form an augmented fifth above B (Example 6-10a), first form a perfect fifth (thinking about Î to 5̂ in B Natural Minor). As Example 6-10b reveals, B and F♯ form a perfect fifth. Then, following Example 6-8, we raise the F♯ by one half step to form an augmented fifth. That pitch is F𝗑 (Example 6-10c).

Example 6-10

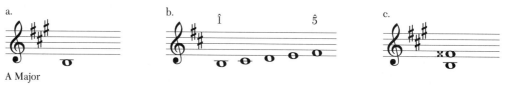

Practice Exercises 6-4

Name each interval. First remove any accidentals that make the interval chromatic. Then assess the quality of the diatonic interval, using the method of Practice Exercises 6-2. (A work area is provided.) Then determine how the chromatic accidental(s) modify the interval's quality.

Name this interval.   First remove the chromatic accidental(s).   Then determine the size and quality of the diatonic interval (as in Practice Exercises 6-2).   Now name the chromatic interval.

Create the intervals requested. For all augmented intervals, first create the major or perfect interval of the same size, and then expand by one half step. For all diminished intervals, first create the minor or perfect interval of the same size, and then contract by one half step.

g. Create an A5 above D.   First create a P5 above D (as in Practice Exercises 6-1).   Then expand into an A5.

h. Create a d7 below B♭.

First create a m7 below B♭ (as in Practice Exercises 6-1).

Then contract into a d7.

i. Create an A6 above G.

First create a M6 above G (as in Practice Exercises 6-1).

Then expand into an A6.

j. Create an A4 below F.

First create a P4 below F (as in Practice Exercises 6-1).

Then expand into an A4.

k. Create a d7 above E♭.

First create a M7 above E♭ (as in Practice Exercises 6-1).°
° We know only one key with tonic E♭—E♭ Major. So start with its M7, and then subtract *two* half steps to find d7.

Then contract into a d7.

l. Create a d5 below C♯.

First create a P5 below C♯ (as in Practice Exercises 6-1).

Then contract into a d5.

Tips for Success

✔ If you have not yet mastered the eighteen key signatures introduced thus far, you will flounder in this chapter. Make it your first priority to review these signatures. In the discussion of Example 6-1, for example, you should have the F Major and F Minor key signatures flashing in your mind, and it should be apparent instantly that D♭ occurs in the F Minor signature, not the F Major signature.

✔ A double sharp may occur only when a pitch is already sharp from the key signature. Likewise, a double flat may occur only when a pitch is already flat from the key signature.

✔ Pay close attention to the procedure you use to solve each problem type. There are several steps involved. Know what to do first, second, third. Know how the procedure changes when you're dealing with a chromatic interval, as compared with a diatonic interval.

✔ Just as all the diatonic pitches of a key can be assembled into a major or natural minor scale, the combination of all diatonic and chromatic pitches can be assembled into a chromatic scale. These scales are introduced in the Appendix.

Compound Meters

Not all meters divide the beat into two parts. In this chapter we explore a family of meters whose beats contain three parts rather than two. When performing these meters, we will count "1 and uh . . ." rather than "1 and . . .".

Simple versus Compound Meter

Though the $\frac{2}{4}$, $\frac{3}{4}$, and $\frac{4}{4}$ meters each contain a different number of beats per measure, these beats share a basic characteristic: they subdivide into halves. We use two eighth notes to fill a quarter-note beat, or a dotted quarter note followed by an eighth note to fill two beats. Because their beats subdivide into halves, $\frac{2}{4}$, $\frac{3}{4}$, and $\frac{4}{4}$ are classified as ***simple meters.***

In ***compound meters***, beats subdivide into thirds rather than into halves. The most common compound meters are $\frac{6}{8}$, $\frac{9}{8}$, and $\frac{12}{8}$, containing two, three, and four beats per measure, respectively. In each case, *three* eighth notes fill a beat. In $\frac{6}{8}$ meter, a measure can hold two groups of three eighth notes (six eighth notes); in $\frac{9}{8}$ meter, a measure can hold three such groups (nine eighth notes); and in $\frac{12}{8}$ meter, a measure can hold four such groups (twelve eighth notes). Example 6-11 compares these compound meters with their simple counterparts and displays how we will count them. The syllables "one and" fill a beat in simple meter, while the syllables "one and uh" fill a beat in compound meter. Observe that measures in both $\frac{3}{4}$ and $\frac{6}{8}$ meter are filled by six eighth notes. In $\frac{3}{4}$, there are three groups of two eighth notes, while in $\frac{6}{8}$ there are two groups of three eighth notes. Beginning each beat with a new beam will remind us of how these two meters differ.

simple meters

compound meters

Example 6-11

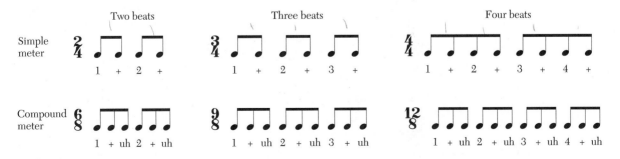

RHYTHM

Filling One Beat in a Compound Meter

What note values can combine to fill a beat in a compound meter? We will often use three eighth notes, or a quarter note followed by an eighth note. These possibilities are emphasized in Example 6-12a. Since three eighth notes fill a beat, so does a dotted quarter note (which in a simple meter exceeds the value of a beat). Example 6-12b displays its use. That example also contains rests. Both quarter and eighth rests are employed in compound meters. In general, use eighth rests to fill in any part of a beat not occupied by a note (for example, ♪𝄾𝄾). Use a quarter rest only when the first two eighths of a beat contain silence (𝄽𝄾 or 𝄽♪ ; never ♪𝄽). Observe that the syllable "uh" is employed for an upbeat consisting of a single eighth note.

Example 6-12

Example 6-12 (continued — image a. Mendelssohn: Song without Words, Op. 19, No. 6; b. Puccini: *Tosca*, Act 1)

It is important to study carefully how measures in the various meters are filled, as demonstrated in Example 6-11. In compound meters, two eighth notes may be combined to form a quarter note, and three eighth notes (a full beat) may be combined to form a dotted quarter note. For a note that lasts for two beats in a compound meter (that is, the combination of two dotted quarter notes), a dotted half note is employed. These relationships are displayed in music notation in Example 6-13.

Example 6-13

Practice Exercises 6-5

Add counting syllables (1 + uh, etc.) to the following melodies. Then perform them.

Each measure below contains a notational error. Rewrite each measure, making an appropriate correction.

Tips for Success

✔ When writing in the counting syllables, think in two phases: (1) where are the beats? and (2) how are the beats subdivided? It may be best to save the upbeat, if present, for last, so that you can see how all the other measures appear and especially what is missing from the last measure.

✔ The notation of rests is idiosyncratic. In some case we do things a certain way simply because that is what has been done for the last several hundred years. Pay attention to the guidelines provided, and be observant when performing music with rests to get accustomed to these conventions.

✔ The Conducting Patterns displayed in the Appendix are suitable for compound meters as well as for simple meters.

ACTIVITIES

Laboratory

L6-1. Play and Sing

a. In this exercise you sing three different ascending fifths: perfect, diminished, and augmented.

- Play a pitch low in your vocal range, and then sing it. Then play the pitch a perfect fifth higher than the starting pitch, and then sing it.
- Now modify the upper pitch so that a diminished fifth results. Play and sing both pitches.
- Then play and sing the perfect fifth again.
- Then modify the upper pitch so that an augmented fifth results. Play and sing both pitches.

Repeat this exercise for other pitches low in your vocal range.

b. Repeat exercise a, this time creating diminished/perfect/augmented fourths and octaves, and diminished/minor/major/augmented seconds, thirds, sixths, and sevenths. Note: The diminished second (e.g., C–D♭♭) sounds the same as a unison!

c. In this exercise you sing three different descending fifths: perfect, diminished, and augmented.

- Play a pitch high in your vocal range, and then sing it. Then play the pitch a perfect fifth lower than the starting pitch, and then sing it.
- Now modify the lower pitch so that a diminished fifth results. Play and sing both pitches.
- Then play and sing the perfect fifth again.
- Then modify the lower pitch so that an augmented fifth results. Play and sing both pitches.

Repeat this exercise for other pitches high in your vocal range.

d. Repeat exercise c, this time creating diminished/perfect/augmented fourths and octaves, and diminished/minor/major/augmented seconds, thirds, sixths, and sevenths.

e. Play each of the intervals below. After you play it, name it (major third, diminished seventh, etc.).

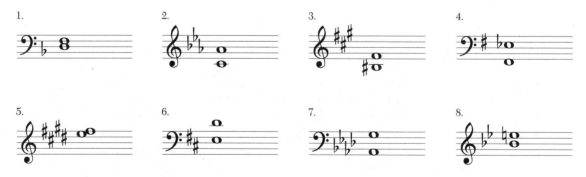

L6-2. Listening

Team up with another student, work with your instructor in class, or make use of the CD-ROM that accompanies this textbook to practice these exercises.

a. *Performer:* Play an interval, either ascending or descending. Name this interval by quality and size. Then play again, modifying one of the interval's two pitches by one half step. (For example, play C up to A, say "Major sixth," then play C♯ up to A.)

Listener: Indicate the quality of the modified interval.

b. *Performer:* Play a major, minor, or diminished triad.

   Listener: Indicate the triad's quality: major, minor, or diminished.

L6-3. Keyboard Album

L6-4. Song Book

b.   Wing-Tra-La

One love-ly Sun-day eve-ning, walk-ing a-long the way,

There was a fine young fel-low do-ing the ver-y same.

c.   Paddy Works on the Railroad

In eight-een hun-dred and for-ty one, I put my cord'-roy breech-es on. I

put my cord'-roy breech-es on To work up-on the rail-way.

d.   Haydn: Symphony No. 99, Mvmt. 1

e.   Beautiful Dreamer

Beau-ti-ful dream-er, wake un-to me Star-light and dew-drops are wait-ing for

thee. Sounds of the rude world heard in the day

Lulled by the moon-light have all passed a-way.

L6-5. Rhythm

a.

b.

c.

d.

e.

L6-6. Improvisation

a. Mix and match the various one-measure segments provided below to create an eight-measure melody in the key of C Major and $\frac{6}{8}$ meter.

Measures 1–4, measure 7   Measures 5–6   Measure 8

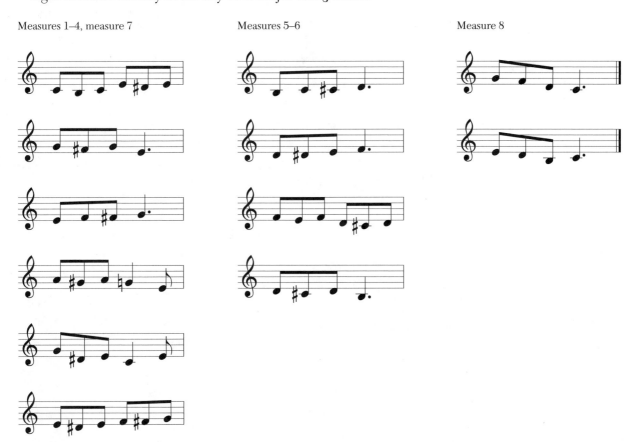

b. Use the segments of exercise L6-6a to create a sixteen-measure melody, freely going back and forth between the first two columns, and closing with a segment from the third column.

L6-7. Score Study

Listen to Selections 1, 2, 3, 4, 6, and 7 in the Scores for Music Analysis section at the back of the textbook. Then answer the questions under the "Chapter 6" headings that accompany these selections.

Name: _____

Instructor: _____

Date: _____

Pitch Exercises

P6-1. Create the diatonic intervals requested. Follow the procedure employed in Practice Exercises 6-1. Staves are provided for this purpose.

°a.   M2 above A♭ is _____

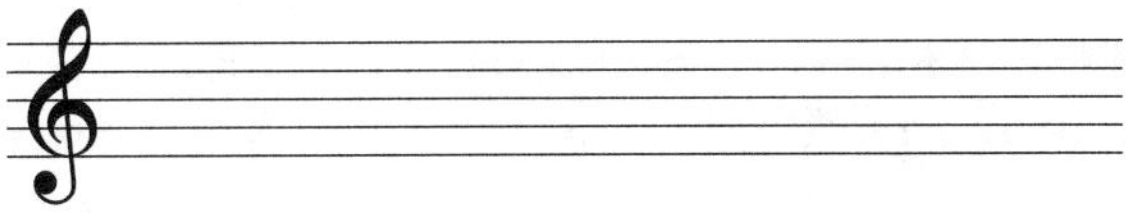

°b.   m3 above A is _____

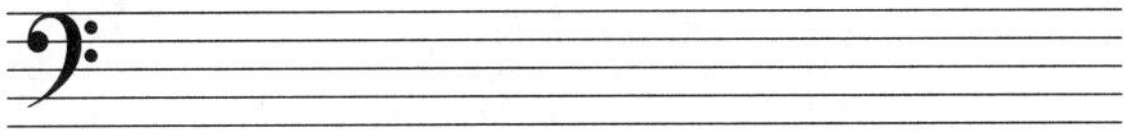

c.   P4 below B♭ is _____

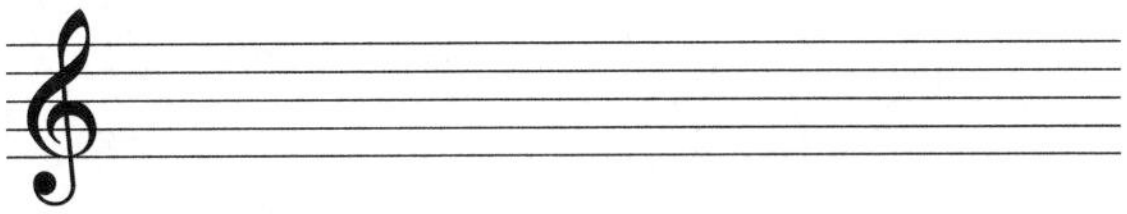

d.   M6 below C is _____

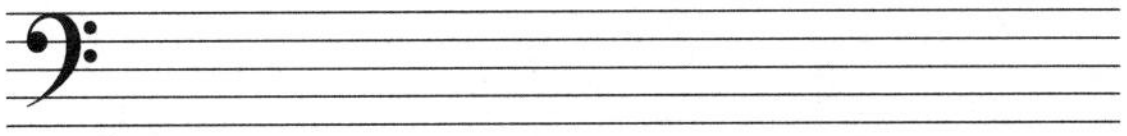

e.   m6 above C is _____

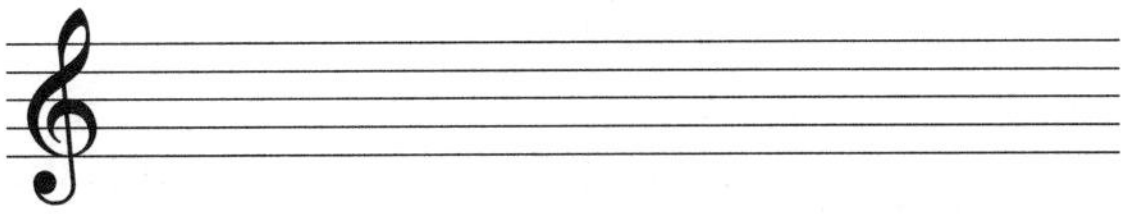

f.   m7 above C♯ is _____

g.   m7 below D is _____

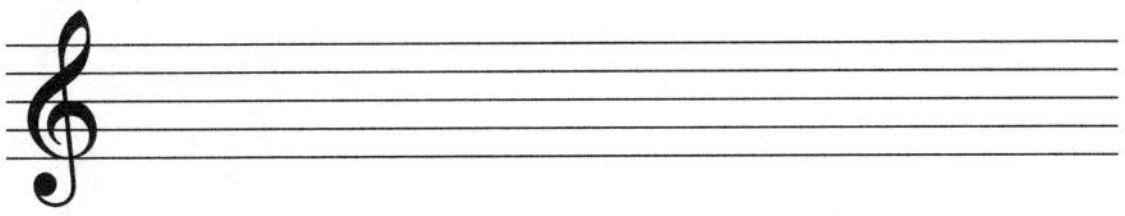

h.   m6 below E♭ is _____

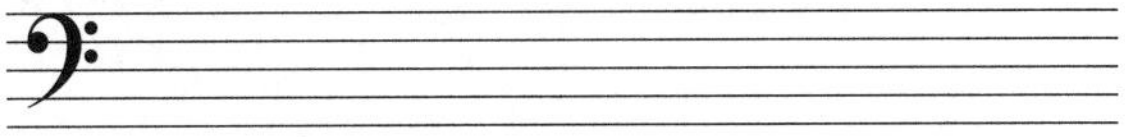

i.   P5 above E is _____

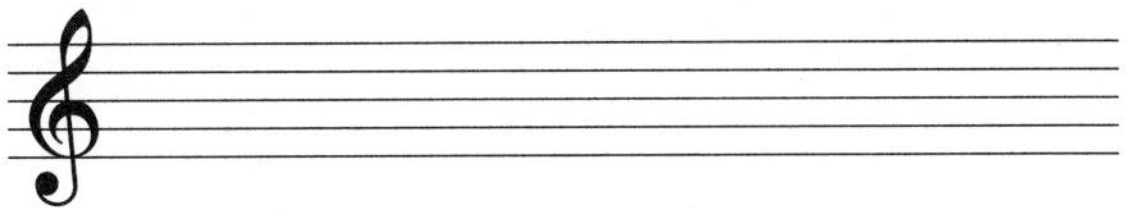

j.   M2 below G is _____

k.   M3 below F♯ is _____

l.   m3 below A is _____

P6-2. Indicate each interval's quality and size (M3, P5, etc.). Follow the procedure employed in Practice Exercises 6-2. Staves are provided for this purpose.

P6-3. Modify the given notehead by the appropriate accidental, so that it corresponds to the key marked on the keyboard diagram.

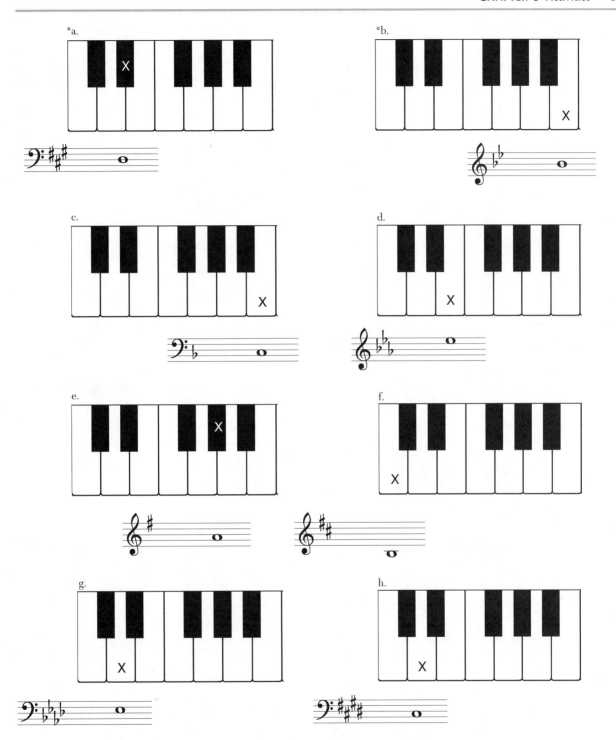

P6-4. Indicate each chromatic interval's quality and size (M3, P5, etc.). Follow the procedure employed in Practice Exercises 6-4 (a through f). Staves are provided for this purpose.

°a.

P6-5. Create the chromatic intervals requested. Follow the procedure employed in Practice Exercises 6-4 (g through l). Staves are provided for this purpose.

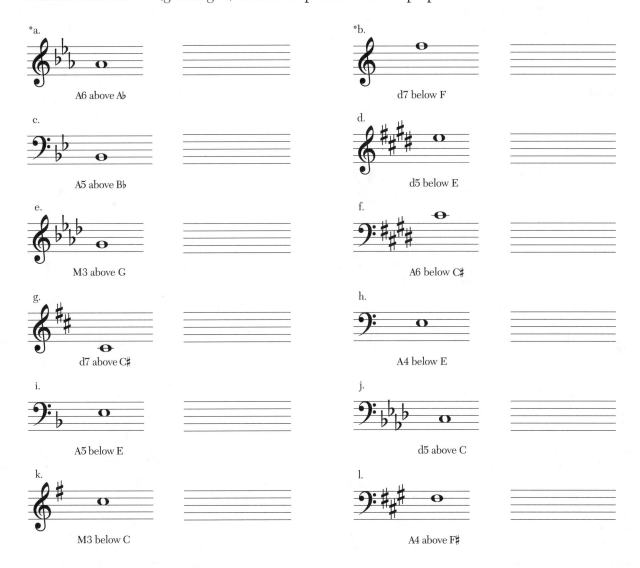

°a. A6 above A♭

°b. d7 below F

c. A5 above B♭

d. d5 below E

e. M3 above G

f. A6 below C♯

g. d7 above C♯

h. A4 below E

i. A5 below E

j. d5 above C

k. M3 below C

l. A4 above F♯

Rhythm Exercises

R6-1. Modify the noteheads indicated by arrows to form measures containing the appropriate number of beats. Wherever possible, incorporate the existing beam notation.

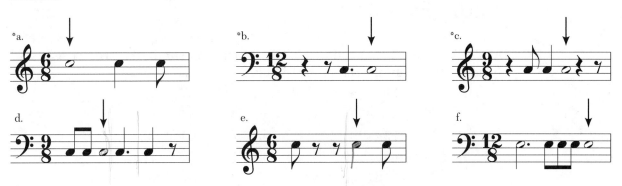

°a.

°b.

°c.

d.

e.

f.

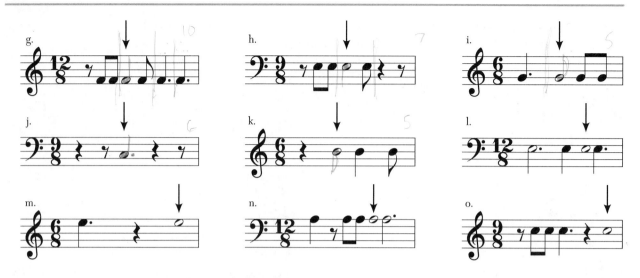

R6-2. Create the melodies indicated by the positioning of the pitch names in relation to the counting numbers. From one note to the next, use only a unison, second, third, or fourth as a melodic interval. Do not add rests.

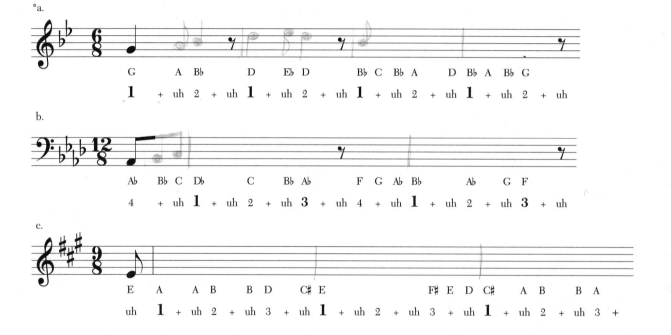

Audio Exercises

A6-1. Two intervals are performed. The quality and size of the first are indicated. Indicate the quality and size of the second.

*a.	M6:	m6	A6		f.	M3:	m3	A3
*b.	m7:	d7	M7		g.	M7:	m7	A7
c.	P5:	d5	A5		h.	m3:	d3	M3
d.	m6:	d6	M6		i.	P4:	d4	A4
e.	M2:	m2	A2		j.	m2:	d2	M2

A6-2. A triad is performed. Indicate its quality.

*a. Major   Minor   Diminished   f. Major   Minor   Diminished

*b. Major   Minor   Diminished   g. Major   Minor   Diminished

  c. Major   Minor   Diminished   h. Major   Minor   Diminished

  d. Major   Minor   Diminished   i. Major   Minor   Diminished

  e. Major   Minor   Diminished   j. Major   Minor   Diminished

A6-3. Circle the music notation that corresponds to the pitches performed.

A6-4. Circle the music notation that corresponds to the rhythm performed.

c.

d.

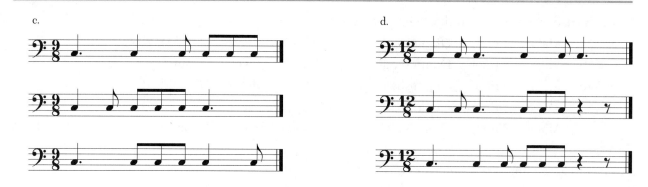

PRACTICE MIDCOURSE EXAM

A Practice Midcourse Examination appears on the pages that follow. Complete this exam in an uninterrupted fifty-minute time period. You will need your CD-ROM for the listening questions, which will be performed twice each.

Do not consult any other section of your textbook when completing the exam. You will need to know from memory such concepts as note names in treble and bass clefs, key signatures, interval and triad qualities, and so on. Though the exam questions for the most part resemble homework exercises, they are stated without any hints regarding how to proceed.

You may use the space below as a work area. Staves and a keyboard diagram are provided.

When you have finished, check your solutions against the answer key on the text's website (http://music.wadsworth.com/damschroder_3e).

Use your CD-ROM for Questions 1–4.

1. A triad is performed. Indicate its quality.

   a. Major   Minor   Diminished

   b. Major   Minor   Diminished

   c. Major   Minor   Diminished

2. A scale is performed. Identify it as a major or natural minor scale.

   a. Major   Natural Minor

   b. Major   Natural Minor

   c. Major   Natural Minor

3. Circle the melody performed.

4. Circle the rhythm performed.

5. Fill in the blanks.

   a. $\hat{7}$ in E Major is the pitch _____. $\hat{3}$ in F Natural Minor is the pitch _____. $\hat{5}$ in A Major is the pitch _____.

   b. The pitch F♯ is scale degree _____ in A Major, scale degree _____ in D Major, and scale degree ___ in C♯ Natural Minor.

   c. The inversion of a major third is a _____ _____. The inversion of a perfect fifth is a _____ _____.

d. The key signature of C Natural Minor contains ___ flats.

e. The key signature of two sharps corresponds both to ___ Major and to ___ Natural Minor.

6. Create the intervals requested.

a.

P5 above B

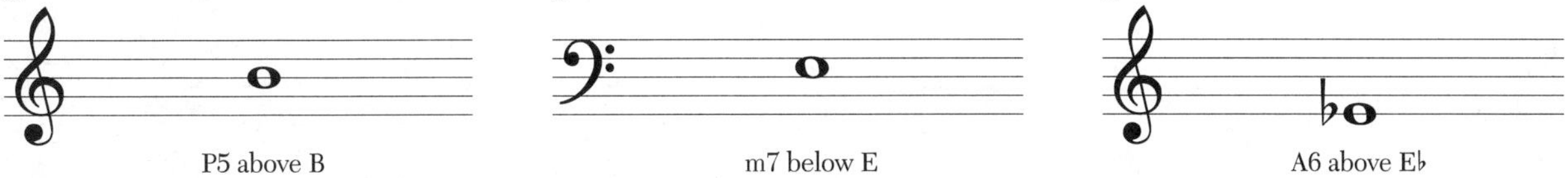

b.

m7 below E

c.

A6 above E♭

7. Name each interval by quality and size.

a.

b.

c.

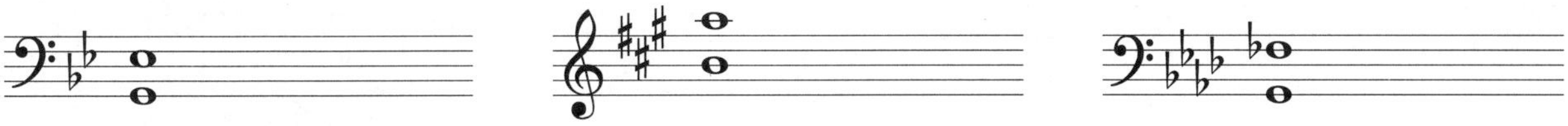

8. Create three ascending scales: D Major; the relative minor of D Major; and the parallel minor of D Major. In each case, employ the appropriate key signature.

D MAJOR   RELATIVE MINOR   PARALLEL MINOR

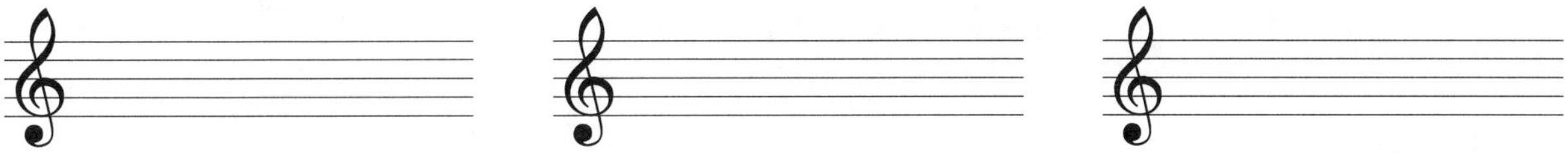

9. Create the triads requested. Employ the appropriate key signatures.

a.

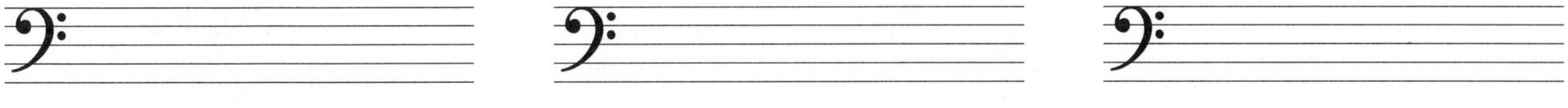

E Major: iii

b.

C Minor: VII

c.

B♭ Major: vii°

10. Provide the appropriate Roman numeral for each triad in both the major and natural minor keys that correspond to the given key signature. (For example: "D Major: V.")

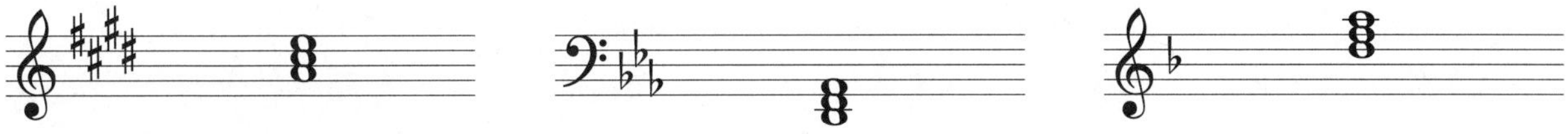

a.

_____ Major: _____

_____ Minor: _____

b.

_____ Major: _____

_____ Minor: _____

c.

_____ Major: _____

_____ Minor: _____

11. If the rhythmic notation contains an error, rewrite the measure with correct notation in the space provided. If there is no error, write "correct" beside that question.

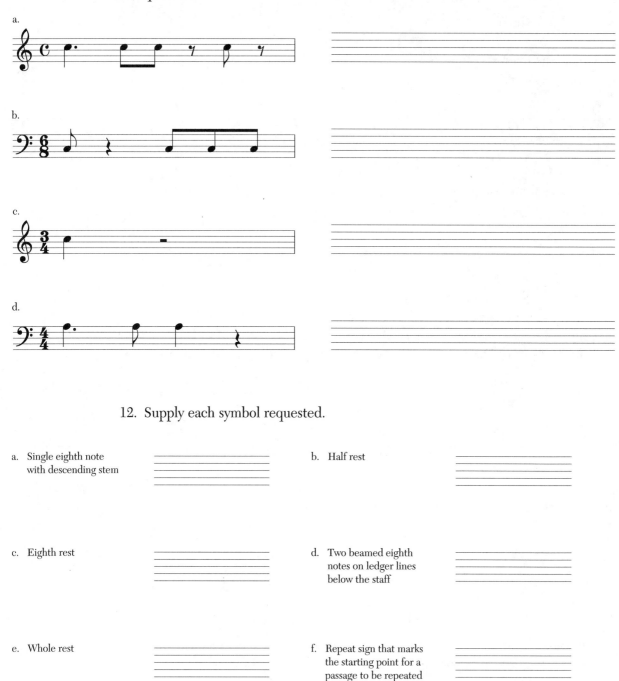

12. Supply each symbol requested.

a. Single eighth note with descending stem

b. Half rest

c. Eighth rest

d. Two beamed eighth notes on ledger lines below the staff

e. Whole rest

f. Repeat sign that marks the starting point for a passage to be repeated

PART II

Chords and Chord Progression

CHAPTER 7

From Triad to Chord

PITCH

Though triads are convenient for thinking about how music is put together, they rarely occur in their natural, unmodified state in compositions. Instead, they are the foundation upon which a composition's chords are built. A chord generally contains more pitches than the triad's three, and these pitches generally are spread wider apart than those of a triad. In this chapter, we learn how to expand triads into chords.

Compound Intervals

Until now, we have worked only within narrow musical spaces. Our intervals and triads have filled spans of an octave or less. The reason for this limitation has been pedagogical, not musical. It is now time to expand our horizons!

Most chordal music is written using pitches from both sides of Middle C. Some of these pitches are conveniently written using the treble clef, and others are conveniently written using the bass clef. Thus the **system**, two staves bound together at the left edge and at each bar line (as in Example 7-1), is a most useful tool. The treble clef controls the system's upper staff, and the bass clef its lower staff. The pitches in vertical alignment on both staves are played at the same time.

system

Example 7-1

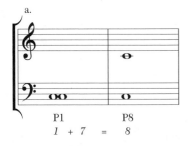

P1   P8
1 + 7 = 8

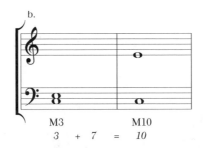

M3   M10
3 + 7 = 10

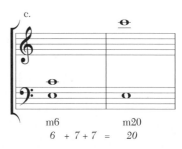

m6   m20
6 + 7 + 7 = 20

Example 7-1a shows a perfect unison and a perfect octave. Though we have used the octave many times, we have never before used both treble and bass clefs to display it. Observe that the octave's size (8) is seven greater than the unison's (1). Example 7-1b shows a major third and a major tenth. Because the tenth is larger than an octave, it is a **compound interval** (in contrast to a **simple interval**, which falls within the span of an octave or less). The major tenth could be called a "compound major third." Observe that since one octave is added to the third to form the tenth, the size of the tenth is seven greater than that of the third. (That is, 3 + 7 = 10.) Also observe that the interval's quality is not affected by the expansion. Example 7-1c shows a minor sixth and a minor twentieth (a compound minor sixth). Since the pitches of the sixth have been separated by two additional octaves, the sizes of the two intervals differ by fourteen. (That is, 6 + 7 + 7 = 20.) Again, the interval's quality is not affected by the expansion.

compound interval

simple interval

Practice Exercises 7-1

Expand each interval by raising its upper pitch by an octave. Name both the given interval and its compound expansion (e.g., P4, P11), using the procedure of Chapter 6.

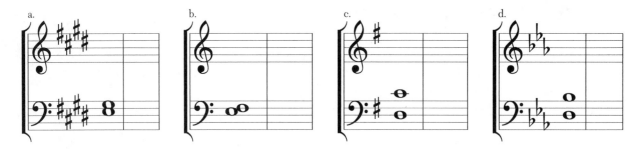

Expand each interval by lowering its lower pitch by an octave. Name both the given interval and its compound expansion (e.g., P4, P11).

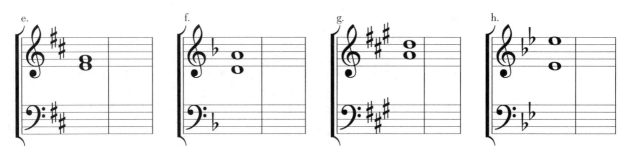

Expand each interval by two octaves, either raising its upper pitch, lowering its lower pitch, or both. Name both the given interval and its compound expansion (e.g., P4, P18).

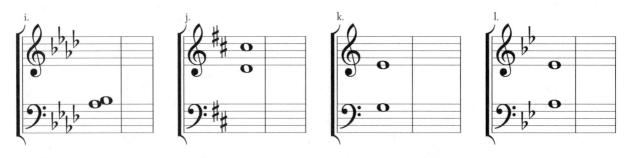

Chords in Root Position

The intervals of a third and a fifth are formed between a root and other triad members. Both of these intervals may be expanded into compound intervals, as shown in Example 7-2. Observe that the intervals may be expanded to varying degrees. In Example 7-2b, the third and fifth of Example 7-2a are expanded into a tenth and a twelfth, respectively. In Example 7-2c, the triad's fifth again appears as a twelfth, while its third is expanded even further, into a seventeenth. Because the chords that we create are all derived from a specific triad (such as that of Example 7-2a), we will often refer to that triad as the ***parent triad.***

Example 7-2

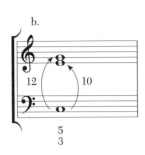
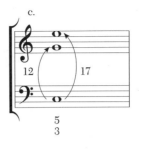

The chords of Example 7-2b and 7-2c contain both a compound third and a compound fifth above the lowest-sounding pitch (called the ***bass***). Musicians convey this information in two different ways. They might say that the chords are in ***root position***, indicating that the parent triad's root serves as the chords' bass. Or, they might say that the chords are in $\frac{5}{3}$ ***position***, indicating which intervals (usually in a compound version) occur above the bass. The symbol $\frac{5}{3}$, in the context of a specific bass note (here C), is the chord's ***figured bass***. The number 5 is always placed above the number 3, even if the compound third is higher than the compound fifth (as in Example 7-2c).

The terms "root" and "bass" will require careful attention as we proceed with chord building. Since in root-position chords the root and the bass are the same (for example, the pitch C in Example 7-2), the distinction is not yet apparent. However, you should begin to think of these terms in the following way:

- The *root* is the lowest-sounding pitch of a parent triad (C in Example 7-2a). We have employed this concept since Chapter 2.
- The *bass* is the lowest-sounding pitch of a chord derived from a parent triad (C in Examples 7-2b and 7-2c). This concept is new to this chapter.

When a chord is inverted (a topic of Chapter 8), its root and its bass are not the same.

Practice Exercises 7-2

Create a chord from the given parent triad by expanding both its third and fifth by one octave. Use the system's lower staff for the bass and upper staff for the remaining notes.

Create a chord from the given parent triad by expanding its third by two octaves and its fifth by one octave. Use the system's lower staff for the bass and upper staff for the remaining notes.

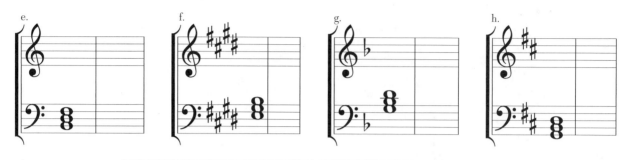

Four-Note Chords

Chords may be written in a variety of notational formats. For example, when using a system to notate choral music, composers generally write two pitches in the treble clef (for the female singers, called sopranos and altos) and two pitches in the bass clef (for the male singers, called tenors and basses). In solo piano music, composers generally assume that the performer will possess a high level of technical skill, so chords often keep both hands busy with a total of six or more pitches played at once. For our purposes, yet another format will prove convenient. We will write three notes on the system's treble-clef staff (for the right hand) and one note on the system's bass-clef staff (for the left hand). With a total of four pitches, such chords offer a fuller sound than the three-note chords of Example 7-2.

double

Since a parent triad contains three—not four—pitches, we must **double** one of these pitches when constructing a four-note chord. The following guidelines describe how to transform a parent triad into a root-position chord:

1. Begin by placing the parent triad's root on the system's bass-clef staff.
2. Place the other two pitches of the parent triad on the system's treble-clef staff.
3. The chord's fourth pitch must be from the parent triad, "doubling" a pitch that is already present. For example, a C in the bass may be doubled by a C one or two octaves higher on the system's treble-clef staff. There are special considerations in major keys: $\hat{7}$ (which we call the **leading tone** because of its strong tendency to ascend to $\hat{8}$) may not be doubled in a V chord, and neither $\hat{4}$ nor $\hat{7}$ (a dissonant combination that we will explore carefully in Chapter 10) may be doubled in a vii° chord.

leading tone

4. The highest of the three pitches on the system's treble-clef staff is called the **soprano**. When a stem is required, it points upward. The other two treble-clef pitches are called the **inner voices**. They share a single stem, which points downward. As already mentioned, the one pitch on the system's bass-clef staff is called the *bass*. Its stem points upward if the notehead is below the middle line, and downward if the notehead is on or above the middle line.

soprano

inner voices

5. All three treble-clef pitches must fall within the span of an octave. That is, from the soprano pitch to the lower of the inner-voice pitches, the maximum distance is an octave. Anything larger would be too wide a span for most hands.

Example 7-3 displays the correct procedure for forming a chord in root position. Example 7-3a shows the parent triad C–E–G. In Example 7-3b, these pitches are distributed using both clefs. In Example 7-3c, the three pitches of Example 7-3b are retained, and each of the three pitches of the parent triad takes a turn as the doubled pitch. Observe that all three pitches in the treble clef are within the span of an octave. Also observe how the stems are affixed.

Example 7-3

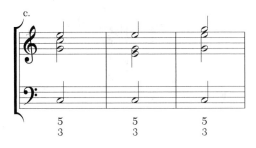

Example 7-4 displays incorrectly formed chords, preceded by their parent triads. In Example 7-4a, the right-hand pitches are too widely spaced, and the stems are incorrectly positioned. In Example 7-4b, E is missing. In Example 7-4c, which represents V in C Major, the leading tone (B) is doubled. In Example 7-4d, the chord contains the pitch B, which is not a member of the parent triad.

Example 7-4

Practice Exercises 7-3

Each of the expansions from triad to chord below contains one or more errors. Name these errors.

Create a four-note chord from the given parent triad. Observe all rules regarding doubling and spacing. Use half notes, with correct stem directions.

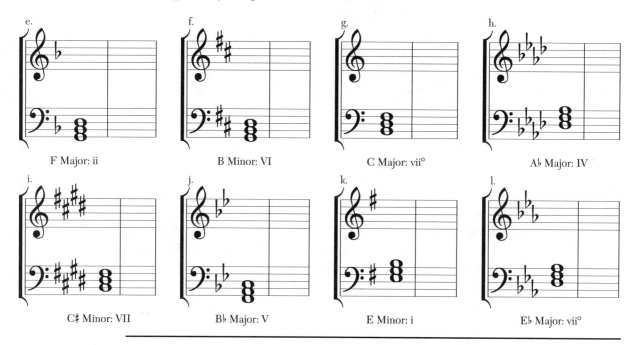

e. F Major: ii f. B Minor: VI g. C Major: vii° h. A♭ Major: IV

i. C♯ Minor: VII j. B♭ Major: V k. E Minor: i l. E♭ Major: vii°

Step-by-Step from Roman Numeral to Chord

Because of the numerous possible positionings and doublings of a chord's pitches, there is no one "right" answer when forming chords. Generally, you will have three pieces of information—the key, the Roman numeral, and the position—from which you could create a number of different correctly formed chords. (In this chapter, only $\frac{5}{3}$ position is employed. Other possibilities are explored in Chapters 8 and 10.) For practice, let's create a VII chord in $\frac{5}{3}$ position in the key of B Minor. The results are shown in Example 7-5.

Step One: Prepare the system by placing the correct key signature on both staves.

Step Two: Write down the parent triad on the lower staff, determining the root by ascending the scale to the scale degree that corresponds to the Roman numeral. (Here, since we are building a VII chord, we ascend to $\hat{7}$.)

Step Three: Position the root on the lower staff and the other pitches on the upper staff.

Step Four: Insert a suitable doubling and add stems.

Example 7-5

Step One   Step Two   Step Three   Step Four

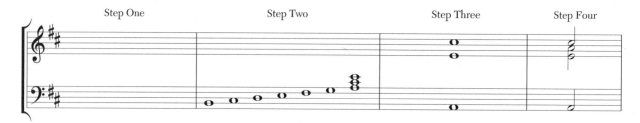

Example 7-6 follows the same procedures in forming a V chord in $\frac{5}{3}$ position in A Major. Because G♯ is A Major's leading tone, it may not be doubled.

Example 7-6

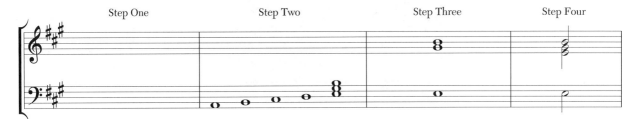

Practice Exercises 7-4

Create the chords indicated by each Roman numeral, figured bass, and key. Follow the four steps displayed in Examples 7-5 and 7-6, using the left side of the system for writing down the key signature and the parent triad, and the right side for presenting a four-note chord in half notes. Remember the special considerations for doubling when the V or vii° chord of major keys is involved.

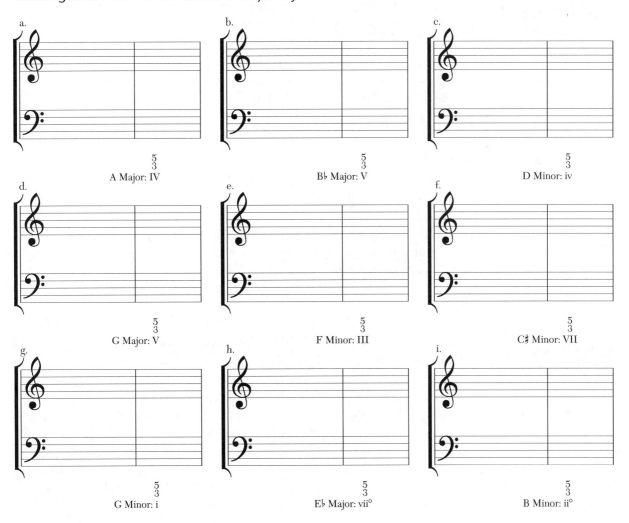

a. $\frac{5}{3}$ A Major: IV

b. $\frac{5}{3}$ B♭ Major: V

c. $\frac{5}{3}$ D Minor: iv

d. $\frac{5}{3}$ G Major: V

e. $\frac{5}{3}$ F Minor: III

f. $\frac{5}{3}$ C♯ Minor: VII

g. $\frac{5}{3}$ G Minor: i

h. $\frac{5}{3}$ E♭ Major: vii°

i. $\frac{5}{3}$ B Minor: ii°

> ## Tips for Success
>
> ✔ $\hat{4}$ and $\hat{7}$ require close attention when they occur in a V or a vii° chord. For now, simply do not double them in those two contexts. In future chapters we will explore their use in greater detail. Because $\hat{4}$ and $\hat{7}$ form a dissonant interval, they attract attention and induce specific musical responses. Composers use these notes in combination often, though carefully.

RHYTHM

Sixteenth Notes and Rests in Simple Meters

Our exploration of how to subdivide the beat continues with sixteenth notes. Four sixteenth notes fill a beat in simple meters such as $\frac{4}{4}$. We will also learn the symbols for rests that coordinate with these partial-beat notes.

Sixteenth Notes

sixteenth notes

Just as the quarter-note beat of simple meters often splits into two eighth notes, these eighth notes may split into two **sixteenth notes**. In all, four sixteenth notes fill a quarter-note beat. *Two* beams or flags cap the stems of darkened noteheads to signify sixteenth notes, as shown in Example 7-7.

Example 7-7

You should count the sixteenth-note subdivisions of the beat whenever sixteenth notes play an important role in a melody. For this purpose, we will use the syllables "1 ee + ee . . .", as demonstrated in Example 7-8.

Example 7-8

Haydn: String Quartet No. 79, Op. 76, No. 5

+ ee   1 ee + ee 2 ee + ee   1 ee + ee 2 ee + ee   1 ee + ee 2 ee + ee   1 ee + ee 2 ee

dotted eighth note

Haydn's melody employs the pattern eighth-sixteenth-sixteenth. Another way to divide the beat is to employ a **dotted eighth note** followed by a single sixteenth note. This combination is demonstrated in Example 7-9. As with all other instances of the augmentation dot, it adds an additional 50 percent to the value of the note to which it is attached. Thus, the dotted eighth note fills three-fourths of a beat. Note carefully how a single sixteenth note is created in beam notation.

Example 7-9

Bellini: *Norma*, Act 1

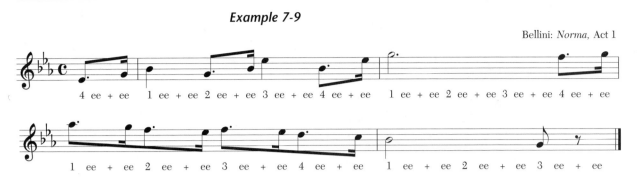

Rests

We have already learned the symbols for a full beat of silence (𝄽) and a half beat of silence (𝄾) in $\frac{2}{4}$, $\frac{3}{4}$, and $\frac{4}{4}$ meters. When one-fourth of a beat is silence, we use a *sixteenth rest* (𝄿). The horizontal components of a sixteenth rest fill the second and third spaces of the staff. When three-fourths of a beat is silence, we use a ***dotted eighth rest*** (𝄾.). Example 7-10 displays their use.

Example 7-10

A sixteenth rest may be employed within a beam that fills a beat. In this case, it may be positioned higher or lower on the staff than is normal. Example 7-11 presents three such sixteenth rests.

Example 7-11

Beethoven: String Quartet No. 12, Op. 127

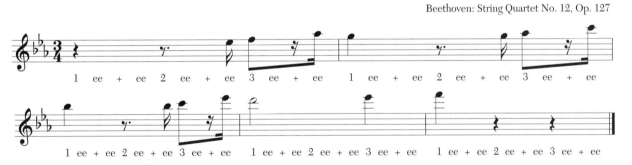

Practice Exercises 7-5

Practice creating music notation by drawing each symbol below twice to the right of its model.

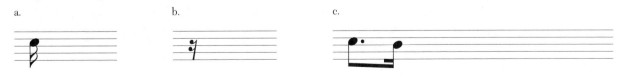

Modify the noteheads indicated by arrows to form measures containing the appropriate number of beats. Wherever possible, incorporate the existing beam notation. Put counting syllables ("1 ee + ee . . .") below the pitches as a reminder of the exact value of each symbol. The following chart should prove useful.

Tips for Success

✔ Counting "1 ee + ee . . ." out loud may seem like a mouthful. But if you can locate exactly where each syllable goes in the context of a complicated rhythm, it is more likely that you will perform the rhythm correctly.

Laboratory

L7-1. Play and Sing

a. In this exercise you test the limits of your vocal range.

- Experiment to find the lowest note in your vocal range. Play and sing notes to the left of Middle C, going stepwise to the left (white keys only) until your voice reaches its lowest pitch ("L").
- Now play L and then a second higher than L, and then sing both pitches.
- Then play L and a compound second (= ninth) higher than L, and then sing both pitches.
- Continue with simple and compound thirds, fourths, fifths, etc., until you reach the upper limit of your vocal range.

b. Repeat exercise a, this time playing the simple interval at the keyboard, but singing the compound interval without first playing it. For example, play a melodic ascending second, sing both pitches, and then *play only the lower pitch* before you sing the two pitches of an ascending ninth.

c. Play a triad with your left hand. Then create and play a four-note chord derived from that triad:

- With your left hand, play the root.
- With your right hand, play the third and fifth, and add a fourth pitch that doubles one of the triad's three pitches.

d. Play each of the chords below. Indicate whether the root, the third, or the fifth is the doubled pitch.

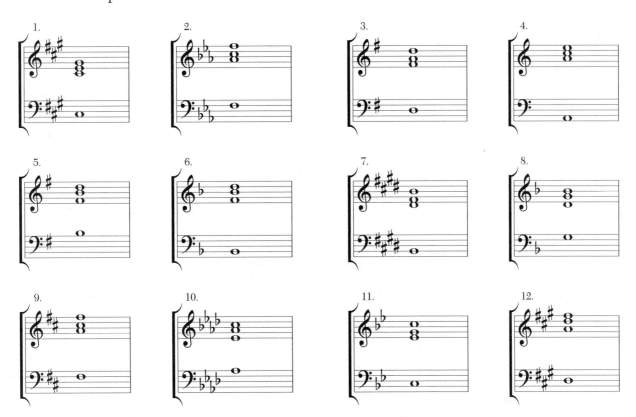

L7-2. Listening

Team up with another student, work with your instructor in class, or make use of the CD-ROM that accompanies this textbook to practice these exercises.

a. *Performer:* Play a simple interval, either ascending or descending. Then play a compound interval, perhaps making it a compound of the simple interval just performed. (For example, play an ascending C–A sixth, then an ascending C–A thirteenth.)

Listener: Indicate whether the second interval is a compound version of the first interval.

b. *Performer:* Play a major, minor, or diminished triad. Then play a four-note chord, perhaps derived from the triad just performed.

Listener: Indicate whether the chord is derived from the triad.

L7-3. Keyboard Album

a. Dvořák; Symphony No. 9 ("From the New World"), Op. 95, Mvmt. 1

b. Mozart: *The Magic Flute,* K. 620, Act 1

c. Berlioz: *The Damnation of Faust,* Op. 24, Part 3

d. Beethoven: Piano Sonata, Op. 31, No. 3, Mvmt. 2

L7-4. Song Book

a. Mozart: *The Magic Flute,* K. 620, Act 1

b.

O Faithful Pine

O faith - ful pine, O faith - ful pine, Green are thy leaves for - ev - er!

c.

Oh! Susanna

I __ come from Al - a - ba - ma with my ban - jo on my knee; I'se __

gwan to Lou' - si - a - na My _____ true lub for to see.

d.

Hupfeld: "As Time Goes By"

You must re - mem - ber this, A kiss is still a kiss, A sigh is just a sigh;

The fun - da - men - tal things ap - ply, As time goes by.

L7-5. Rhythm

a.

b.

c.

d.

e.

L7-6. Improvisation

a. In this improvisation, the hands build chords in various configurations. Several choices for I and V chords in C Major are provided below, though you need not limit yourself to these. Fill each of eight measures with one whole-note chord or two half-note chords, according to the following plan:

measures 1 through 4:   I
measures 5 and 6:   V
measures 7 and 8:   I

b. Repeat exercise a in other major keys.

If you create an improvisation that especially pleases you, write it down. Perhaps at your next class your instructor will ask you to perform it for the class.

L7-7. Score Study

Listen to Selections 1, 3, 5, and 6 in the Scores for Music Analysis section at the back of the textbook. Then answer the questions under the "Chapter 7" headings that accompany these selections.

Name: _____

Instructor: _____

Date: _____

Pitch Exercises

P7-1.
1. Name the given interval (m7, etc.). Follow the procedure of Chapter 6.
2. Expand each interval by one or two octaves, as indicated. You may raise the higher pitch, lower the lower pitch, or (for a two-octave expansion) do both.
3. Name each interval that you have created (m14, etc.).

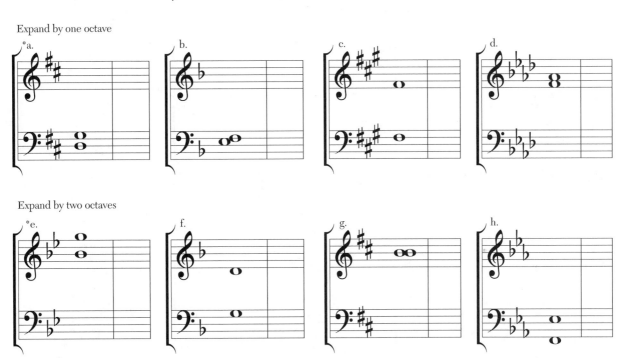

Expand by one octave

Expand by two octaves

P7-2. For each chord below, add a fourth note that appropriately doubles one of the given notes. (Remember that the three notes in the treble clef must all fall within one octave.) Then add stems to convert each notehead into a half note.

Hint: Remember that in the major mode, the leading tone ($\hat{7}$) is not doubled in a V chord, and neither $\hat{4}$ nor $\hat{7}$ is doubled in a vii° chord.

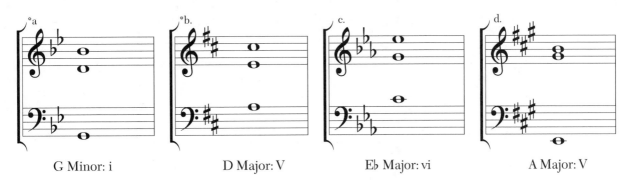

G Minor: i   D Major: V   E♭ Major: vi   A Major: V

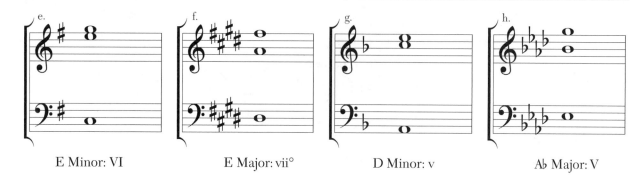

E Minor: VI   E Major: vii°   D Minor: v   A♭ Major: V

P7-3. Create the chords indicated by each Roman numeral, figured bass, and key. Follow the four steps outlined in this chapter, using the left side of the system for writing down the key signature and the parent triad, and the right side for presenting a four-note chord in half notes. Remember the special considerations for doubling when the V or vii° chord of major keys is involved.

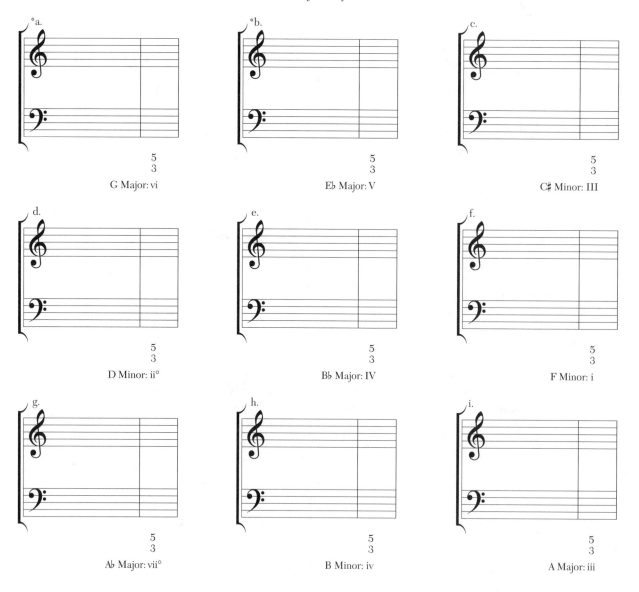

Name: _____

Instructor: _____

Date: _____

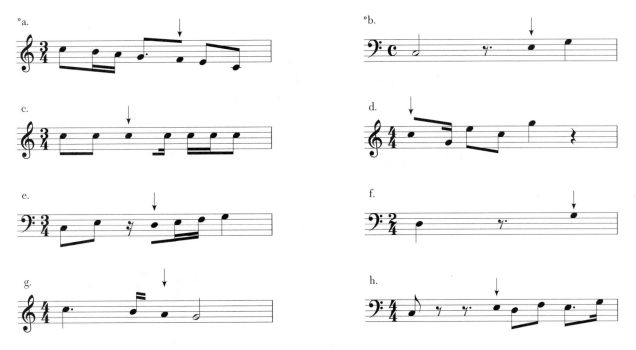

j.

5
3

A Minor: VII

k.

5
3

D Major: V

l.

5
3

G Minor: VI

Rhythm Exercises

R7-1. Modify the noteheads indicated by arrows to form measures containing the appropriate number of beats. Wherever possible, incorporate the existing beam notation.

Hint: Put counting syllables ("1 ee + ee . . .") below the pitches as a reminder of the exact value of each symbol.

°a.

°b.

c.

d.

e.

f.

g.

h.

R7-2. Create the melodies indicated by the positioning of the pitch names in relation to the counting numbers. From one note to the next, use only a unison, second, third, or fourth as a melodic interval. Do not add rests.

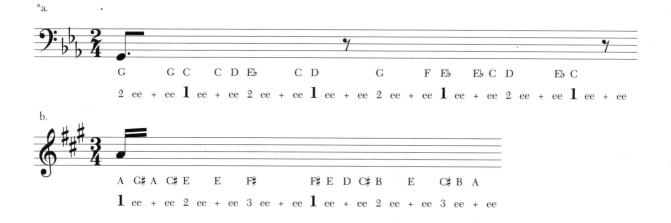

°a.

G   G C   C D E♭   C D   G   F E♭   E♭ C D   E♭ C
2 ee + ee **1** ee + ee 2 ee + ee **1** ee + ee 2 ee + ee **1** ee + ee 2 ee + ee **1** ee + ee

b.

A G♯ A C♯ E   E   F♯   F♯ E D C♯ B   E   C♯ B A
1 ee + ee 2 ee + ee 3 ee + ee **1** ee + ee 2 ee + ee 3 ee + ee

Audio Exercises

A7-1. Two intervals are performed—one simple, the other compound. Is the second a compound of the first? (For example, for the C–A sixth followed by the C–A thirteenth, answer "Yes." But for the C–A sixth followed by the C–G twelfth, answer "No.")

°a.	Yes	No	f.	Yes	No
°b.	Yes	No	g.	Yes	No
c.	Yes	No	h.	Yes	No
d.	Yes	No	i.	Yes	No
e.	Yes	No	j.	Yes	No

A7-2. A major, minor, or diminished triad is performed. Then a root-position chord is performed. Does the pitch content of the chord match that of the parent triad?

°a.	Yes	No	f.	Yes	No
°b.	Yes	No	g.	Yes	No
c.	Yes	No	h.	Yes	No
d.	Yes	No	i.	Yes	No
e.	Yes	No	j.	Yes	No

A7-3. Circle the music notation that corresponds to the pitches performed.

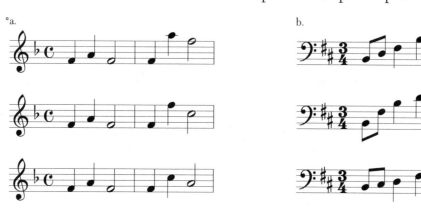

°a.

b.

Name: _____

Instructor: _____

Date: _____

A7-4. Circle the music notation that corresponds to the rhythm performed.

CHAPTER 8

Chordal Inversion

PITCH

Just as an interval can be inverted, so too can a triad or a chord. Because three—rather than two—pitches are involved, a triad has two inversions. In this chapter, we build inverted triads and chords, expanding upon the strategies developed in Chapter 7.

Chords in First and Second Inversion

Because a triad contains three pitches, it has two inversions. The **first inversion** is formed by moving a triad's *root* an octave higher. Example 8-1b shows this transformation applied to the parent triad of Example 8-1a. Because the first inversion of a triad always contains a sixth and a third above the bass, the term $\frac{6}{3}$ **position** is often used to describe its construction. (By convention, the symbol $\frac{6}{3}$ sometimes appears in an abbreviated form, as 6.) As with the expansions of chords in $\frac{5}{3}$ position in Chapter 7, various arrangements of the pitches above the bass are possible when forming inverted chords. Examples 8-1c and 8-1d show two possible arrangements, including suitable doublings. In these examples, E is the bass, but C remains the root, because these chords are derived from the C-major parent triad shown in Example 8-1a.

first inversion

$\frac{6}{3}$ **position**

Example 8-1

The **second inversion** is formed by moving a triad's *root* and *third* an octave higher. Example 8-2b shows this transformation applied to the parent triad of Example 8-2a. Because the second inversion of a triad always contains a sixth and a fourth above the bass, the term $\frac{6}{4}$ **position** is often used to describe its construction. As with the expansions shown in Example 8-1c and 8-1d, various arrangements of the pitches above the bass are possible when forming chords. Examples 8-2c and 8-2d show two possible arrangements, including suitable doublings. In these examples, G is the bass, but C remains the root, because these chords are derived from the C-major parent triad shown in Example 8-2a.

second inversion

$\frac{6}{4}$ **position**

Example 8-2

Practice Exercises 8-1

Convert each of the following triads into first inversion ($\frac{6}{3}$ position), first using simple intervals, and then expanding into a four-note chord through the use of compound intervals and a doubling.

Convert each of the following triads into second inversion ($\frac{6}{4}$ position), first using simple intervals, and then expanding into a four-note chord through the use of compound intervals and a doubling.

Consonance and Dissonance

When sounding on its own, the perfect fourth generally functions as a dissonance. When heard in the context of other pitches, however, the perfect fourth may represent the perfect fifth (whose inversion it is) and thus function as a consonance. In Example 8-3a, a chord in $\frac{6}{4}$ position follows chords in $\frac{5}{3}$ and $\frac{6}{3}$ positions. They all have the same root, C. The perfect fourth of this $\frac{6}{4}$ chord is consonant. In contrast, the fourth in Example 8-3b is dissonant. With D also present, this fourth merely displaces the third that belongs in the G–B–D chord. The notes cannot be interpreted as the second inversion of any triad. In this text, the perfect fourth will be used only as a consonance in chord construction. Though you should be aware that there are other uses for the perfect fourth that justify its classification as a dissonance, those contexts will not be explored here.

Example 8-3

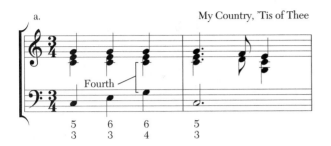

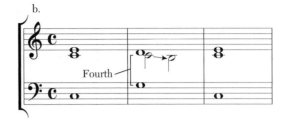

Chord Construction

The strategies of chord construction introduced in Chapter 7 apply to inverted chords as well. Here are some additional points to consider:

1. The bass (the single pitch positioned on the system's bass-clef staff) reflects the chord's inversion. In a chord in $\frac{5}{3}$ position (root position), the parent triad's root is the bass; in a chord in $\frac{6}{3}$ position (first inversion), the parent triad's third is the bass; and in a chord in $\frac{6}{4}$ position (second inversion), the parent triad's fifth is the bass.
2. When a chord is in root position, its fifth may be omitted. In that case, the upper voices will include only the third and doublings of the root and/or third.
3. When a chord is inverted, all of its members must be present.

Example 8-4 displays the correct procedure for forming a chord in first inversion. In Example 8-4a, the parent triad C–E–G is inverted, forming the $\frac{6}{3}$ position. To retain this position, E must remain the lowest-sounding pitch. In Example 8-4b, these pitches are distributed using both clefs. In Example 8-4c, the three pitches of Example 8-4b are retained, and each of the three pitches of the parent triad takes a turn as the doubled pitch. Observe that all three pitches in the treble clef are within the span of an octave. Also observe how the stems are affixed.

Example 8-4

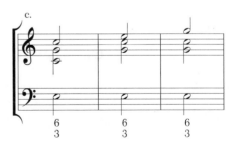

Practice Exercises 8-2

Convert each of the following triads into a four-note chord in root position. For practice, omit the fifth. Use half notes.

a. 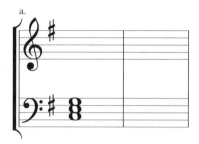   b.    c.

Convert each of the following triads into a four-note chord in first inversion. Use half notes.

d.    e.    f.

Convert each of the following triads into a four-note chord in second inversion. Use half notes.

g.    h.    i.

Step-by-Step from Roman Numeral to Chord

Given a key, a Roman numeral, and a position (conveyed via figured-bass numbers), you should be able to create a chord. For practice, let's create a IV chord in $\frac{6}{4}$ position in the key of F Major. The results are shown in Example 8-5.

Step One: Prepare the system by placing the correct key signature on both staves.

Step Two: Write down the parent triad on the lower staff, determining the root by ascending the scale to the scale degree that corresponds to the Roman numeral. (Here, since we are building a IV chord, we ascend to $\hat{4}$.)

Step Three: If a $\frac{6}{3}$ or $\frac{6}{4}$ chord is required, invert the parent triad accordingly. (Here, since we require $\frac{6}{4}$, we place both B♭ and D above F.)

Step Four: Position the bass on the lower staff and the other pitches on the upper staff. The fifth may be omitted if the chord is in $\frac{5}{3}$ position.

Step Five: Insert suitable doubling(s) and add stems.

Example 8-5

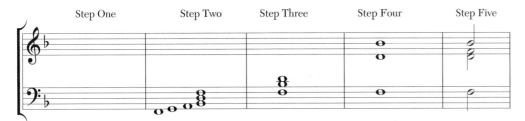

Example 8-6 follows the same procedure in forming a V chord in $\frac{5}{3}$ position in E♭ Major. Here the fifth has been omitted, and the root has been tripled! Because D is E♭ Major's leading tone, it may not be doubled. If the fifth is omitted, the root must be tripled.

Example 8-6

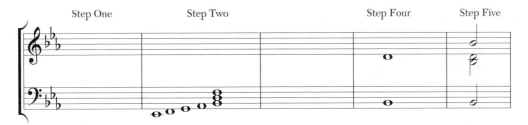

Practice Exercises 8-3

Create the chords indicated by each Roman numeral, figured bass, and key. Follow the five steps displayed in Examples 8-5 and 8-6, using the left side of the system for writing down the key signature and the parent triad, inverting if necessary, and the right side for presenting a four-note chord in half notes. Remember the special considerations for doubling in the V or vii° chord of major keys. For practice, omit the fifth when the chord is in $\frac{5}{3}$ position.

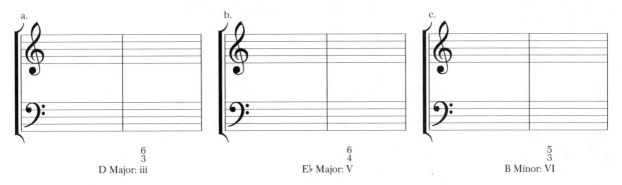

a. $\frac{6}{3}$ D Major: iii   b. $\frac{6}{4}$ E♭ Major: V   c. $\frac{5}{3}$ B Minor: VI

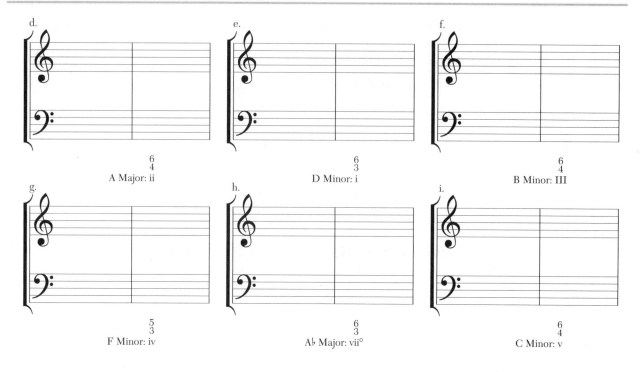

d.

A Major: ii
$\begin{smallmatrix}6\\4\end{smallmatrix}$

e.

D Minor: i
$\begin{smallmatrix}6\\3\end{smallmatrix}$

f.

B Minor: III
$\begin{smallmatrix}6\\4\end{smallmatrix}$

g.

F Minor: iv
$\begin{smallmatrix}5\\3\end{smallmatrix}$

h.

A♭ Major: vii°
$\begin{smallmatrix}6\\3\end{smallmatrix}$

i.

C Minor: v
$\begin{smallmatrix}6\\4\end{smallmatrix}$

Tips for Success

✔ The distinction between *bass* and *root* can be troublesome. For example, in creating a V chord in $\begin{smallmatrix}6\\3\end{smallmatrix}$ position in C Major, one does NOT proceed by ascending to $\hat{5}$ and then placing a sixth and third above that note. (The resulting chord would be G–B–E.) That is a $\begin{smallmatrix}6\\3\end{smallmatrix}$ chord with *bass* G, not with *root* G. Instead, one ascends to $\hat{5}$ (G), builds the parent triad with *root* $\hat{5}$ (G–B–D), and then inverts this parent triad to create a chord in $\begin{smallmatrix}6\\3\end{smallmatrix}$ position (B–D–G).

RHYTHM

Sixteenth Notes and Rests in Compound Meters

In the compound meters we have learned, six sixteenth notes will fill a beat. In this chapter we explore rhythms created using these subdivisions of the beat.

Sixteenth Notes in Compound Meters

The quarter note, which represents the beat in simple meters such as $\frac{2}{4}$, can be subdivided into four sixteenth notes. The dotted quarter note, which represents the beat in compound meters such as $\frac{6}{8}$, can be divided into six sixteenth notes. Example 8-7 compares the subdivision of beats in simple and compound meters.

Example 8-7

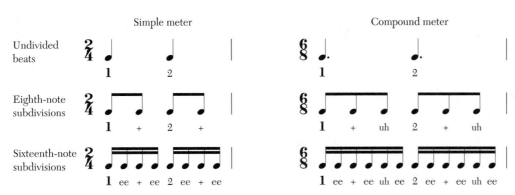

Whenever such subdivisions are employed in a compound meter, you should count "1 ee + ee uh ee . . .", as displayed in Example 8-7. Though somewhat of a tongue twister, these syllables convey the relative weight of each part of the beat. The "uh" syllable should be employed only in compound meters. Though some musicians count simple meter as "1 ee + uh . . .", that strategy confuses the clear distinctions laid out in Example 8-7. The syllables adopted for this text are employed in Example 8-8.

Example 8-8

Mozart: *Così fan tutte,* Act 2

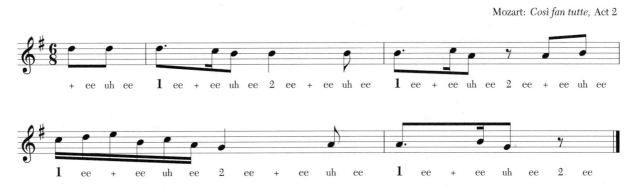

Rests

A sixteenth rest fills one-sixth of a beat in a compound meter such as $\frac{6}{8}$, while an eighth rest fills two-sixths and a dotted eighth rest fills three-sixths of a beat. Though this arithmetic is straightforward, the ways in which composers use such rests is a bit idiosyncratic. If you count "1 ee + ee uh ee . . .", as suggested, then you can think of a sixteenth rest as one syllable, an eighth rest as two syllables, and a dotted eighth rest as three syllables. In Example 8-9a, a dotted eighth rest occurs at the beginning of the first beat. It is counted as "1 ee +". The three sixteenth notes that follow finish the first beat. In Example 8-9b, an eighth rest is followed by a sixteenth rest. Even though this is the same time value as a dotted eighth rest (again, three syllables: "+ ee uh"), Beethoven here employs two separate rests. Finally, in Example 8-9c, a sixteenth rest begins the measure (one syllable: "1") and three rests occur in succession later in the measure (total value of four syllables: "ee 2 ee +"). These principles pertain to the $\frac{9}{8}$ and $\frac{12}{8}$ meters as well.

Example 8-9

Beethoven: String Quartet, Op. 59, No. 2, Mvmt. 1

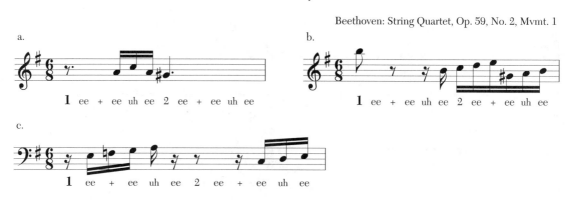

The idiosyncrasies of rest notation are attempts by composers to help musicians read music notation quickly and accurately. Though a quarter rest fills the same time value as a sixteenth-eighth-sixteenth-rest combination (Example 8-9c), only the latter notation reveals where the second beat begins.

Practice Exercises 8-4

Modify the noteheads indicated by arrows to form measures containing the appropriate number of beats. Wherever possible, incorporate the existing beam notation. Put counting syllables ("1 ee + ee uh ee . . .") below the pitches as a reminder of the exact value of each symbol. The following chart should prove useful.

Sixteenth note or rest	♬	♪	One syllable
Eighth note or rest	♪	𝄾	Two syllables
Dotted eighth note or rest	♪.	𝄾·	Three syllables
Quarter note or rest	♩	𝄽	Four syllables
Dotted quarter note	♩.		Six syllables
Half note	𝅗𝅥		Eight syllables

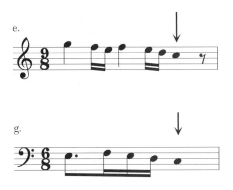

Tips for Success

✔ It is prudent to be careful when performing rhythms by counting out loud. "1 ee + ee uh ee . . ." may seem like a mouthful. But if you can locate exactly where each syllable goes in the context of a complicated rhythm, it is more likely that you will perform the rhythm correctly.

Laboratory

L8-1. Play and Sing

a. Play a triad that is low in your vocal range, and then play and sing its three pitches: "Root," "Third," and "Fifth." Now play and sing the first inversion of this triad: "Third," "Fifth," and (higher) "Root." Now play and sing the second inversion of this triad: "Fifth," (higher) "Root," and (higher) "Third." Repeat for other triads low in your vocal range. (Make sure to include triads of major, minor, and diminished qualities among your choices.)

b. Repeat Exercise L8-1a, this time playing only the lowest pitch of each inversion before singing all three pitches.

c. Play a triad with your left hand. Then create and play a four-note chord in first inversion derived from that triad:
   • With your left hand, play the triad's third.
   • With your right hand, play the root and fifth, and add a fourth pitch that doubles one of the triad's three pitches.

d. Play a triad with your left hand. Then create and play a four-note chord in second inversion derived from that triad:
   • With your left hand, play the triad's fifth.
   • With your right hand, play the root and third, and add a fourth pitch that doubles one of the triad's three pitches.

e. Play each of the chords below. Indicate whether the chord is in root position, first inversion, or second inversion.

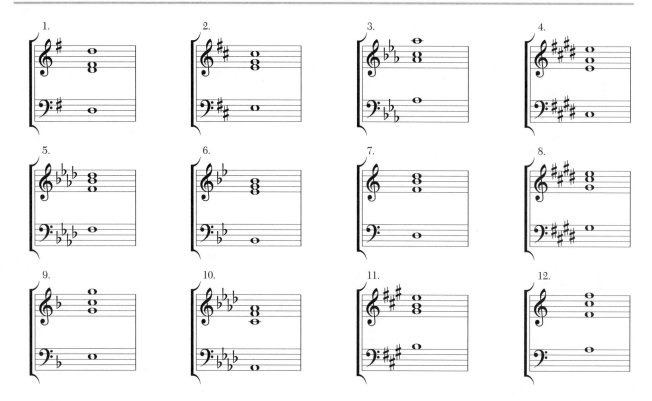

L8-2. Listening

Team up with another student, work with your instructor in class, or make use of the CD-ROM that accompanies this textbook to practice these exercises.

a. *Performer:* Play the three pitches of a triad in ascending order (for example, A–C–E). Then play either that triad's first or second inversion (either C–E–A or E–A–C).

   Listener: Indicate whether the first or the second inversion has been performed.

b. *Performer:* Play a major, minor, or diminished triad in first inversion. Then play a four-note chord, perhaps derived from the inverted triad just performed.

   Listener: Indicate whether the chord is derived from the inverted triad.

c. *Performer:* Play a major, minor, or diminished triad in second inversion. Then play a four-note chord, perhaps derived from the inverted triad just performed.

   Listener: Indicate whether the chord is derived from the inverted triad.

L8-3. Keyboard Album

Beethoven: Piano Sonata, Op. 27, No. 1, Mvmt. 4

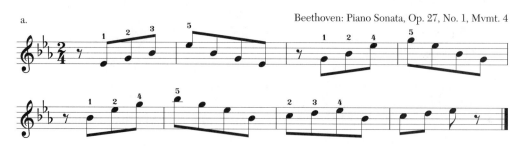

b.

Handel: *Royal Fireworks Music*

c.

Schubert: *Fierrabras*, D. 796, Act 1

St. Patrick's Day

d.

L8-4. Song Book

a.

Mozart: String Quartet No. 17 ("Hunting"), K. 458, Mvmt. 1

b.

Handel: *Royal Fireworks Music*

c.

The Cowboy

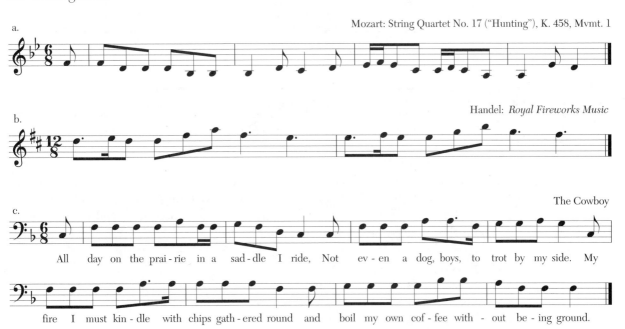

All   day on the prai - rie in a   sad - dle I ride,   Not   ev - en a dog, boys, to trot by my side.   My

fire   I   must kin - dle   with chips gath - ered round   and   boil my own cof - fee with - out   be - ing ground.

d.   Get Along Little Dogies

Whoo-pie ti - yi-yo, ___ get a - long lit-tle do - gies, It's your mis-for-tune and none of my own. Whoo-pee

ti - yi - yo, ___ get a - long lit - tle do - gies, You know that Wy - o - ming will be your new home.

L8-5. Rhythm

a.

b.

c.

d.

e.

L8-6. Improvisation

a. In this improvisation, the hands build chords in various inversions. Several choices for I and V chords in C Major are provided below, though you need not limit yourself to these. Fill each of eight measures with one whole-note chord or two half-note chords, according to the following plan:

measure 1:   I in root position
measures 2 and 3:   I in root position or either inversion
measure 4:   I in root position
measures 5 and 6:   V in first or second inversion
measures 7 and 8:   I in root position

I IN C MAJOR
(ROOT POSITION)   I IN C MAJOR (INVERSIONS)   V IN C MAJOR (INVERSIONS)

b. Repeat Exercise L8-6a in other major keys.

If you create an improvisation that especially pleases you, write it down. Perhaps at your next class your instructor will ask you to perform it for the class.

L8-7. Score Study

Listen to Selections 2 and 6 in the Scores for Music Analysis section at the back of the textbook. Then answer the questions under the "Chapter 8" headings that accompany these selections.

Name: _____

Instructor: _____

Date: _____

Pitch Exercises

P8-1. Convert each of the following triads into first inversion ($\frac{6}{3}$ position) and second inversion ($\frac{6}{4}$ position). Retain the use of simple intervals.

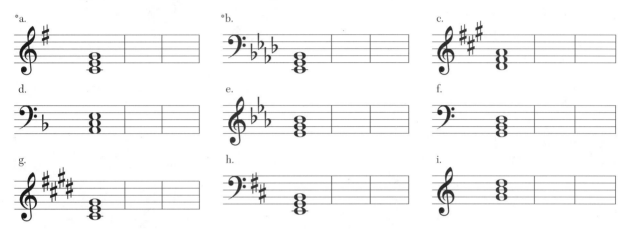

P8-2. For each chord below, add a fourth note that appropriately doubles one of the given notes. (Remember that the three notes in the treble clef must all be played by the right hand.) Then add stems to convert each notehead into a half note.

Hint: Remember that in the major mode, the leading tone ($\hat{7}$) may not be doubled in a V chord, and neither $\hat{4}$ nor $\hat{7}$ may be doubled in a vii° chord. Take this into account in chords c, d, f, and g.

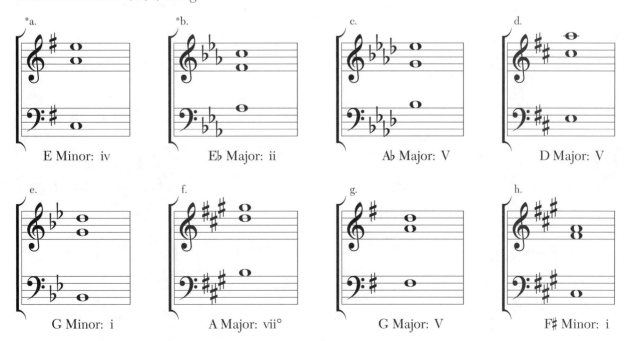

P8-3. Create the chords indicated by each Roman numeral, figured bass, and key. Follow the five steps outlined in this chapter, using the left side of the system for writing down the key signature and the parent triad, and inverting it if necessary. Use the right side for presenting a four-note chord in half notes. Remember the special considerations for doubling when the V or vii° chord of major keys is involved. For practice, when a chord is in $\frac{5}{3}$ position, omit the fifth.

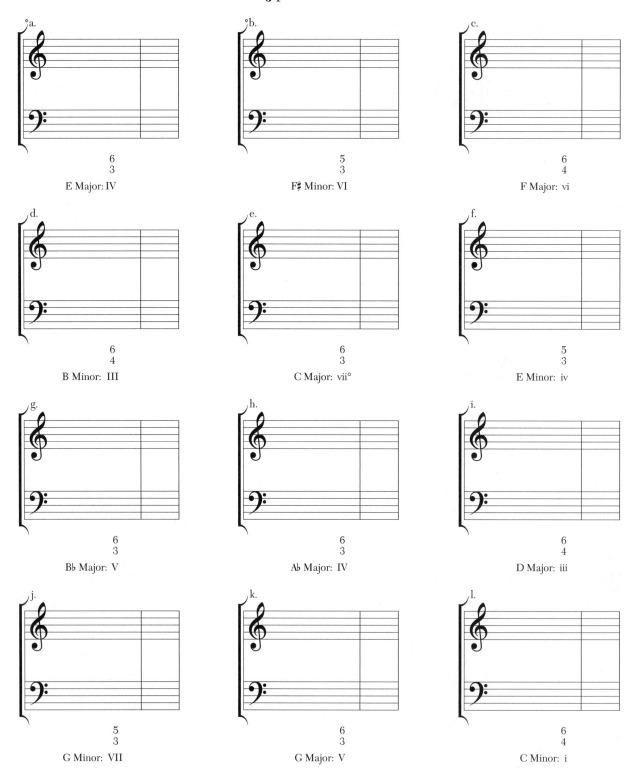

Name: _____

Instructor: _____

Date: _____

Rhythm Exercises

R8-1. Modify the noteheads indicated by arrows to form measures containing the appropriate number of beats. Wherever possible, incorporate the existing beam notation.

Hint: Put counting syllables ("1 ee + ee uh ee . . .") below the pitches as a reminder of the exact value of each symbol.

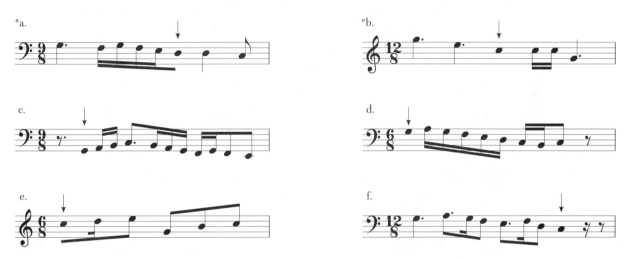

R8-2. Create the melodies indicated by the positioning of the pitch names in relation to the counting numbers. From one note to the next, use only a unison, second, third, or fourth as a melodic interval. Do not add rests.

Audio Exercises

A8-1. The three pitches of a major, minor, or diminished triad are performed, first in ascending order and then together. Then the three pitches of this triad's first or second inversion are performed, first in ascending order and then together. Identify the inversion. (Hint: Remember that the parent triad's third is the first inversion's lowest pitch, and that the parent triad's fifth is the second inversion's lowest pitch.)

a. First inversion Second inversion   f. First inversion Second inversion

b. First inversion Second inversion   g. First inversion Second inversion

c. First inversion Second inversion   h. First inversion Second inversion

d. First inversion Second inversion   i. First inversion Second inversion

e. First inversion Second inversion   j. First inversion Second inversion

A8-2. An inverted triad is performed. Then a four-note chord is performed. Is the chord derived from the inverted triad?

a. Yes No   f. Yes No

b. Yes No   g. Yes No

c. Yes No   h. Yes No

d. Yes No   i. Yes No

e. Yes No   j. Yes No

A8-3. Circle the music notation that corresponds to the pitches performed.

a.

b.

c.

d.

Name: _____

Instructor: _____

Date: _____

A8-4. Circle the music notation that corresponds to the rhythm performed.

CHAPTER 9

Chordal Analysis

Composition and analysis are complementary activities. In Chapters 7 and 8, we learned how to build a chord from a given figured bass and Roman numeral. Now we learn how to determine the figured bass and Roman numeral for a given chord.

Figured-Bass Analysis

Just as sentences are made up of appropriate successions of words, musical phrases and periods (which we will explore in later chapters) are made up of appropriate successions of chords. What a sentence conveys depends on the meaning and positioning of its words. Likewise, what a phrase conveys depends partly upon the identity and arrangement of its component chords. The processes of chord creation that we explored in Chapters 7 and 8—going from parent triad to full-fledged chord in any inversion—can be reversed: for any chord in a composition, we should be able to determine the parent triad and the inversion in which it has been positioned. (Of course, some complex chords are not covered in this text and will not appear in our exercises.)

You should think of figured-bass numbers as an inventory of the pitches positioned above the bass. This requires careful attention. A common mistake among beginners is to consider only the three notes written on the system's upper staff. Remember that all four pitches of a chord sound together, and that the one pitch on the lower staff is the bass, from which *all* the intervals indicated by the figured bass are calculated.

Four chords are presented in Example 9-1, along with appropriate figured-bass numbers. Arrows show all of the intervals that are formed with the bass. The figured bass is not affected by which pitch is doubled. Though one could write "8" if the bass is doubled by one of the upper-staff pitches, that is not usually done. And one would not write "$\frac{5}{3}$" or "$\frac{5}{3}$" if the fifth or third is doubled. $\frac{5}{3}$, $\frac{6}{3}$, and $\frac{6}{4}$ are your only figured-bass choices at this point. You should never write $\frac{3}{5}$, $\frac{6}{6}$, or $\frac{4}{6}$, even if the compound third or fourth is the highest pitch. Observe that, though the three upper-staff pitches of Example 9-1c have the form of a triad (line-line-line), the chord is nevertheless in $\frac{6}{4}$ position, because the figured-bass numbers are calculated from the bass, G, not from the lower inner voice, C. Finally, observe that the number 5 is used even when the fifth is omitted (Example 9-1d).

Example 9-1

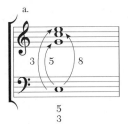

a.

$\frac{5}{3}$

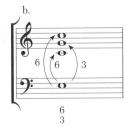

b.

$\frac{6}{3}$

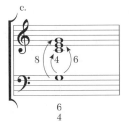

c.

$\frac{6}{4}$

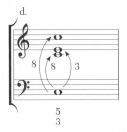

d.

$\frac{5}{3}$

Practice Exercises 9-1

Place the appropriate figured-bass numbers below each chord: $\frac{5}{3}$, $\frac{6}{3}$, or $\frac{6}{4}$.

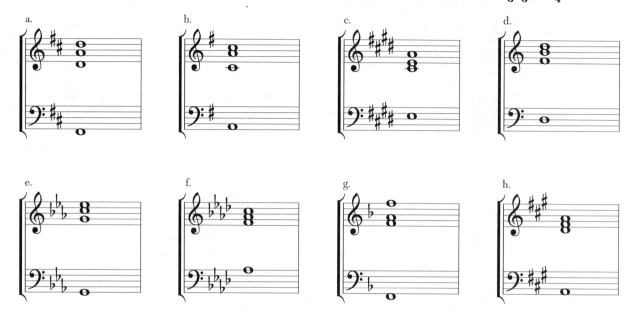

Roman-Numeral Analysis

The figured-bass analysis takes the chord "as is," assessing the interval content of the chord's existing configuration. In contrast, the Roman-numeral analysis depends on the root, which might be positioned anywhere within the chord. At first, it is best to take the time to write down the parent triad from which the chord is derived, and then assess that triad's location within the prevailing key. Example 9-2 displays the four steps of this process for three different chords. Though every key signature pertains to two different keys, here we shall regard the first two chords of the example as being in major keys, and the third chord as being in a minor key.

Step One: Write down one notehead for each component pitch of the chord, omitting doublings. Keep the noteheads as close to one another as possible.

Step Two: If Step One results in the parent triad (or in just a root and third if the fifth has been omitted), move on to Step Three. If the result is instead a $\frac{6}{3}$ or a $\frac{6}{4}$ configuration, move one or two notes down an octave so that the parent triad (line-line-line or space-space-space) results.

Step Three: Determine the scale degree of the parent triad's root within the scale of the prevailing key.

Step Four: Write down the Roman numeral that corresponds to the scale degree determined in Step Three. Pay careful attention to the chord's quality. (Review Example 4-8.)

Example 9-2

The above procedure should always yield the correct result. When you understand it thoroughly, you may take a shortcut by determining the root directly from the figured bass, as follows:

If the chord is in $\frac{5}{3}$ position, the bass is the root.

For example,   5   G
              3   E
                   C ← Root

If the chord is in $\frac{6}{3}$ position, the pitch that is the sixth above the bass is the root.

For example,   6   C ← Root
              3   G
                   E

If the chord is in $\frac{6}{4}$ position, the pitch that is the fourth above the bass is the root.

For example,   6   E
              4   C ← Root
                   G

Practice Exercises 9-2

First name the key that corresponds to the key signature. Then place the appropriate figured-bass numbers below each chord: $\frac{5}{3}$, $\frac{6}{3}$, or $\frac{6}{4}$. Then use the work area provided to form the chord's parent triad, determine the root, and write down the chord's Roman numeral (I, ii°, vi, etc.).

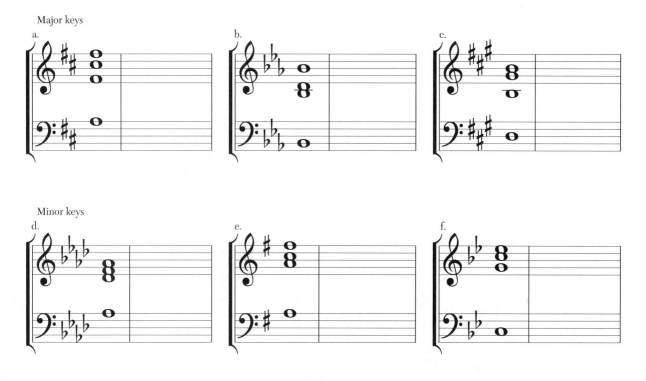

Major keys

a.　　　　b.　　　　c.

Minor keys

d.　　　　e.　　　　f.

Naming Chords

Musicians often discuss chord progressions using Roman numerals (for example, "a I–V–I progression"). We may instead refer to chords using a set of conventional names, such as "tonic" for I. Example 9-3 shows the complete set of names in two separate arrays: first in numerical order, and then in a symmetrical arrangement that might prove more useful when memorizing these terms. For most chords, the name is the same in both major and minor keys. But observe that for the chord built on $\hat{7}$, the name varies according to whether the key is major or minor. Only in major keys is $\hat{7}$ separated from $\hat{8}$ by a half step, the one case in which the label "leading tone" is appropriate.

Example 9-3

Major Keys		Minor Keys	Name
I	or	i	Tonic
ii	or	ii°	Supertonic
iii	or	III	Mediant
IV	or	iv	Subdominant
V	or	v	Dominant
vi	or	VI	Submediant
vii°			Leading tone (major keys)
		VII	Subtonic (minor keys)

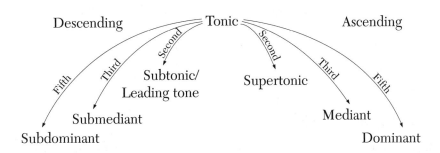

Practice Exercises 9-3

Provide the chord names (tonic, supertonic, etc.) for the six chords of Practice Exercises 9-2.

a. _____   d. _____

b. _____   e. _____

c. _____   f. _____

Tips for Success

✔ The distinction between bass and root is critical to the analytical procedures introduced in this chapter. The figured bass is an inventory of pitches above the bass, the bottom note of the chord. For this, take the chord as is. There is no need to move notes around, because the bass is easy to find just by glancing at the chord: it is the lowest pitch. In contrast, the Roman numeral requires that you know which pitch functions as the root. That pitch could reside anywhere within the chord, and you have to find it.

✔ Memorize all of the material of Example 9-3 without delay. Most of its content was introduced in earlier chapters.

Triplets

Having established two separate categories of meter—simple and compound—we now discover that the boundaries between them are not rigid. It is possible to divide a beat in a simple meter into three equal parts, as would be typical in a compound meter. We call the three notes that fill such a beat a triplet.

Triplets

The distinction we make between simple meters and compound meters is a useful one. When a melody emerges in a composer's mind, its beats will generally divide into either two or three parts (1 + 2 + . . . , or 1 + uh 2 + uh . . .). Sometimes a text that a composer sets to music will dictate one or the other of these choices. For example, it would be appropriate to use a simple meter for:

> **Twin**-kle,   **twin**-kle   **lit**-tle   **star.**

It would be unsatisfactory to put the same words into a compound-meter context, as:

> **Twin**-kle, twin-   **kle** lit-tle   **star.**

triplet

Because the way in which the beat subdivides is a characteristic feature of music, it is especially intriguing when, on occasion, a beat in a simple meter divides into three *equal* parts. Unlike combinations of an eighth note and two sixteenth notes, which maintain the midpoint of the beat as a moment of articulation (Examples 9-4a and 9-4b), a **triplet** (Example 9-4c) is a true division into thirds. The number "3" that appears alongside the beam indicates that the three eighth notes of a triplet are to be performed in the time normally occupied by two eighth notes in a simple meter. The duration of the beat, however, does not change.

Example 9-4

Performance Strategies for Triplets

Though the concept of triplets is straightforward, you may find it difficult to perform a triplet correctly. Two different sorts of mistakes are common:

1. You may forget that the eighth notes of the triplet are not of the same duration as ordinary eighth notes in a simple meter. They are faster! The three eighth notes of a triplet must all occur in the amount of time normally occupied by only two eighth notes.

2. You may have trouble making the three notes of a triplet sound for the same duration. Since the music before a triplet will reinforce the midpoint of the beat, it is very tempting to perform the second note of a triplet at that midpoint, and then squeeze the third note in before the beat is over, or to perform the first two notes of a triplet within the first half of the beat so that the third note occurs at the midpoint. There are other notational schemes for those rhythms (Examples 9-4a and 9-4b)! A triplet is a different phenomenon. Nothing happens at the midpoint of the beat.

As a practice exercise, say the words "E-ven" (for two-part division) and "Tri-an-gle" (for three-part division) while clapping the beats (marked by ✲ below) in the following configurations:

		E-	ven	E-	ven	E-	ven
✲	✲	✲		✲		✲	

		Tri-	an-	gle	Tri-	an-	gle	Tri-	an-	gle
✲	✲	✲			✲			✲		

		E-	ven	Tri-	an-	gle	E-	ven
✲	✲	✲		✲			✲	

Eventually convert to the conventions already presented for two- and three-part divisions of the beat—that is, "1 + . . ." and "1 + uh . . .", as displayed in Example 9-5.

Example 9-5

Schubert: Piano Sonata, D. 664, Mvmt. 1

___

Practice Exercises 9-4

Practice creating music notation by drawing each triplet symbol below twice to the right of its model.

a.

b.

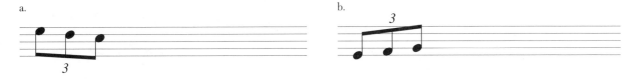

Create the melody indicated by the positioning of the pitch names in relation to the counting numbers. From one note to the next, use only a unison, second, third, or fourth as a melodic interval. Do not add rests.

c.

C	D	E	C	F	E	D	E	C	B	A	G	A	B	D	C
1	+	2	+	3	+	uh	4	+	1	+	uh 2	+	3	+	4	+

Tips for Success

✔ Do not underestimate the difficulty of performing triplets. Have your instructor or a more experienced student listen to you perform melodies or rhythms containing triplets to confirm that you are performing them correctly.

Laboratory

ACTIVITIES

L9-1. Play and Sing
a. With help from the keyboard as necessary, practice singing C–E–G, C–E–A, and C–F–A. Imagine ascending the C Major scale as you sing:
   C D E *F* *G*,   *C* D E *F* G *A*,   *C* D E *F* G *A*.
   Practice until you do not need assistance from the keyboard.
b. The collage of chords on the facing page contains two tonic chords, two supertonic chords, two mediant chords, and so forth, in F Major. Match up each pair, then play the chords in pairs until you have played all fourteen chords.

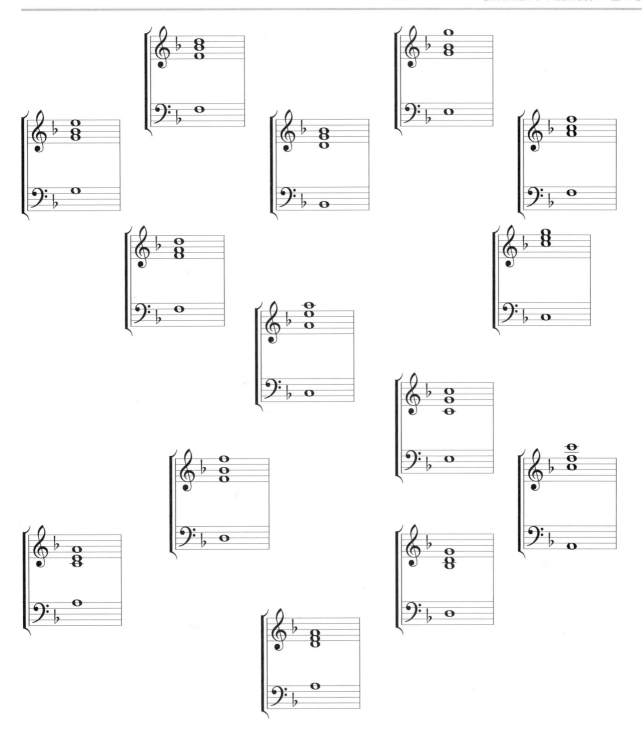

L9-2. Listening

Team up with another student, work with your instructor in class, or make use of the CD-ROM that accompanies this textbook to practice these exercises.

a. *Performer:* Play C–E–G, or C–E–A, or C–F–A.
   Listener: Indicate whether a chord in root position, a chord in first inversion, or a chord in second inversion has been performed.

b. *Performer:* Play two chords in the key of C Major—perhaps two different inversions of the same harmony.
   Listener: Indicate whether the chords represent the same harmony in C Major.

L9-3. Keyboard Album

a.

Schubert: *Schwanengesang,* "Ständchen," D. 957, No. 4

b.

Debussy: *Pour le piano,* Sarabande

c.

Verdi: *Aida,* Act 2

d.

Dvořák: Symphony No. 9 ("From the New World"), Op. 95, Mvmt. 4

L9-4. Song Book

a.

Brahms: Piano Concerto No. 2, Mvmt. 1

b.

Ride the Pony

Ride and ride the po - ny A mile an hour _____ on - ly.

Jump o - ver the tree - stump, Down falls the ba - by.

c.

Tying Knots in the Devil's Tail

A - way up high in the Si - er - ra Peaks, Where the yel - low jack pines grow tall,

Sand - y Bob and Bus - ter Jiggs Had a round - up camp last fall.

d.

Friend - ship thou Char - mer of the mind, Thou sweet de - lud - ing

ill, The bright - est min - utes Mor - tals find, And sharp - est Hours we feel.

L9-5. Rhythm

a.

b.

c.

d.

e.

L9-6. Improvisation

a. In this improvisation, the hands build chords in various inversions. Several choices for i, iv, and v chords in A Natural Minor are provided below, though you need not limit yourself to these. Fill each of eight measures with one whole-note chord or two half-note chords, according to the following plan:

measure 1:	i in root position
measure 2:	i in root position or either inversion
measures 3 and 4:	v in root position or either inversion
measure 5:	i in root position or either inversion
measure 6:	iv in root position or either inversion
measures 7 and 8:	i in root position

i IN A NATURAL MINOR   iv IN A NATURAL MINOR   v IN A NATURAL MINOR

b. Repeat exercise a in other natural minor keys.

If you create an improvisation that especially pleases you, write it down. Perhaps at your next class your instructor will ask you to perform it for the class.

L9-7. Score Study

Listen to Selections 2, 3, 4, and 5 in the Scores for Music Analysis section at the back of the textbook. Then answer the questions under the "Chapter 9" headings that accompany these selections.

Name: _____

Instructor: _____

Date: _____

Pitch Exercises

P9-1.
1. Below each three-note chord, indicate its figured-bass numbers: $\frac{6}{3}$ or $\frac{6}{4}$.
2. To the right, form its parent triad.
3. Underneath the parent triad, indicate the major or minor key that corresponds to the key signature, and provide the chord's Roman numeral (I, ii°, vi, etc.) and name (tonic, supertonic, submediant, etc.).

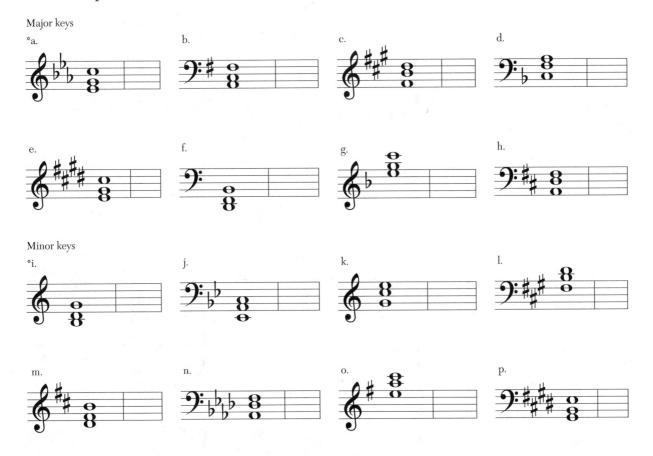

Major keys

°a.   b.   c.   d.

e.   f.   g.   h.

Minor keys

°i.   j.   k.   l.

m.   n.   o.   p.

P9-2.
1. Below each four-note chord, indicate its figured-bass numbers: $\frac{5}{3}$, $\frac{6}{3}$, or $\frac{6}{4}$.
2. To the right, form its parent triad, using either treble or bass clef.
3. Underneath the parent triad, indicate the major or minor key that corresponds to the key signature, and provide the chord's Roman numeral (I, ii°, vi, etc.) and name (tonic, supertonic, submediant, etc.).

Major keys

Minor keys

Name: _____

Instructor: _____

Date: _____

p.

q.

r.

P9-3. Fill in the blanks.

*a.   In the key of C Major, the pitch ___ is the third of the subdominant triad.

*b.   In the key of A Major, the pitch E is the _____ of the dominant triad.

*c.   In the key of ___ Natural Minor, the pitch G is the fifth of the tonic triad.

d.   In the key of D Major, the pitch F♯ is the root of the ___ triad.

e.   In the key of C Natural Minor, the pitch ___ is the third of the tonic triad.

f.   In the key of A♭ Major, the pitch G is the _____ of the leading-tone triad.

g.   In the key of ___ Natural Minor, the pitch C is the fifth of the submediant triad.

h.   In the key of C♯ Natural Minor, the pitch F♯ is the fifth of the _____ triad.

i.   In the key of D Natural Minor, the pitch ___ is the third of the subdominant triad.

j.   In the key of E Natural Minor, the pitch B is the _____ of the dominant triad.

k.   In the key of ___ Major, the pitch B♭ is the third of the supertonic triad.

l.   In the key of G Major, the pitch B is the fifth of the _____ triad.

m.   In the key of F Natural Minor, the pitch ___ is the root of the subtonic triad.

n.   In the key of F♯ Natural Minor, the pitch E is the _____ of the mediant triad.

o.   In the key of ___ Major, the pitch G is the third of the tonic triad.

Rhythm Exercises

R9-1. Create the melodies indicated by the positioning of the pitch names in relation to the counting numbers. From one note to the next, use only a unison, second, third, or fourth as a melodic interval. Do not add rests.

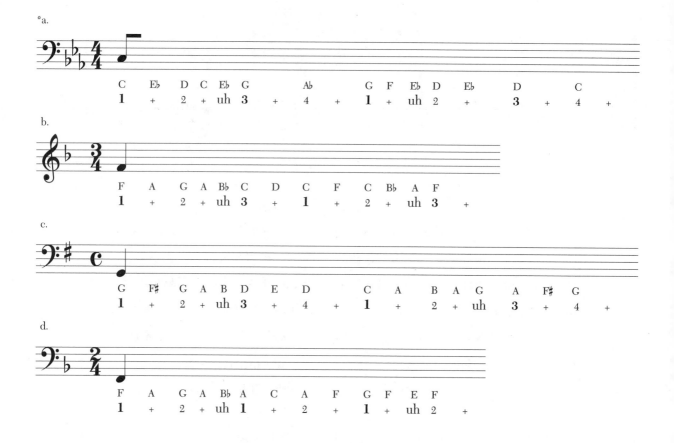

°a.

C	Eb	D	C	Eb	G		Ab		G	F	Eb	D		Eb		D		C	
1	+	2	+	uh	3	+	4	+	1	+	uh	2	+	3	+	4	+

b.

F	A	G	A	Bb	C	D	C	F	C	Bb	A	F
1	+	2	+	uh	3	+	1	+	2	+	uh	3	+

c.

G	F#	G	A	B	D	E	D		C	A	B	A	G	A	F#	G	
1	+	2	+	uh	3	+	4	+	1	+	2	+	uh	3	+	4	+

d.

F	A	G	A	Bb	A	C	A	F	G	F	E	F
1	+	2	+	uh	1	+	2	+	1	+	uh	2	+

Audio Exercises

A9-1. Either C–E–G, C–E–A, or C–F–A is performed. Indicate whether what you hear is in root position, first inversion, or second inversion.

°a. A C triad in root position   An A triad in first inversion   An F triad in second inversion

°b. A C triad in root position   An A triad in first inversion   An F triad in second inversion

c. A C triad in root position   An A triad in first inversion   An F triad in second inversion

d. A C triad in root position   An A triad in first inversion   An F triad in second inversion

e. A C triad in root position   An A triad in first inversion   An F triad in second inversion

f. A C triad in root position   An A triad in first inversion   An F triad in second inversion

g. A C triad in root position   An A triad in first inversion   An F triad in second inversion

h. A C triad in root position   An A triad in first inversion   An F triad in second inversion

i. A C triad in root position   An A triad in first inversion   An F triad in second inversion

j. A C triad in root position   An A triad in first inversion   An F triad in second inversion

Name: _____

Instructor: _____

Date: _____

A9-2. Two chords are performed. Indicate whether they represent the same harmony in C Major.

*a.	Yes	No	f.	Yes	No
*b.	Yes	No	g.	Yes	No
c.	Yes	No	h.	Yes	No
d.	Yes	No	i.	Yes	No
e.	Yes	No	j.	Yes	No

A9-3. Circle the music notation that corresponds to the pitches performed.

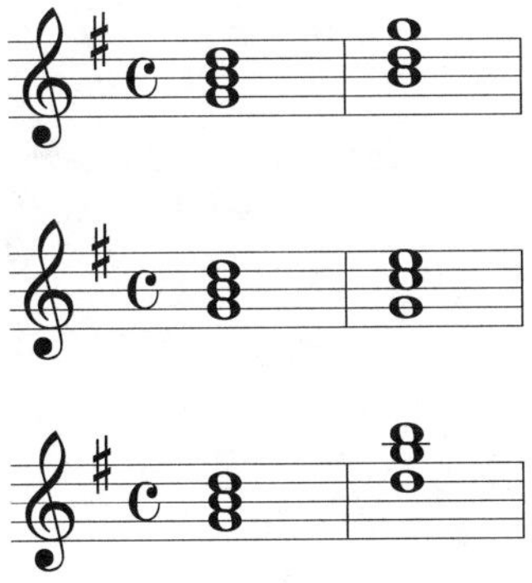

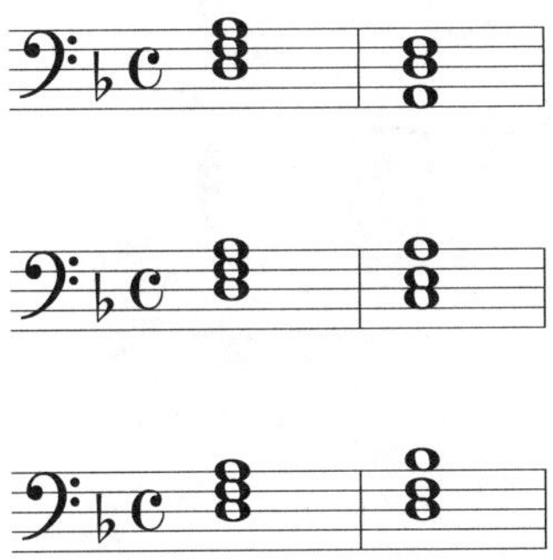

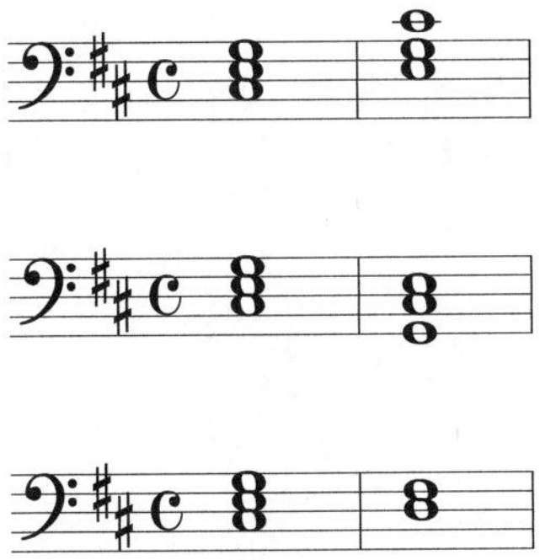

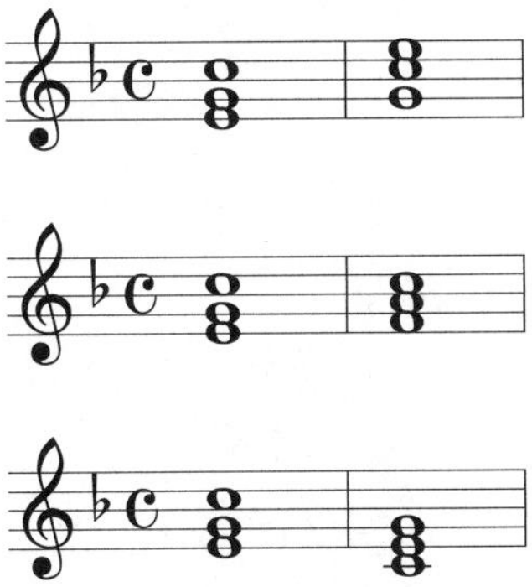

A9-4. Circle the music notation that corresponds to the rhythm performed.

CHAPTER 10

The Leading Tone in Chords and Scales

The leading tone, $\hat{7}$ in major keys, plays a special role in music. Its tendency to "lead" to the tonic ($\hat{8}$) makes it a most useful pitch. This natural tendency to ascend is enhanced when both $\hat{4}$ and $\hat{7}$ sound together, forming a $\frac{\hat{4}}{\hat{7}}$ diminished fifth or $\frac{\hat{7}}{\hat{4}}$ augmented fourth. One of these intervals will always occur in the dominant seventh chord, a dissonant four-note chord that is built upon the same foundation as $V\frac{5}{3}$. Because natural minor lacks a leading tone, opportunities for dynamic motion toward tonic are limited. Yet for centuries composers have inserted the leading tone into minor-key contexts. The resulting pitch collections have been assembled into harmonic minor and melodic minor scales.

Dissonance in the Leading-Tone Chord

When we classify intervals as consonant or dissonant, we are not saying that some are "good" and others are "bad." A dissonant interval is not necessarily something to be avoided. Instead, it is something to be careful with, because dissonance generates a powerful force toward resolution that must be harnessed in an appropriate way. Though there are many contexts for the use of dissonance in music, we shall focus on just two in this introductory text: those that occur in the leading-tone chord and in the dominant seventh chord.

If you play an ascending major scale only through $\hat{7}$, you will understand why $\hat{7}$ is called the leading tone, for it strongly tends toward tonic ($\hat{8}$). This tendency is enhanced in the vii° chord, when $\hat{7}$ and $\hat{4}$ occur simultaneously, forming the interval of a diminished fifth (d5) or its inversion, the augmented fourth (A4). (Remember from Chapter 6 that the diminished fifth is one half step smaller than a perfect fifth; the augmented fourth is one half step larger than a perfect fourth.) Example 10-1 shows how the dissonant diminished fifth resolves by contracting to a third, while the dissonant augmented fourth resolves by expanding to a sixth. In both cases, $\hat{7}$ leads to $\hat{8}$ (leading tone to tonic) and $\hat{4}$ leads to $\hat{3}$.

Example 10-1

d5 to M3

C Major: vii°   I

A4 to m6

C Major: vii°   I

Note: In the first tonic chord, the pitch E is doubled at the unison. That is, both D and F in the leading-tone chord move to the same E in the tonic chord. Observe how stems are applied in such situations.

Practice Exercises 10-1

Each chord below serves as vii° in some major key. Below each chord, indicate the major key indicated by the key signature, the chord's figured-bass numbers ($\frac{5}{3}$, $\frac{6}{3}$, or $\frac{6}{4}$), and which pitches serve as $\hat{4}$ and $\hat{7}$ (remembering to include a sharp or flat if indicated by the key signature). Then fill in the noteheads that correspond to $\hat{4}$ and $\hat{7}$. Finally, to the right of the notehead corresponding to $\hat{4}$, draw a filled-in notehead corresponding to $\hat{3}$, and to the right of the notehead corresponding to $\hat{7}$, draw a filled-in notehead corresponding to $\hat{8}$.

a. _____ Major f.b.: _____ $\hat{4}$ = _____ $\hat{7}$ = _____

b. _____ Major f.b.: _____ $\hat{4}$ = _____ $\hat{7}$ = _____

c. _____ Major f.b.: _____ $\hat{4}$ = _____ $\hat{7}$ = _____

d. _____ Major f.b.: _____ $\hat{4}$ = _____ $\hat{7}$ = _____

e. _____ Major f.b.: _____ $\hat{4}$ = _____ $\hat{7}$ = _____

f. _____ Major f.b.: _____ $\hat{4}$ = _____ $\hat{7}$ = _____

The Dominant Seventh Chord

dominant seventh chord

The resolutional force generated when $\hat{4}$ and $\hat{7}$ occur together is so desirable for creating forward momentum that composers devised a way to employ it even in the major dominant chord, which also contains the leading tone. By adding $\hat{4}$ to the three pitches of the dominant triad, a ***dominant seventh chord*** results. Example 10-2 shows that this chord merges all the pitches of both the V and vii° triads, forming a four-note chord with figured bass $\frac{7}{5}$. (By convention, the symbol $\frac{7}{5}$ sometimes appears in an abbreviated form, as 7.)

Example 10-2

As in the leading-tone chord, the resolutional tendencies generated by the dominant seventh chord include $\hat{4}$ to $\hat{3}$ and $\hat{7}$ to $\hat{8}$. Example 10-3 shows several samples of this resolution. Neither $\hat{4}$ nor $\hat{7}$ should be doubled when they occur together in a leading-tone or dominant seventh chord. Observe especially that, as with chords in $\frac{5}{3}$ position, the fifth may be omitted in a chord in $\frac{7}{5}$ position (Example 10-3c). Since its third and seventh (scale degrees $\hat{7}$ and $\hat{4}$ in the key) form a dissonant diminished fifth or augmented fourth, the root should be doubled in such cases.

Example 10-3

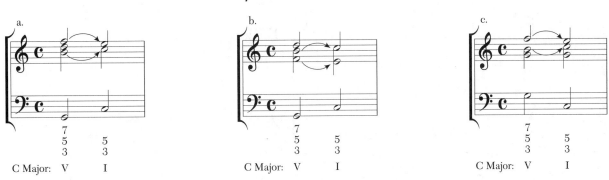

Practice Exercises 10-2

Create the chords requested, using four half notes (three in the treble clef, one in the bass clef). Employ the appropriate key signatures. If you omit the fifth (the only pitch that may be omitted), double the root. (Why?)

d.

$\begin{smallmatrix}7\\5\\3\end{smallmatrix}$
F Major: V

e.

$\begin{smallmatrix}7\\5\\3\end{smallmatrix}$
E Major: V

f.

$\begin{smallmatrix}7\\5\\3\end{smallmatrix}$
B♭ Major: V

Below each chord, indicate the major key indicated by the key signature, the chord's Roman numeral (V or vii°) and figured-bass numbers ($\begin{smallmatrix}5\\3\end{smallmatrix}$, $\begin{smallmatrix}6\\3\end{smallmatrix}$, $\begin{smallmatrix}6\\4\end{smallmatrix}$, or $\begin{smallmatrix}7\\5\\3\end{smallmatrix}$), and which pitches serve as $\hat{4}$ and $\hat{7}$ (remembering to include a sharp or flat if indicated by the key signature). Then fill in the noteheads that correspond to $\hat{4}$ and $\hat{7}$. Finally, to the right of the notehead corresponding to $\hat{4}$, draw a filled-in notehead corresponding to $\hat{3}$, and to the right of the notehead corresponding to $\hat{7}$, draw a filled-in notehead corresponding to $\hat{8}$.

g.

_____ Major   R.n. _____   f.b.: _____

$\hat{4}$ = _____ $\hat{7}$ = _____

h.

_____ Major   R.n. _____   f.b.: _____

$\hat{4}$ = _____ $\hat{7}$ = _____

i.

_____ Major   R.n. _____   f.b.: _____

$\hat{4}$ = _____ $\hat{7}$ = _____

j.

_____ Major   R.n. _____   f.b.: _____

$\hat{4}$ = _____ $\hat{7}$ = _____

k.

_____ Major   R.n. _____   f.b.: _____

$\hat{4}$ = _____ $\hat{7}$ = _____

l.

_____ Major   R.n. _____   f.b.: _____

$\hat{4}$ = _____ $\hat{7}$ = _____

Harmonic Minor

The absence of the leading tone contributes to the solemn, reserved character of natural minor. Melodies such as "Greensleeves" (Example 10-4) employ the seven diatonic pitches of natural minor in wonderful ways.

Example 10-4

Greensleeves

Yet in the context of chord progressions, the leading tone's absence is a liability. Without the resolution of the leading tone to tonic, characteristic of V–I, V⁷–I, and vii°–I in major keys, the natural minor counterpart seems to lack conviction. For this reason, it is common for composers to substitute the dominant or leading-tone chord of the parallel major key. Compare the sense of closure in the two versions of an excerpt by Schumann in Example 10-5a. E–G–B is the dominant chord generated by the diatonic pitches of A Natural Minor. By substituting the dominant chord of the parallel major key—A Major's E–G♯–B—a more satisfying progression is achieved.

The leading tone becomes even more vital when the dominant seventh chord is employed. Try, for example, adding D just above B in the next-to-last chord of the two excerpts in Example 10-5a. With E–G♯–B, D sounds fine (Example 10-5b). As $\hat{4}$, D creates dissonant tension against $\hat{7}$ (G♯, the leading tone). D resolves to tonic's third, C; and G♯ to the tonic root, A. In contrast, with E–G–B, the D is an awkward presence (Example 10-5c). The chord does not possess as strong a sense of forward momentum.

Example 10-5

Schumann: *Album for the Young*, Op. 68, The Wild Horseman

A Natural Minor (*not* how Schumann composed it)

With G♯ replacing the G of A Natural Minor (Schumann's version)

Because the substitution of the leading tone for the subtonic pitch is so prevalent in music written in minor keys, the version of minor that results has been given a name: ***harmonic minor***. Example 10-6 displays A Harmonic Minor and C Harmonic Minor scales. Since these scales contain a pitch that is not diatonic in the context of the natural minor key signature (which is retained), the label ↑ $\hat{7}$ (read "raised seven") is used in place of $\hat{7}$. This modification must be made by inserting the appropriate accidental beside the notehead. In some keys, $\hat{7}$ is raised using a sharp. In other keys, $\hat{7}$ is raised using a natural. All accidentals affect all noteheads written on that particular line or space until the next bar line, at which point the key signature's full power resumes.

harmonic minor

Example 10-6

A Harmonic Minor

C Harmonic Minor

Most minor-key compositions employ both the subtonic pitch (a whole step below tonic) and the leading tone (a half step below tonic). For example, the mediant chord will generally be built using the subtonic pitch (for example, C–E–**G** in A Minor), while the dominant chord, when it precedes tonic, will almost always contain the leading tone (for example, E–**G♯**–B).

Practice Exercises 10-3

Create the scales requested. Use the key signature of natural minor, and make the adjustment in the seventh scale degree manually by placing the appropriate accidental to the left of the notehead that will represent ↑ $\hat{7}$.

a. A Harmonic Minor, ascending

b. D Harmonic Minor, descending

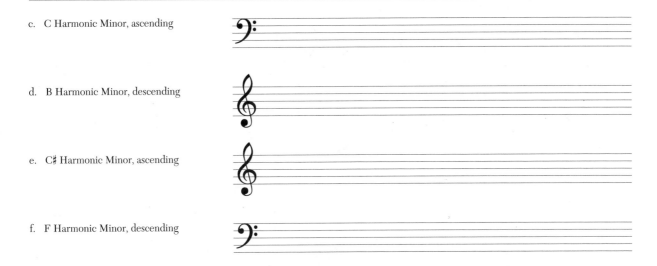

c. C Harmonic Minor, ascending

d. B Harmonic Minor, descending

e. C♯ Harmonic Minor, ascending

f. F Harmonic Minor, descending

Melodic Minor

The interval formed by the diatonic sixth scale degree (6̂) and the leading tone (↑7̂) in the harmonic minor scale is an augmented second, one half step larger than a major second. It is a harsh dissonance that will rarely occur in a melodic context such as a stepwise ascent from 5̂ to 8̂. In compositions written in minor keys, the sixth scale degree of the parallel major key is often borrowed, along with the seventh scale degree, to avoid this awkward melodic interval, forming another variant of natural minor called ***melodic minor***. Its scale differs from natural minor's in that both the sixth and seventh scale degrees of the parallel major key are borrowed during the ascent. During the descent, the scale reverts to natural minor, because the leading tone's ascending function is not called upon when a melodic line descends. Example 10-7 displays A Melodic Minor and C Melodic Minor scales.

melodic minor

Example 10-7

A Melodic Minor

C Melodic Minor

Of the scales we have explored—major, natural minor, harmonic minor, and melodic minor—only the melodic minor has differing ascending and descending forms. Example 10-8 displays these four scales for tonic C. The pitches that require the addition of an accidental are circled. Remember that, depending on the key, you will sometimes raise a pitch with a natural (for example, C Minor's 7̂, B♭, becomes B♮) and sometimes with a sharp (for example, A Minor's 7̂, G, becomes G♯). In some other minor keys, introduced in the Appendix, a double sharp would be required. Those keys will not be explored in this chapter.

Example 10-8

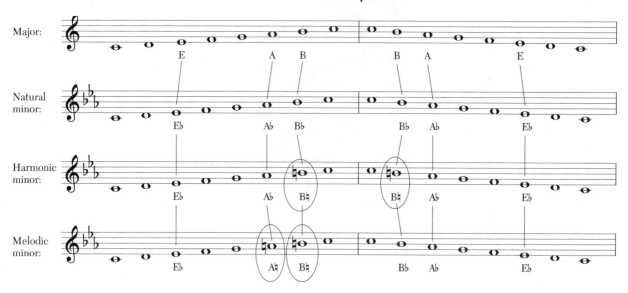

Practice Exercises 10-4

Create the scales requested, using the appropriate key signatures and accidentals.

a. F Major, ascending

b. F Natural Minor, ascending

c. F Harmonic Minor, ascending

d. F Melodic Minor, ascending

e. E Major, descending

f. E Natural Minor, descending

g. E Harmonic Minor, descending

h. E Melodic Minor, descending

Identify each scale (A Major, D Harmonic Minor, etc.).

i. _____

j. _____

k. _____

l. _____

m. _____

n. _____

Tips for Success

✔ Half of the material presented in Example 10-8 is a review of concepts from earlier chapters. Make sure that you memorize *all* of the information in this example, and remember that in some keys a sharp, rather than a natural, may be required.

✔ Like the $\frac{5}{3}$ position, the $\frac{7}{5}{3}$ position of V is classified as a root position. To learn about the inversions of $\frac{7}{5}{3}$, see Seventh Chords and Their Inversions in the Appendix.

✔ Chord construction and analysis involving the altered pitches of the harmonic and melodic minor scales are topics of Chapter 12.

✔ Though $\hat{7}$ is a member of the iii chord in major keys, its function in that context is not the same as in V and vii° chords. Therefore, doubling $\hat{7}$ is not prohibited in that context.

✔ Composers sometimes add a seventh to chords besides V. However, in this and the next two chapters only V will appear with a seventh. To learn about seventh chords on other scale degrees, see Seventh Chords and Their Inversions in the Appendix.

RHYTHM

Syncopation

In any meter, some beats are strong and others are weak. Syncopation occurs when the positioning of a melody's pitches counters that pattern. In this chapter we explore syncopation resulting from a creative ordering of the symbols of rhythmic notation we have employed in earlier chapters.

Metrical Syncopation

Meter is the framework upon which the rhythmic life of music unfolds. It sets up our expectations regarding when musical events will occur. Because of meter, we expect that the first beat of a measure will be the strongest and that what happens on a beat will be stronger than what happens between beats. The purposeful contradiction of these expectations—making strong that which is normally weak, or making weak that which is normally strong—is a powerful tool for enhancing musical expression. **syncopation** *Syncopation* is a temporary contradiction of the meter. It is often accomplished without any special symbols of rhythmic notation. For example, the melody of Example 10-9 is built entirely of eighth notes, quarter notes, and half notes. Three times, a half note is positioned on beat 2 of a common-time measure. The meter would generally dictate that beat 3 be stronger than beat 2. Beethoven confounds our expectations. His melody is distinctive because he has positioned a half note in an atypical position.

Example 10-9

Beethoven: Trio, Op. 11

Submetrical Syncopation

In Beethoven's melody (Example 10-9), the first, second, and fourth beats are the sites of action. This arrangement occurs at the submetrical level as well. When we say "1 ee + ee", we emphasize the "1" and the "+" more than the "ee" segments of the beat. Twice in Example 10-10, Mozart makes the first "ee" of the beat stronger than the "+". In measures 1 and 3, the first, second, and fourth segments of beat 1 are the sites of action. The melody is formed entirely from standard note values: sixteenth notes, eighth notes, dotted eighth notes, and a quarter note. It is *where* these notes occur that creates the feeling of syncopation.

Example 10-10

Mozart: *The Marriage of Figaro*, Act 2

Our study of syncopation will continue in Chapter 11, where a new symbol (the tie) opens up even greater opportunities for enhanced expression.

Practice Exercises 10-5

Position counting syllables (1 ee + ee . . . or 1 ee + ee uh ee . . .) in the appropriate positions beneath the noteheads (as in Example 10-10). Then perform each rhythm.

Tips for Success

✔ When performing syncopated rhythms, the counting syllables must continue at a uniform pace, as always. These syllables represent the normalcy of the meter, which a syncopated rhythm counters.

Laboratory

L10-1. Play and Sing

a. Play the four pitches of a dominant seventh chord, close together and low in your vocal range. (For example, play A–C♯–E–G or C–E–G–B♭.) Then play and sing its four pitches: "Root," "Third," "Fifth," and "Seventh." Then play and sing other dominant seventh chords low in your vocal range.

b. Repeat Exercise L10-1a, this time playing only the lowest pitch before singing all four pitches.

c. Place the little finger of your left hand above A (a third or a tenth below Middle C, depending on your vocal range) and the next three fingers above B, C, and D. Place the second finger of your right hand above the adjacent E and the next three fingers above F, G♯, and A. (Let your thumbs dangle back a bit.) Now play each of these keys in succession from left to right, forming an A Harmonic Minor scale ascending from $\hat{1}$ to $\hat{8}$. Then play the scale descending from $\hat{8}$ to $\hat{1}$.

d. Play the ascending and descending A Harmonic Minor scales again, but this time, pause after each pitch and sing it. That is, play A, then sing A; play B, then sing B; and so on. You may sing on the neutral syllable "la," sing the pitch names ("A," "B," "C," etc.), or sing the scale degree numbers ("$\hat{1}$," "$\hat{2}$," "$\hat{3}$," etc., singing $\uparrow\hat{7}$ as "sharp").

e. Repeat exercises c and d, now performing ascending and descending A Melodic Minor scales. (Remember that the ascending and descending scales are not the same.)

f. Repeat exercises c–e for other minor keys.

L10-2. Listening

Team up with another student, work with your instructor in class, or make use of the CD-ROM that accompanies this textbook to practice these exercises.

a. *Performer:* Play a four-note chord, either a major triad with octave (for example, G–B–D–G) or a major triad with minor seventh (for example, G–B–D–F).
Listener: Indicate whether a chord in $\frac{5}{3}$ or $\frac{7}{5}{3}$ position has been performed.

b. *Performer:* Play a scale, both ascending and descending. Select the scale from among the following choices: major, natural minor, harmonic minor, or melodic minor.
Listener: Indicate which scale type has been performed: major, natural minor, harmonic minor, or melodic minor.

L10-3. Keyboard Album

a. Berlioz: *Béatrice et Bénédict*, Act 1

b. Bach: Suite for Orchestra, BWV 1067, Ouverture

c. Franck: Symphony, Mvmt. 1

d. Beethoven: String Quartet No. 2, Op. 18, No. 2, Mvmt. 4

L10-4. Song Book

a. Grieg: *Peer Gynt*, Act 1

b. Come All Ye Fair and Tender Maidens

Come all ye fair and ten-der maid-ens, take warn-ing how you court young

men,   one night they may shine   like stars a - bove you,   to love you that night   but ne'er a - gain.

c.

Tom Dooley

Hang down   your head Tom   Doo - ley,   Hang down   your head   and   cry,

Hang down   your head Tom   Doo - ley,   Poor boy,   you're bound   to   die.

d.

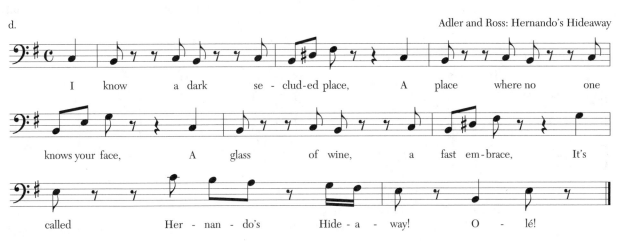

Adler and Ross: Hernando's Hideaway

I   know   a dark   se - clud-ed place,   A   place   where no   one

knows your face,   A   glass   of wine,   a   fast em - brace,   It's

called   Her - nan - do's   Hide - a - way!   O - lé!

L10-5. Rhythm

a.

b.

c.

d.

e.

L10-6. Improvisation

a. In this improvisation, the I, IV, and V⁷ chords in C Major are employed. Samples of each are provided below, though you need not limit yourself to these. Fill each of eight measures with one whole-note chord or two half-note chords, according to the following plan:

measure 1:	I in root position
measure 2:	I in root position or first inversion
measure 3:	IV in root position
measure 4:	I in root position
measures 5 and 6*:	V⁷
measures 7* and 8:	I in root position

    *Place F in the soprano in measure 6. F is $\hat{4}$, which creates a diminished fifth against inner-voice B (= $\hat{7}$). What soprano pitch must occur in the I chord that begins measure 7?

b. Repeat exercise L10-6a in other major keys.

    If you create an improvisation that especially pleases you, write it down. Perhaps at your next class your instructor will ask you to perform it for the class.

L10-7. Score Study

Listen to Selections 1, 5, 6, and 7 in the Scores for Music Analysis section at the back of the textbook. Then answer the questions under the "Chapter 10" headings that accompany these selections.

Name: _____

Instructor: _____

Date: _____

Pitch Exercises

P10-1. Create the chords indicated by each Roman numeral, figured bass, and key. Use the left side of the system for writing down the key signature and the parent dominant seventh chord (line-line-line-line or space-space-space-space). Use the right side for presenting a four-note chord in half notes (three notes in the treble clef; one note in the bass clef). Remember that neither the third nor the seventh of a dominant seventh chord may be doubled.

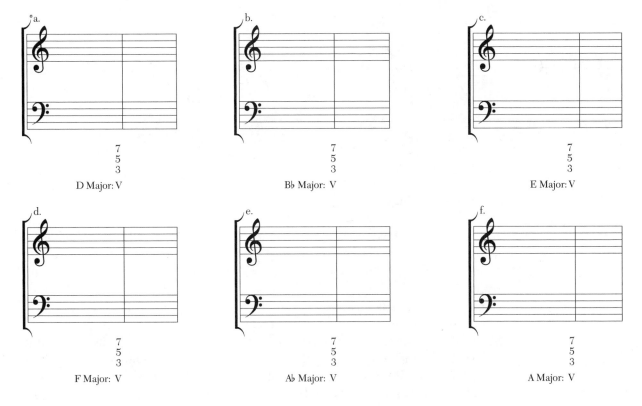

P10-2.

1. Below each four-note chord, indicate its figured bass: $\frac{5}{3}$, $\frac{6}{3}$, $\frac{6}{4}$, or $\frac{7}{5}$.

2. To the right, form its parent triad or parent dominant seventh chord, in either the treble or bass clef.

3. Underneath the parent triad or chord, indicate the major key that corresponds to the key signature and provide the chord's Roman numeral (V or vii°) and name (dominant or leading tone).

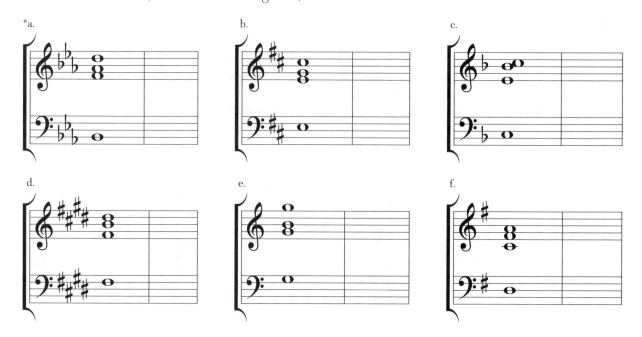

P10-3. Each chord below contains the interval of a diminished fifth or augmented fourth.

1. Name the major key indicated by the key signature. Determine which pitches correspond to $\hat{4}$ and $\hat{7}$. (For example, in C Major you would identify F as $\hat{4}$ and B as $\hat{7}$.)

2. Fill in the noteheads of these two pitches with your pencil. (For example, in C Major you would fill in the F and B noteheads.)

3. Show how the diminished fifth or augmented fourth resolves by drawing filled-in noteheads for the resolution pitches to the right of the two noteheads you have already filled in. Remember that $\hat{4}$ resolves downward by step to $\hat{3}$, and $\hat{7}$ resolves upward by step to $\hat{8}$. (For example, in C Major you would write an E to the right of F, and a C to the right of B.)

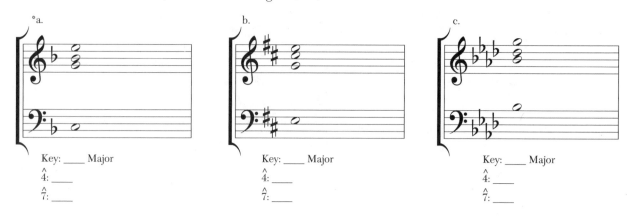

Name: _____

Instructor: _____

Date: _____

d.

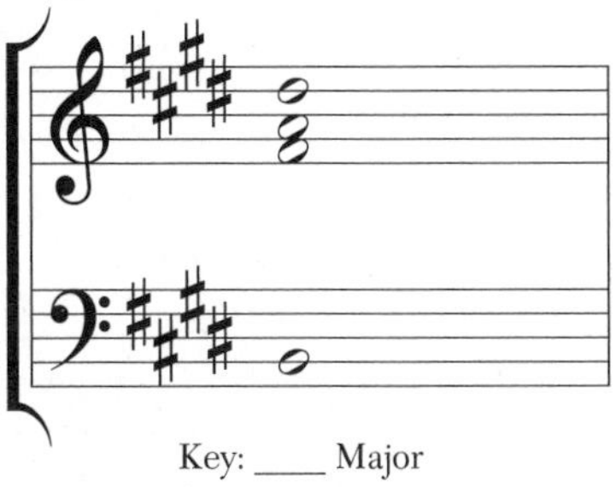

Key: ____ Major
4̂: ____
7̂: ____

e.

Key: ____ Major
4̂: ____
7̂: ____

f.

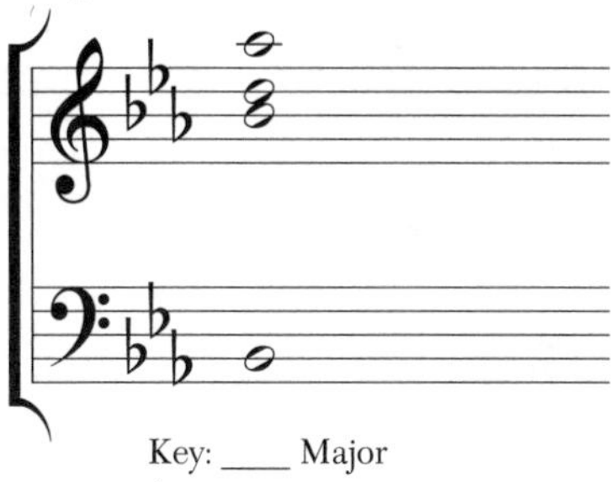

Key: ____ Major
4̂: ____
7̂: ____

P10-4. Create each of the scales requested. Use natural minor key signatures, and label each pitch with its scale degree number (including ↑6̂ and ↑7̂ where appropriate). Remember that some accidentals may need to be inserted.

°a.   D Melodic Minor, ascending

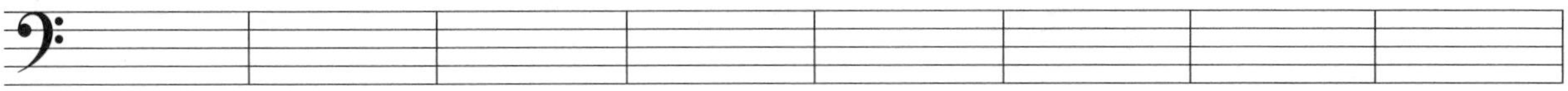

°b.   F Harmonic Minor, descending

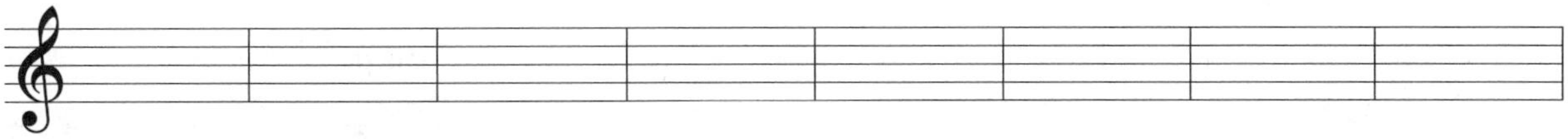

c.   B Melodic Minor, descending

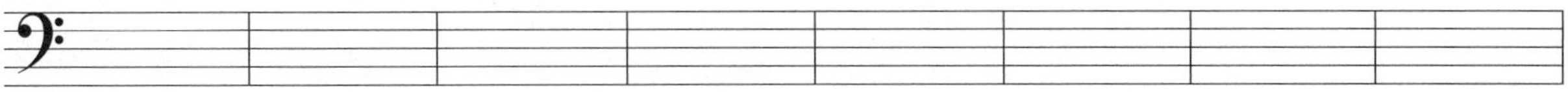

d.   F♯ Harmonic Minor, ascending

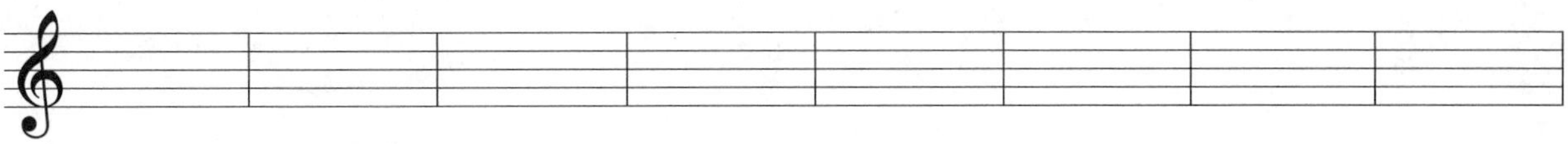

e.   C Melodic Minor, ascending

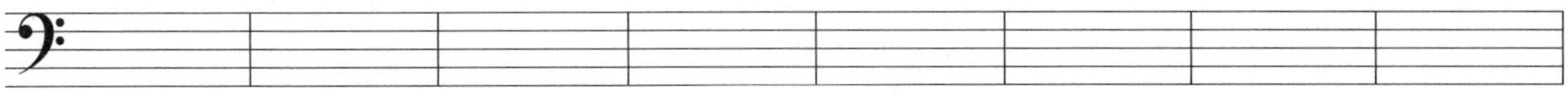

f.   A Harmonic Minor, descending

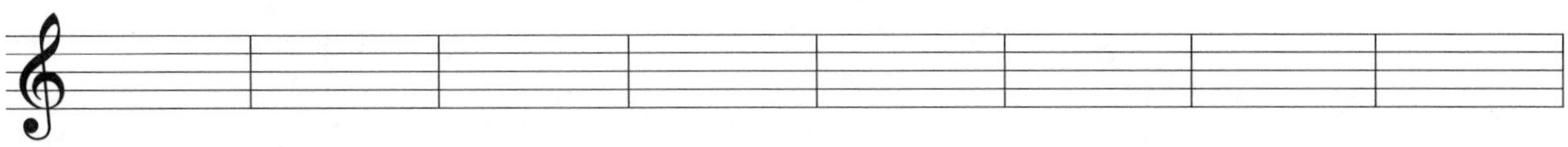

g. F♯ Melodic Minor, descending

h. G Harmonic Minor, ascending

i. C♯ Melodic Minor, ascending

P10-5. Name the key in which each melody below has been composed, including the form of minor (for example, C Melodic Minor or F Harmonic Minor). You may use the staves provided as a work area to form ascending and/or descending scales. (Note: Because these melodies are excerpts from larger compositions, they will not necessarily end on a pitch of the tonic triad.)

°a.   Beethoven: Trio No. 2, Op. 1, No. 2, Mvmt. 3

b.   Berlioz: *Béatrice et Bénédict*, Act 1

c.   Berlioz: *Béatrice et Bénédict*, Act 1

Name: _____

Instructor: _____

Date: _____

d.

Beethoven: String Quartet No. 5, Op. 18, No. 5, Mvmt. 1

This melody employs both D and D♯. D plays an embellishing role, as a neighbor to C. (D♯ would not be a good neighbor for C, since it is an augmented second away.) For your answer, consider D♯, not D, to be part of the scale.

Rhythm Exercises

R10-1. For each melody below, place counting syllables in correct alignment below the noteheads. In exercise a, use "1 + 2 + . . .". In exercise b, use "1 ee + ee 2 ee + ee . . .". In exercise c, use "1 ee + ee uh ee 2 ee + ee uh ee . . .".

a.

b.

c.

R10-2. Create the melodies indicated by the positioning of the pitch names in relation to the counting numbers. From one note to the next, use only a unison, second, third, or fourth as a melodic interval. Do not add rests.

°a.

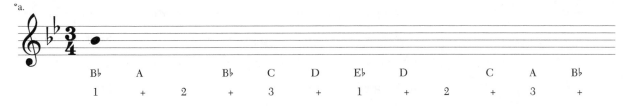

B♭	A	B♭	C	D	E♭	D	C	A	B♭
1	+	2	+	3	+	1	+	2	+	3	+

b.

	D	D		F♯	A	A		G	F♯	F♯		E	C♯	E		D
	1	ee	+	ee	2	ee	+	ee	1	ee	+	ee	2	ee	+	ee

c.

	C		D	E♭	D	G					F		G	A♭	G		C
	1	ee	+	ee	uh	ee	2	ee	+	ee	uh	ee	1	ee	+	ee	uh	ee	2	ee	+	ee	uh	ee

Audio Exercises

A10-1. A four-note chord in $\frac{5}{3}$ position (e.g., C–E–G–C) or in $\frac{7}{5}{3}$ position (e.g., C–E–G–B♭) is performed. Indicate which of these two choices is performed.

*a. $\frac{5}{3}$ $\frac{7}{5}{3}$ f. $\frac{5}{3}$ $\frac{7}{5}{3}$

*b. $\frac{5}{3}$ $\frac{7}{5}{3}$ g. $\frac{5}{3}$ $\frac{7}{5}{3}$

c. $\frac{5}{3}$ $\frac{7}{5}{3}$ h. $\frac{5}{3}$ $\frac{7}{5}{3}$

d. $\frac{5}{3}$ $\frac{7}{5}{3}$ i. $\frac{5}{3}$ $\frac{7}{5}{3}$

e. $\frac{5}{3}$ $\frac{7}{5}{3}$ j. $\frac{5}{3}$ $\frac{7}{5}{3}$

A10-2. A scale is performed, both ascending and descending. Indicate the type of scale performed.

*a.	Major	Natural Minor	Harmonic Minor	Melodic Minor
*b.	Major	Natural Minor	Harmonic Minor	Melodic Minor
c.	Major	Natural Minor	Harmonic Minor	Melodic Minor
d.	Major	Natural Minor	Harmonic Minor	Melodic Minor
e.	Major	Natural Minor	Harmonic Minor	Melodic Minor
f.	Major	Natural Minor	Harmonic Minor	Melodic Minor
g.	Major	Natural Minor	Harmonic Minor	Melodic Minor
h.	Major	Natural Minor	Harmonic Minor	Melodic Minor
i.	Major	Natural Minor	Harmonic Minor	Melodic Minor
j.	Major	Natural Minor	Harmonic Minor	Melodic Minor

Name: _____

Instructor: _____

Date: _____

A10-3. Circle the music notation that corresponds to the pitches performed.

°a.

b.

c.

d.

A10-4. Circle the music notation that corresponds to the rhythm performed.

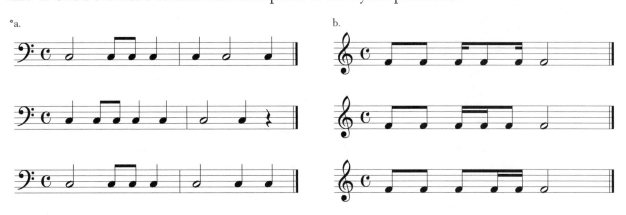

°a.

b.

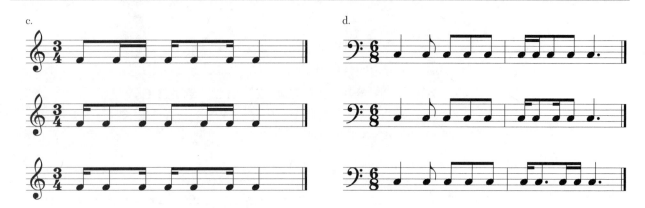

CHAPTER 11

Chord Progression in Major Keys

PITCH

Individual chords are the building blocks of music. Composers assemble collections of chords to follow one another in forming musical formations called phrases. Certain successions of chords, called cadences, produce a sense of closure at the ends of phrases. Different successions of chords create cadences of various types, each with a distinguishing name: authentic cadence, half cadence, plagal cadence, and deceptive cadence.

Phrases and Cadences in the Parallel Period

Music is often composed in segments called **phrases**, which are groups of measures shaped by clearly perceptible beginnings and endings. For example, the melody will often descend at the end of a phrase, accompanied by a **cadence**: a succession of chords that invokes a sense of closure. Though a phrase is often four or eight measures in length, composers sometimes write phrases of other lengths.

phrases

cadence

When two phrases work together as a pair, they form a **period**. In the period shown in Example 11-1, each phrase is four measures in length. As you listen to this example, consider why you sense that measure 5 begins a new phrase, even though there is no obvious visual clue to indicate the end of the first phrase in measure 4.

period

Example 11-1

Mozart: Sonata, K. 331, Mvmt. 1

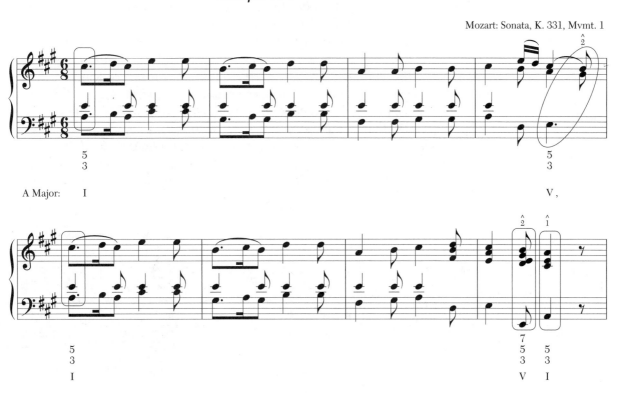

A Major: I

5
3

V,

5
3

I

7
5
3

5
3

V   I

One reason measure 5 seems like the beginning of a new phrase is that Mozart repeats the music of the opening measures in measure 5 through the first chord of measure 7. A period whose two phrases begin in the same way is called a **parallel period**. What distinguishes the two phrases from one another is how each ends. In the first phrase, the melody and its accompanying chords lead to $\hat{2}$, the fifth of the V chord. Though they end the phrase adequately, neither gives a sense of completion. The composition *must* continue. In the second phrase, the melody and its accompanying chords lead to $\hat{1}$, the root of the I chord. Both $\hat{1}$ and I provide a sense of completion. In this case, they conclude the period, but not the composition. When the two phrases of a period are structured so that the first phrase requires a second phrase to follow, they are called **antecedent** and **consequent phrases**. Only the consequent phrase resolves fully. A cadence from a root-position V chord to a root-position I chord, as in measure 8 of the excerpt, is called an **authentic cadence**. Though the cadence at the end of the antecedent phrase may adequately conclude the chordal progression of that phrase, it does not possess the finality of an authentic cadence. A cadence on a root-position V chord, as in measure 4, is called a **half cadence**.

Example 11-2 shows the characteristic features of a parallel period, here demonstrated with two four-measure phrases.

parallel period

antecedent phrase

consequent phrase

authentic cadence

half cadence

Example 11-2

measure	1	2	3	4	5	6	7	8
	Melody . . .				Repeat of melody . . .			
	I			V,	I		V	I
				Half			Authentic	
				cadence			cadence	

___Antecedent phrase___/   ___Consequent phrase___/
_____Parallel period_____/

The authentic cadence that ends Example 11-1 derives part of its finality from the fact that the soprano pitches of the last four chords lead downward by step to $\hat{1}$ in coordination with the cadence on I. When $\hat{1}$ resides in both the soprano and bass at the end of a phrase, the cadence is called *perfect*. The ending of Mozart's period is a **perfect authentic cadence**. Later in the composition, Mozart concludes a similar phrase on $\hat{3}$ instead of $\hat{1}$ in the soprano, as shown in Example 11-3. Even though the chordal progression is V-I, this cadence is an **imperfect authentic cadence** because a scale degree other than $\hat{1}$ ends the melody. (The dissonant G♯ and B that appear above the bass pitch A at this cadence are remnants of the preceding V chord. At the very end of the measure, the consonant A and C♯, chord members of I, arrive.) Only when a phrase ends on tonic may the cadence be perfect. A half cadence is never perfect.

perfect authentic cadence

imperfect authentic cadence

Example 11-3

Mozart: Sonata, K. 331, Mvmt. 1

A Major: V   I

Practice Exercises 11-1

a. Beneath each chord in the progression below, indicate its figured bass and Roman numeral. If the same analysis symbols pertain to more than one consecutive chord, write the analysis only once, and draw horizontal lines to show the point to which it extends: for example,

$$6 \text{———}$$
$$3 \text{———}$$
$$\text{ii} \text{———}$$

Hint: The Roman numeral is determined from the root, not the bass. If the chord is in $\frac{6}{3}$ or $\frac{6}{4}$ position, you must follow the procedure introduced in Chapter 9 to determine which pitch functions as the root.

F Major: $\overset{5}{\underset{3}{\text{I}}}$

b. Fill in the blanks.

The composition above contains two p_____s. A(n) _____

cadence occurs at measure 4. Thus measures 1 through 4 form a(n)

_____ _____. A(n) _____

_____ cadence occurs at measure 8. Thus measures 5 through 8

form a(n) _____ _____. All together, measures 1 through

8 form a p_____ _____.

Plagal and Deceptive Cadences

An authentic cadence, V to I, gives a strong sense of closure at the end of a phrase. The leading tone ($\hat{7}$, the third of the V chord) resolves by step to $\hat{1}$. When the dominant seventh chord is used, $\hat{4}$—a dissonant augmented fourth or diminished fifth against the leading tone—resolves by step to $\hat{3}$. (See the last measure of Example 11-1.)

In contrast, the progression from IV to I lacks both the leading tone and the capacity to include a dissonant interval that would resolve to pitches of the tonic chord. When this progression occurs at the end of a phrase, a ***plagal cadence*** results.

plagal cadence

The plagal cadence offers a solemn alternative to the V–I authentic cadence. The plagal cadence rarely occurs except in the immediate context of an authentic cadence.

A plagal cadence appears in the "Amen" endings of many Protestant hymns, after the verse has concluded with an authentic cadence. As with the authentic cadence, the plagal cadence is perfect if the soprano pitch of the I chord is $\hat{1}$, and imperfect if it is $\hat{3}$ or $\hat{5}$. Example 11-4 shows a perfect plagal cadence that follows after a perfect authentic cadence in a Protestant hymn, and an imperfect plagal cadence in a nocturne by Chopin. This phrase by Chopin both begins and ends the nocturne. The squiggly lines that appear to the left of the first and last chords instruct the performer to **arpeggiate** the pitches of the chords—that is, to play each note in rapid succession from bottom to top.

arpeggiate

Example 11-4

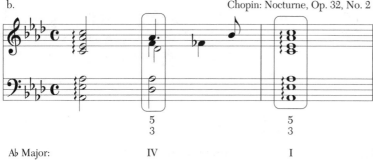

In Example 11-5, from Handel's opera *Xerxes*, there is a surprise. The melodic line of the phrase starts on $\hat{8}$ and proceeds through all the scale degrees down to $\hat{2}$, which is supported by V (measure 5). With this precedent—and because a phrase earlier in the movement began with the same descent and concluded with a perfect authentic cadence—$\hat{1}$ supported by I is the expected continuation. Handel instead moves the bass from $\hat{5}$ to $\hat{6}$, supporting the IV chord in $\frac{6}{3}$ position where we had expected I. This type of cadence, where IV in $\frac{6}{3}$ position or VI in $\frac{5}{3}$ position (or some other substitute for the root-position tonic) is used, is called a **deceptive cadence**. It is the least final of the basic cadence types. The chord that substitutes for I typically leads into another succession of chords that ends in a perfect authentic cadence, as in measure 8 of Example 11-5.

deceptive cadence

Example 11-5

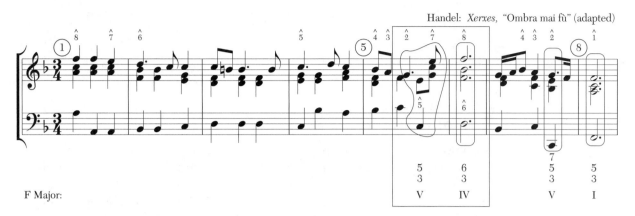

Example 11-6 provides a summary of the basic cadence types.

Example 11-6

Next-to-last chord	Last chord	Last soprano pitch	Cadence type
V	I	$\hat{1}$	Perfect Authentic
V	I	$\hat{3}$ or $\hat{5}$	Imperfect Authentic
Anything except V	V	any chord member	Half
IV	I	$\hat{1}$	Perfect Plagal
IV	I	$\hat{3}$ or $\hat{5}$	Imperfect Plagal
V	Anything except I	any chord member	Deceptive

Practice Exercises 11-2

a. Beneath each chord in the progression below, indicate its figured bass and Roman numeral.

b. Fill in the blanks.

The first phrase of the composition above ends in measure 4 with a(n)

_____ cadence. The second phrase ends in measure 8 with a(n)

_____ _____ cadence.

Tips for Success

✔ Composers employ a variety of styles when applying stems, dependent in part on how many notes are used to create a chord. This chapter samples some of these styles.

✔ Some notes do not belong to any harmony. Their function may be passing, neighboring, delaying, or anticipating. Guidance will be provided in sorting out the harmonic from the nonharmonic notes in the form of circles enclosing the notes that are members of a given harmony (as in Examples 11-1, 11-3, and 11-5).

✔ Remember to distinguish chordal quality (major, minor, or diminished) in the way you write a Roman numeral, and to distinguish authentic and plagal cadences as either perfect or imperfect.

Ties

Sometimes the precise notation of the starting point and duration of a pitch cannot be indicated using a single symbol of rhythmic notation. In such cases, the time value is indicated by binding two adjacent noteheads together using a symbol—the tie—that tells the performer to continue a single pitch without break for the combined time value of the two noteheads. Ties are often used to create a syncopated rhythm.

The Tie

For his opera *Norma,* Bellini imagined a beautiful melody. He probably sang it, and maybe even played it at a piano. Before writing it down, he decided that the appropriate meter would be $\frac{9}{8}$ and the key B♭ Major. Then he proceeded by writing down notation for pitch and rhythm. As he imagined it, the melody's second and fourth measures contain a beat that is divided into two parts: *1-ee-+-ee-uh* followed by *ee.* How does one show $\frac{5}{6}$ of a beat in a compound meter? Neither a sixteenth note, nor an eighth note, nor a quarter note, nor a dotted quarter note corresponds to this time value. Instead of inventing new and ever more complex symbols for all possible time values, we combine the value of two or more noteheads, using a ***tie***, a curved line that connects two adjacent noteheads. Bellini's melody appears in Example 11-7. Observe that $\frac{5}{6}$ of a beat is represented by a quarter note ($\frac{4}{6}$ of a beat) tied to a sixteenth note ($\frac{1}{6}$ of a beat). Observe also that the tie is placed on the side of the noteheads opposite the side of the stems.

Example 11-7

Bellini: *Norma*, Act 1

1 ee + ee uh ee   1 ee + ee uh ee

Practice Exercises 11-3

Connect each pair of noteheads below with a tie. Remember that a tie is placed on the side of the notehead *opposite* the side of the stems.

a.   b.   c.

d. Add ties to the melody below wherever possible. A total of four ties should be employed. *Note:* When a tie connects two noteheads whose stems go in opposite directions, the tie may be placed either above or below the noteheads.

Ties for Syncopation

A tie allows even the first beat of a measure to be involved in syncopation. In Example 11-8, the G that begins in the second half of measure 6, beat 2, continues through the first half of measure 7, beat 1. The notehead for the pitch is written twice: at the end of measure 6, and at the beginning of measure 7. A tie connects the unstemmed sides of these noteheads. The sound persists *without rearticulation* for the combined time value of both noteheads.

Example 11-8

Beethoven: Piano Sonata, Op. 10, No. 2, Mvmt. 1

The tie, a symbol of rhythmic notation, should not be confused with another musical symbol, the **slur**, which is a performance indication pertaining either to legato (smooth) connections among pitches, or to phrasing (the grouping of notes into coherent units). The short curved line connecting C and B♭ and the two long curved lines in Example 11-8 are slurs. A tie, in contrast, always connects two *adjacent* noteheads that represent *the same* pitch.

slur

A tie is employed twice in Example 11-9 to connect pitches that begin in one measure and continue into the next. The example also demonstrates a tie used for a pitch whose duration resides entirely within a single measure (C♯ in measure 2). Though a dotted quarter note would convey the same information, composers often prefer to use a tie. The clarity of this example's notation results from the careful application of ties and beams. The location of each beat is easy to see from the notation. Especially when one wants to counteract the natural tendencies of the meter, it is important for the performer to have a clear sense of where each beats falls.

Example 11-9

Bach: Fugue, *The Well-Tempered Clavier*, Vol. 2, No. 14

Practice Exercises 11-4

Add a tie wherever possible. Remember that a tie is placed on the side of the notehead *opposite* the side of the stems, though when a tie connects two noteheads whose stems go in opposite directions, the tie may be placed either above or below the noteheads.

a.   b.   c.

d. Add ties to the melody below wherever possible.

Dvořák: Symphony No. 8, Op. 88, Mvmt. 4

Tips for Success

✔ When performing a rhythm that uses a tie, remember that the two component noteheads correspond to a *single* musical sound. Do *not* rearticulate that sound at the point where the duration of the first notehead ends and the second notehead begins.

✔ Whether or not ties are employed, every measure will contain exactly enough rhythmic content to fill it, in accordance with the amount of content the time signature indicates a measure is supposed to contain. (An upbeat before measure 1 and the last measure are the only exceptions.) A safe rule of thumb to use when writing rhythmic notation is: "*Beam each beat separately.*" This safeguard both helps performers, because the underlying metrical framework will be easier to see, and helps you, because it will be easier for you to check your work. By beaming each beat separately, you can then use ties to show the duration of a pitch that begins during one beat and extends into the next—both when that next beat is within the same measure and when it begins the following measure.

Laboratory

L11-1. Play and Sing

a. Play each of the phrases below. After you play it, name the cadence that ends the phrase.

b. Perform the progressions of exercise a again, this time singing the bass line (perhaps an octave higher, depending on your vocal range) as you play.

L11-2. Listening

Team up with another student, work with your instructor in class, or make use of the CD-ROM that accompanies this textbook to practice these exercises.

a. *Performer:* Play either IV–I or V^7–I.
   Listener: Indicate whether IV–I or V^7–I has been performed.
b. *Performer:* Play either V^7–I or V^7–vi.
   Listener: Indicate whether V^7–I or V^7–vi has been performed.

L11-3. Keyboard Album

Brahms: Symphony No. 1, Op. 68, Mvmt. 4

Beethoven: Symphony No. 7, Mvmt. 1

Donizetti: *Lucia di Lammermoor*, Act 1

Dvořák: Symphony No. 9 ("From the New World"), Op. 95, Mvmt. 3

L11-4. Song Book

a.   Beethoven: Symphony No. 9 ("Choral"), Op. 125, Mvmt. 4

b.   Schubert: Piano Sonata, D. 960, Mvmt. 2

c.   Beethoven: Fantasia for Piano, Chorus, and Orchestra, Op. 80

d.   Berlioz: *Les Troyens*, Act 1

L11-5. Rhythm

a.

b.

c.

d.

e.

L11-6. Improvisation

a. In this improvisation, use I, IV, V, and V^7 chords in C Major to create a parallel period. Fill each of eight measures with one whole-note chord or two half-note chords, according to the following plan:

measure 1:	I in root position
measures 2 and 3:	your choice
measure 4:	V in root position (half cadence)
measure 5:	same as measure 1
measure 6:	your choice
measure 7:	V^7 with $\hat{2}$ in the soprano
measure 8:	I in root position, with $\hat{1}$ in the soprano (perfect authentic cadence)

b. Repeat exercise a in other major keys.

If you create an improvisation that especially pleases you, write it down. Perhaps at your next class your instructor will ask you to perform it for the class.

L11-7. Score Study

Listen to Selections 3, 5, and 6 in the Scores for Music Analysis section at the back of the textbook. Then answer the questions under the "Chapter 11" headings that accompany these selections.

Name: _____

Instructor: _____

Date: _____

Pitch Exercises

P11-1.

1. Below the key signature, indicate the major key in which the phrase is written.
2. Analyze each chord of the phrase by writing down its figured bass and Roman numeral in the space underneath the system.

    Hint: The Roman numeral is determined from the root, *not* the bass. If the chord is in $\frac{6}{3}$ or $\frac{6}{4}$ position, you must follow the procedure introduced in Chapter 9 to determine which of the upper-staff pitches functions as the root.

3. Indicate the type of cadence that ends each phrase: perfect authentic, imperfect authentic, perfect plagal, imperfect plagal, half, or deceptive.

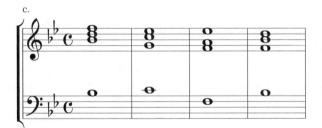

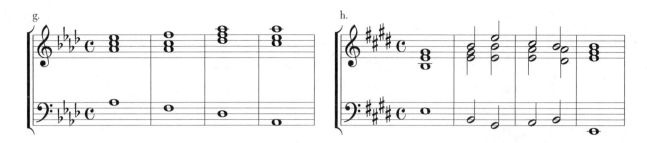

P11-2. Analyze the following examples from music literature in the same way you did with the phrases of exercise P11-1. The chords of these examples are constructed using a variety of strategies that contrast the standard procedure of this text. Observe that composers often embellish a chord with "nonharmonic" pitches. The notes that form each chord are circled. The notes outside the circles should not be acknowledged in the chordal analysis, for their function is melodic, *not* harmonic. When a chord is repeated or expanded through arpeggiation, write down its analytical symbols only once, and use horizontal lines to indicate their duration. For example:

```
5————————
3————————

I————————
```

°a.   Beethoven: Septet for Strings and Winds, Op. 20, Mvmt. 3

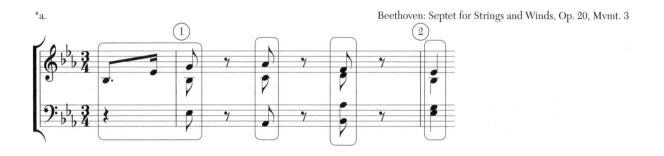

b.   Schubert: Symphony No. 6, D. 589, Mvmt. 2

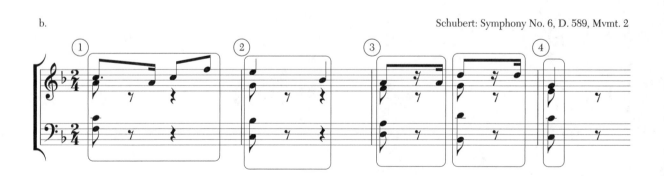

Name: _____

Instructor: _____

Date: _____

c.   Bach: Chorale No. 26, "O Ewigkeit, du Donnerwort"

Note: Bach has doubled a dissonant pitch (B♭) in the chord on beat 2 of measure 1.
Observe that it resolves correctly in the lower staff (B♭-A = 4̂ - 3̂). In the upper staff,
however, B♭ leads to C.

d.   Schubert: Écossaise, D. 529, No. 6

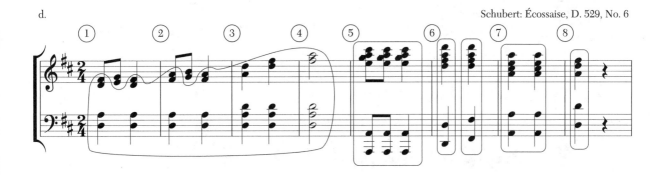

e.   Rossini: *The Barber of Seville*, Act 1

Note: There are two cadences in this excerpt. The first occurs at bass G in measure 7.
The second occurs at bass B♭ in measure 10.

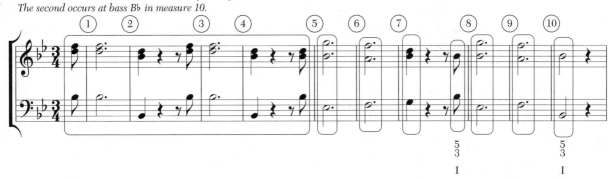

f.   Bach: Chorale No. 293, "Was Gott tut, das ist wohlgetan"

g.

Note: There are two cadences in this excerpt, at the downbeats of measures 4 and 8.

Mozart: Sonata for Piano, K. 331, Mvmt. 3

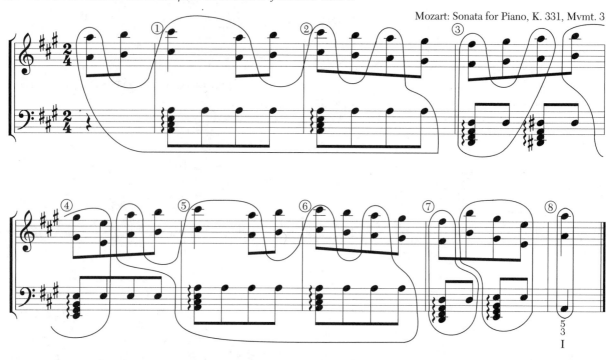

Rhythm Exercises

R11-1. Create the melodies indicated by the positioning of the pitch names in relation to the counting numbers. From one note to the next, use only a unison, second, third, or fourth as a melodic interval. Do not add rests.

Note: *Beam each beat separately.* If a pitch continues from one beat into the next or over a bar line, *write its notehead twice* and use a tie to connect the two noteheads. In exercise a, the A that straddles beats 3 and 4 of measure 1 could be displayed either as a quarter note, or as two eighth notes connected by a tie.

°a.

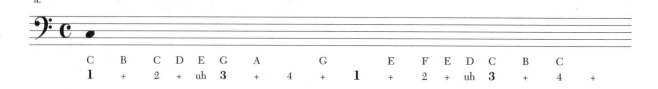

b.

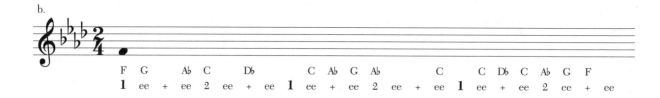

Name: _____

Instructor: _____

Date: _____

c.

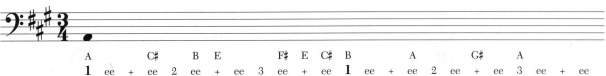

| A | C♯ | B | E | | F♯ | E | C♯ | B | | A | | G♯ | | A |
| 1 | ee | + | ee | 2 | ee | + | ee | 3 | ee | + | ee | 1 | ee | + | ee | 2 | ee | + | ee | 3 | ee | + | ee |

Audio Exercises

A11-1. One of two chord progressions—IV–I or V⁷–I—is performed. Indicate which.

*a. IV–I   V⁷–I   f. IV–I   V⁷–I

*b. IV–I   V⁷–I   g. IV–I   V⁷–I

c. IV–I   V⁷–I   h. IV–I   V⁷–I

d. IV–I   V⁷–I   i. IV–I   V⁷–I

e. IV–I   V⁷–I   j. IV–I   V⁷–I

A11-2. One of two chord progressions—V⁷–I or V⁷–vi—is performed. Indicate which.

*a. V⁷–I   V⁷–vi   f. V⁷–I   V⁷–vi

*b. V⁷–I   V⁷–vi   g. V⁷–I   V⁷–vi

c. V⁷–I   V⁷–vi   h. V⁷–I   V⁷–vi

d. V⁷–I   V⁷–vi   i. V⁷–I   V⁷–vi

e. V⁷–I   V⁷–vi   j. V⁷–I   V⁷–vi

A11-3. Circle the music notation that corresponds to the pitches performed.

*a.

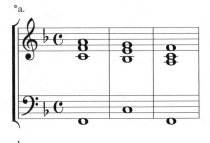
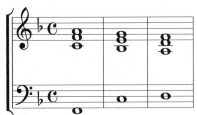

b.

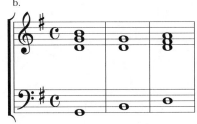
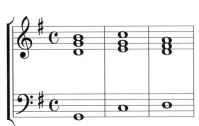

c.

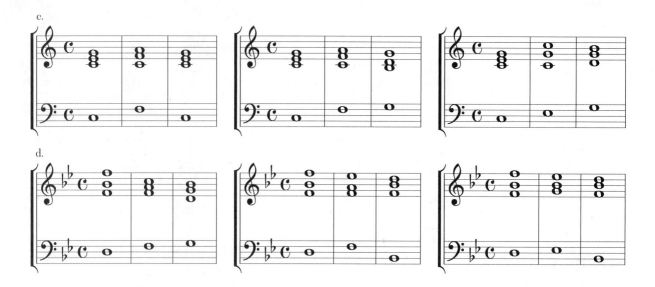

d.

A11-4. Circle the music notation that corresponds to the rhythm performed.

°a.

b.

c.

d.

Chapter 12

Chord Progression in Minor Keys

The minor key signatures are designed to select the diatonic pitches of natural minor. Yet composers often make substitutions using pitches of the harmonic minor or melodic minor scale. It is common for phrases written in a minor key to contain at least one pitch borrowed from the parallel major key. In this chapter, we practice making such borrowings and acknowledging them in our analyses.

Figured-Bass Analysis in Minor Keys

A figured-bass number does not change when an accidental is employed beside the note corresponding to that number. However, the accidental will be acknowledged beside the number. As suggested in Chapter 9, you should think of figured bass as an inventory of the pitches that occur above the bass. Since the use of pitches from harmonic and melodic minor will expand the total pitch collection from seven (the diatonic pitches of natural minor) to nine, the figured bass must distinguish between the two forms of the sixth and seventh scale degrees—for example, A♭ or A♮, and B♭ or B♮ in the key of C Minor. Always keep in mind what the key signature indicates. The figured-bass numbers for these diatonic pitches are not modified. Only the two pitches borrowed from the parallel major key require an accidental beside their numbers, and only when they occur above the bass. (As always, the bass does not receive a figured-bass number. The numbers indicate only what is *above* the bass.)

Five chords are presented in Example 12-1, along with appropriate figured-bass numbers. In the first chord, C is the fifth above bass F. Thus its figure appears as "5." The third above the bass, A♮, is ↑6̂ of the ascending C Melodic Minor scale. In this case, the "3" of the figured bass must be modified to distinguish this pitch from A♭, which might be used on other occasions. You must place a natural to the left or right of the number 3. Or, by convention, when the accidental applies to the number 3, the number may be omitted. That is, "♮" always means "♮3." The second chord—the first inversion of the first chord—requires special attention. What is altered? The bass itself! The figures assess only what is *above* the bass. And above this bass A♮ is a diatonic third (C) and a diatonic sixth (F). Thus the figured bass is simply $\frac{6}{3}$. To write $\frac{6}{3♮}$ would be wrong, because the number 3 here refers to the third above the bass—that is, C—and not to A♮. The third and fourth chords are similar to the first and second chords, respectively, now with ↑7̂ instead of ↑6̂. In the fifth chord, B♮ (a sixth above the bass) is the altered pitch. Thus, the figured bass is $\frac{6♮}{3}$.

Example 12-1

		7	7	
5 or 5	6	5 or 5	6	6♮
♮3 ♮	3	3♮ ♮	3	3

Practice Exercises 12-1

Add appropriate accidentals beside the appropriate noteheads so that each chord corresponds to the figured-bass analysis below it.

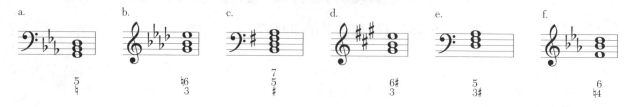

Provide figured-bass numbers for each chord below. When appropriate, include the accidental beside the corresponding number. (*Hint:* Remember that when the accidental modifies the *bass* pitch, it will not appear in the figured-bass analysis.)

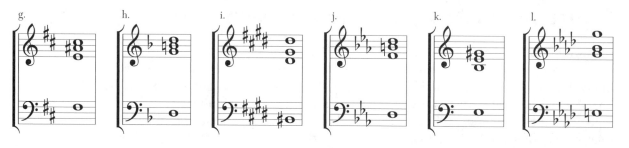

Roman-Numeral Analysis in Minor Keys

In minor keys, nine of the twelve pitches per octave are used in chord formation: the seven diatonic pitches, plus ↑6̂ and ↑7̂. We will employ a total of ten different parent triads in a minor key: the seven diatonic triads that we explored in Chapter 4, plus the subdominant, dominant, and leading-tone triads borrowed from the parallel major key. The new subdominant triad employs ↑6̂ of the melodic minor scale; the new dominant and leading-tone triads employ ↑7̂ of the harmonic and melodic minor scales. To only one of these ten triads will a seventh sometimes be added: the dominant triad borrowed from the parallel major key.

The Roman-numeral analysis must distinguish these chords from one another. For example, consider the two subdominant triads in the key of A Minor, shown in Example 12-2. The diatonic subdominant pitches are D, F, and A, which form a triad of minor quality. (Review Example 4-8.) When ↑6̂ is employed, the triad's quality is major, just as it is in the parallel major key, A Major. These two forms of the subdominant have different Roman-numeral labels: iv and IV, respectively.

Example 12-2

A Minor: iv   IV

The two dominant triads of minor keys differ in the same way as do the two subdominant triads. Their Roman-numeral labels are shown in Example 12-3a. For the subtonic/leading-tone triads, the root, not the third, is the altered pitch. These triads are shown in Example 12-3b, along with appropriate Roman-numeral labels. Note that all of the Roman numerals we will employ were presented in Example 4-8. The difference is that in that example there was a clear division between triads that occur only in major keys and triads that occur only in minor keys. Now, some of the triads formerly found only in major keys will occur in minor keys as well.

Example 12-3

As in our previous analytical work, the Roman numeral of any chord is the same as that of its parent triad. Thus, as demonstrated in Chapter 9, the first step of analysis is reducing a chord to its parent triad (retaining any added accidentals when you move noteheads closer together to form the triad). You must then assess whether that triad is major, minor, or diminished. Once each chord is analyzed, you may then view the chord progression of a phrase and identify the cadence employed at its conclusion. Either a minor or a major dominant may occur at a half cadence, but only the major dominant will be employed in the context of an authentic or deceptive cadence. Example 12-4 displays the full range of altered chords introduced in this chapter, along with appropriate analytical symbols. In some keys, sharps would be used instead of naturals in the figured bass.

Example 12-4

Practice Exercises 12-2

Beneath each triad, indicate the minor key that corresponds to the key signature and provide the appropriate Roman numeral and name. Your choices are iv, IV, v, V, VII, and vii°; and subdominant, dominant, subtonic, and leading tone.

a.   b.   c.   d.

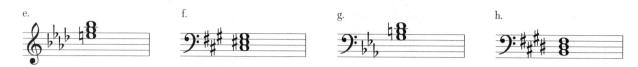

Create the chords indicated by each Roman numeral, figured bass, and key.

1. Prepare the system by writing in the correct natural minor key signature.

2. From the information provided by the Roman numeral, write the parent triad on the left side of the lower staff. Include the seventh if the number 7 appears in the figured bass. For IV, V, and vii°, add the required accidental. (For iv, v, and VII, no accidental is required.)

3. Invert the parent triad if the figured bass is $\frac{6}{3}$ or $\frac{6}{4}$ (either with or without accidentals).

4. On the right side of the system, position the bass on the lower staff and the other pitches on the upper staff. (The fifth may be omitted if the chord is in root position.) Remember to take along the accidental if you added one in Step 2.

5. Insert suitable doubling(s). Do not double the leading tone ($\uparrow\hat{7}$) or, when it occurs in the same chord as the leading tone, $\hat{4}$. If you double $\uparrow\hat{6}$ in a IV chord, make sure that you employ the appropriate accidental twice.

6. Add stems to form half notes.

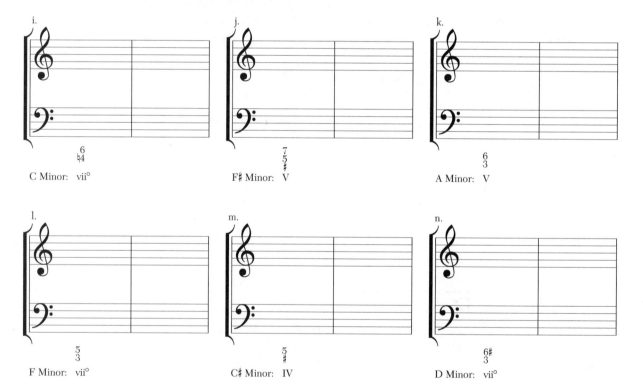

Analyze each chord below.

1. Below each chord, indicate its figured bass, including any required accidental. Remember that if the bass is the modified pitch, an accidental should *not* be placed beside one of the numbers.

2. To the right, form its parent triad, remembering to take along the accidental if one is present. (One chord is in root position and does not require any adjustment.)

3. Underneath the parent triad, indicate the minor key that corresponds to the key signature, and provide the chord's Roman numeral and name (tonic, supertonic, etc.). Remember that the subtonic chord (VII) is built on $\hat{7}$, while the leading-tone chord (vii°) is built on ↑$\hat{7}$.

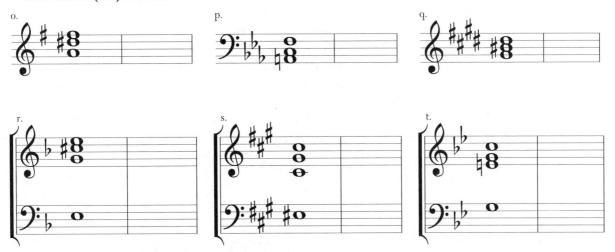

Analyze the following chord progression.

1. Below the key signature, indicate the minor key in which the phrase is written.

2. Analyze each chord of the phrase by writing down its figured-bass numbers and Roman numeral in the space underneath the system. Use care with accidentals and chord-quality designations (iv vs. IV, etc.).

    Hint: The Roman numeral is determined from the root, not the bass. If the chord is in $\frac{6}{3}$ or $\frac{6}{4}$ position, you must follow the procedure introduced in Chapter 9 to determine which of the upper-staff pitches functions as the root.

3. Indicate the type of cadence that ends the phrase: perfect authentic, imperfect authentic, perfect plagal, imperfect plagal, half, or deceptive.

Tips for Success

✔ Keep in mind that much of your work in this chapter is closely related to concepts you have learned in earlier chapters. What is different is the occasional presence of an accidental. In Roman-numeral analysis, the presence of an accidental within a chord will require a switch from iv, v, or VII to IV,

V, or vii°, respectively. In figured-bass analysis, the presence of an accidental within a chord will require that you place an accidental beside one of the figured-bass numbers *only* if that accidental appears beside one of the upper notes of the chord, **not** the bass. Conversely, in chord construction you know that an accidental is required if you see the Roman numeral IV, V, or vii°, or if an accidental appears beside one of the figured-bass numbers. If the accidental corresponds to the bass pitch, the only indication of its presence will be the quality indicated by the Roman numeral. In this text, only $\hat{6}$ or $\hat{7}$ will be modified by an accidental.

✔ Though a careful study of voice leading (how one chord connects with the next) is beyond the scope of this textbook, take note of one interesting aspect of voice leading in exercise u, above. The second chord contains the augmented fourth $\frac{C\#}{G}$. Whereas G resolves by descending to F, as expected, the leading tone, C♯, jumps to A! This is possible only because the soprano provides a D to resolve the C♯. Because the resolution chord is inverted, A must be present. That is an obligation that supersedes the requirement for the leading tone to resolve upward.

✔ The topics we have explored in the past twelve chapters are a foundation, as the title of this textbook suggests. If you are eager to continue the study of music begun here, your college probably offers a sequence of courses on tonal harmony, for which you are now well qualified to enroll. In the meantime, there are additional materials available for study in the Appendix: Pop Music Symbols (including symbols for the seventh chords introduced in the Seventh Chords and Their Inversion segment of the Appendix) and Transposition. In addition, you may go to the text's website (http://music.wadsworth.com/damschroder_03) and download some supplementary materials on the harmonization of melodies. (These materials appeared in earlier editions of this textbook.)

RHYTHM

Meters with Half-Note Beats

The meters we have used thus far employ the quarter note or the dotted quarter note to represent the beat. We now explore three meters—$\frac{2}{2}$, $\frac{3}{2}$, and $\frac{4}{2}$—that employ the half note for this purpose.

$\frac{2}{2}$, $\frac{3}{2}$, and $\frac{4}{2}$ Meters

In the simple meters $\frac{2}{4}$, $\frac{3}{4}$, and $\frac{4}{4}$, the quarter note represents the beat. In the compound meters $\frac{6}{8}$, $\frac{9}{8}$, and $\frac{12}{8}$, the dotted quarter note represents the beat. Another family of simple meters employs the half note as the representative of the beat. A measure in $\frac{2}{2}$ meter contains two half notes, while in the $\frac{3}{2}$ and $\frac{4}{2}$ meters measures contain three and four half notes, respectively. Example 12-5 displays each.

Example 12-5

Subdivisions of the beat are easier to write down in these new meters because fewer filled-in noteheads, beams, and flags are required, as Example 12-6 demonstrates. Performances of the two versions shown in this example should sound identical if equivalent tempos are maintained.

Example 12-6

The $\frac{2}{2}$ meter has a special name, ***alla breve***. In English it is often called ***cut time***. Just as we have used the symbol **C** to represent $\frac{4}{4}$ meter, we may use the symbol **¢** to represent cut time. Example 12-7 demonstrates its use.

alla breve

cut time

Example 12-7

Practice Exercises 12-3

For each of the rhythms in the left column, write an equivalent notation in the right column using the meter indicated.

Longer Note and Rest Values

dotted whole note

double whole note

double whole rest

Some new rhythmic symbols may be employed in the $\frac{3}{2}$ and $\frac{4}{2}$ meters. The ***dotted whole note*** (Example 12-8a) fills three beats in the $\frac{3}{2}$ or $\frac{4}{2}$ meter, while the ***double whole note*** (Example 12-8b) fills four beats in the $\frac{4}{2}$ meter. The whole rest is used for a full measure of rest in the $\frac{2}{2}$ or $\frac{3}{2}$ meter, as it is in the other meters we have studied. In the $\frac{4}{2}$ meter, however, a ***double whole rest*** (Example 12-8c) is used for an entire measure of silence.

Example 12-8

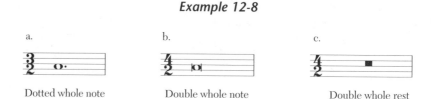

Dotted whole note   Double whole note   Double whole rest

Practice Exercises 12-4

Practice creating music notation by drawing each symbol below twice to the right of its model.

a.

b.

c.

Modify the noteheads indicated by arrows, if appropriate, to form measures containing the appropriate number of beats.

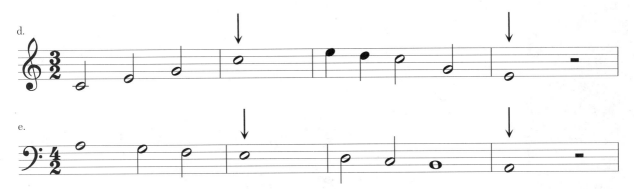

Add a rest at each point marked by an arrow to form measures containing the appropriate number of beats.

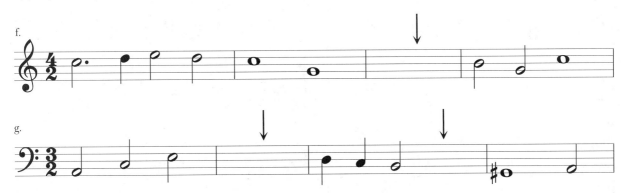

> ## Tips for Success
>
> ✔ Review the appropriate counting syllables for all nine meters mentioned in this chapter. The Conducting Patterns presented in the Appendix may be used in any two-, three-, or four-beat context.
> ✔ Though the meters introduced in these twelve chapters are among the most commonly used, numerous other meters exist. You may want to explore some of these meters in the Additional Meters section of the Appendix.

Laboratory

L12-1. Play and Sing

a. Play each of the phrases below. After you play it, name the cadence that ends the phrase.

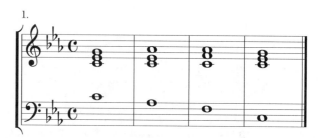

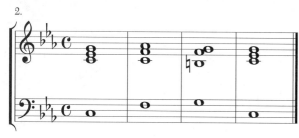

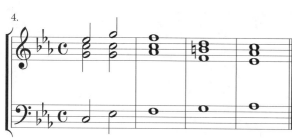

b. Perform the progressions of exercise a again, this time singing the bass line (perhaps an octave higher, depending on your vocal range) as you play.

L12-2. Listening

Team up with another student, work with your instructor in class, or make use of the CD-ROM that accompanies this textbook to practice these exercises.

a. *Performer:* Play either iv–i or V^7–i.
   Listener: Indicate whether iv–i or V^7–i has been performed.
b. *Performer:* Play either V^7–i or V^7–VI.
   Listener: Indicate whether V^7–i or V^7–VI has been performed.

L12-3. Keyboard Album

a.   Berlioz: *Les Troyens*, Act 3

b.   Brahms: *Academic Festival Overture*

c.   Franck: Symphony, Mvmt. 3

d.   Berlin: "Puttin' On the Ritz"

L12-4. Song Book

a.   Haydn: Symphony No. 104 ("London"), Mvmt. 4

b.   Tchaikovsky: *Mazeppa* (The Battle of Poltava), Act 3

c.   Towne and Hadjidakis: Never on Sunday

Oh, you can kiss me on a   Mon - day, a Mon - day, a   Mon - day is ver - y, ver - y   good,

Or you can kiss me on a   Tues - day, a Tues - day, a   Tues - day, in fact I wish you   would.

d.   Wagner: *Tannhäuser*, Act 2

L12-5. Rhythm

L12-6. Improvisation

a. In this improvisation, use i, iv, V, and V^7 chords in A Minor to create a parallel period. Fill each of eight measures with one whole-note chord or two half-note chords, according to the following plan:

measure 1:	i in root position
measures 2 and 3:	your choice
measure 4:	V in root position (half cadence)
measure 5:	same as measure 1
measure 6:	your choice
measure 7:	V^7 with $\hat{2}$ in the soprano
measure 8:	i in root position, with $\hat{1}$ in the soprano (perfect authentic cadence)

b. Repeat exercise a in other minor keys.

　　If you create an improvisation that especially pleases you, write it down. Perhaps at your next class your instructor will ask you to perform it for the class.

L12-7. Score Study

Listen to Selections 1, 4, and 7 in the Scores for Music Analysis section at the back of the textbook. Then answer the questions under the "Chapter 12" headings that accompany these selections.

Name: _____

Instructor: _____

Date: _____

Pitch Exercises

P12-1. Create the chords indicated by each Roman numeral, figured bass, and key.
1. Prepare the system by writing in the correct natural minor key signature.
2. From the information provided by the Roman numeral, write the parent triad on the left side of the lower staff. Include the seventh if the number 7 appears in the figured bass. For IV, V, and vii°, add the required accidental. (For iv, v, and VII, no accidental is required.)
3. Invert the parent triad if the figured bass is $\frac{6}{3}$ or $\frac{6}{4}$ (either with or without accidentals).
4. On the right side of the system, position the bass on the lower staff and the other pitches on the upper staff. (The fifth may be omitted if the chord is in root position.) Remember to take along the accidental if you added one in Step 2.
5. Insert suitable doubling(s). Do not double the leading tone ($\uparrow\hat{7}$) or, when it occurs in the same chord as the leading tone, $\hat{4}$. If you double $\uparrow$ 6 in a IV chord, make sure that you employ the appropriate accidental *twice*.
6. Add stems to form half notes.

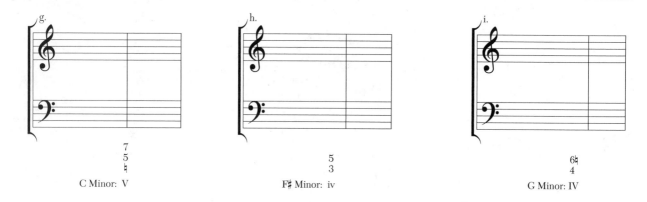

P12-2. Analyze each chord below.

1. Below each three-note chord, indicate its figured bass, including any required accidental. Remember that if the *bass* is the modified pitch, an accidental should *not* be placed beside one of the numbers.
2. To the right, form its parent triad, remembering to take along the accidental if one is present. (A few chords are in root position and do not require any adjustments.)
3. Underneath the parent triad, indicate the minor key that corresponds to the key signature, and provide the chord's Roman numeral and name (tonic, supertonic, etc.). Remember that the subtonic chord (VII) is built on $\hat{7}$, while the leading-tone chord (vii°) is built on ↑$\hat{7}$.

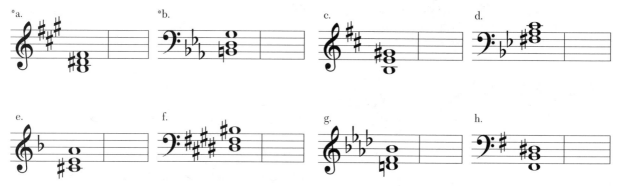

P12-3. Analyze each chord below.

1. Below each four-note chord, indicate its figured bass, including any required accidental. Remember that if the *bass* is the modified pitch, an accidental should *not* be placed beside one of the numbers.
2. To the right, form its parent triad or parent dominant seventh chord, remembering to take along the accidental if one is present.
3. Underneath the parent triad or chord, indicate the minor key that corresponds to the key signature, and provide the chord's Roman numeral and name (tonic, supertonic, etc.). Remember that the subtonic chord (VII) is built on $\hat{7}$, while the leading-tone chord (vii°) is built on ↑$\hat{7}$.

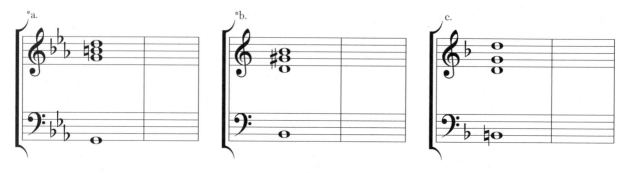

Name: _____

Instructor: _____

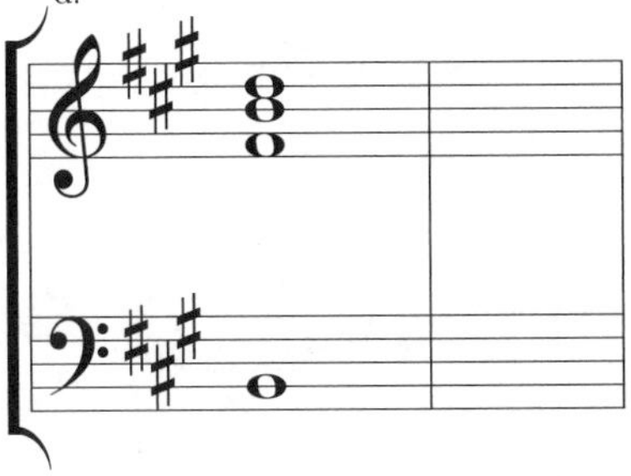

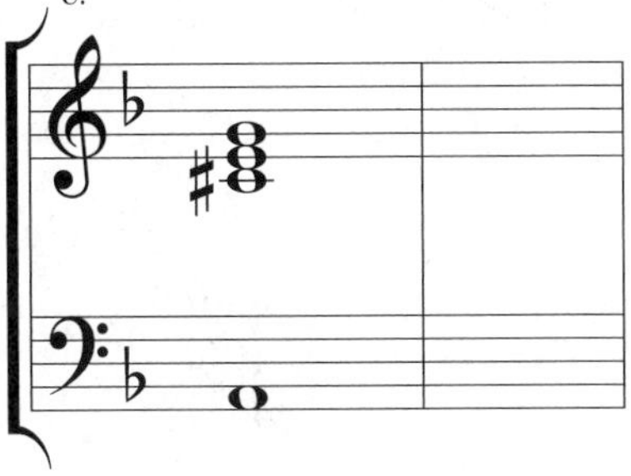

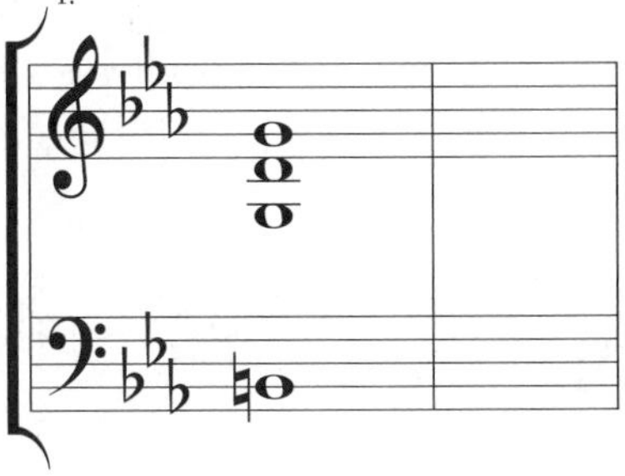

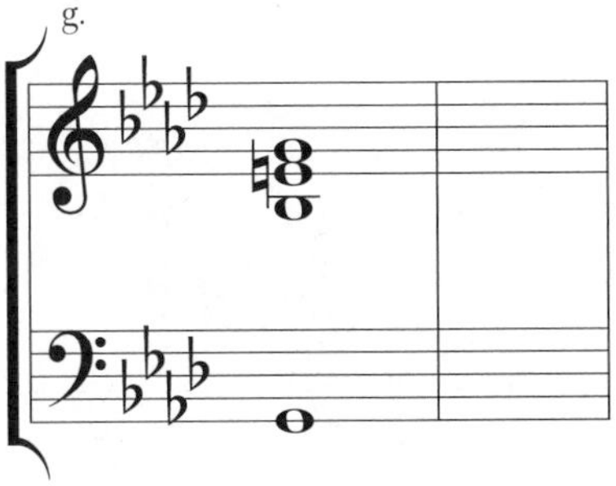

Date: _____

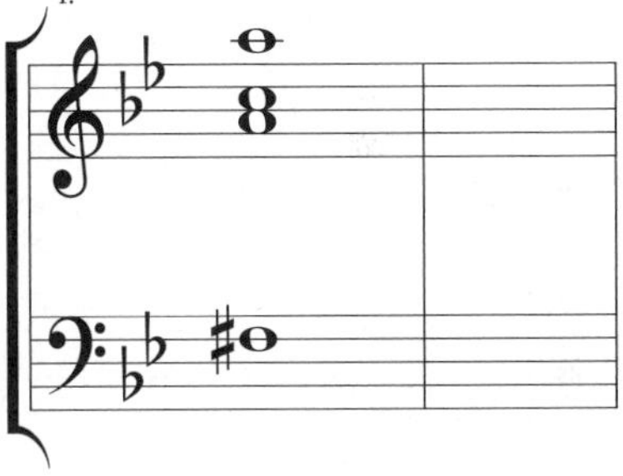

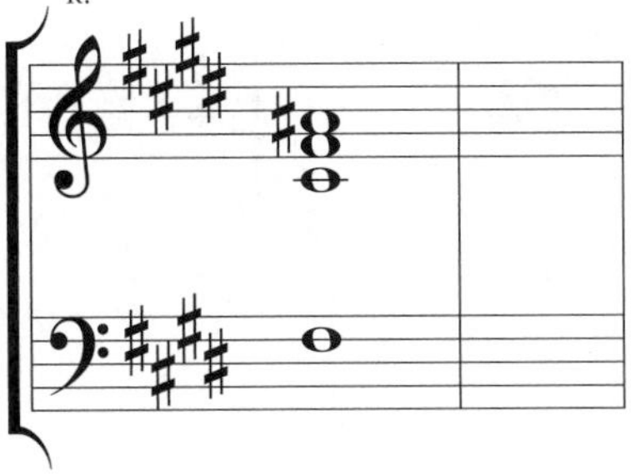

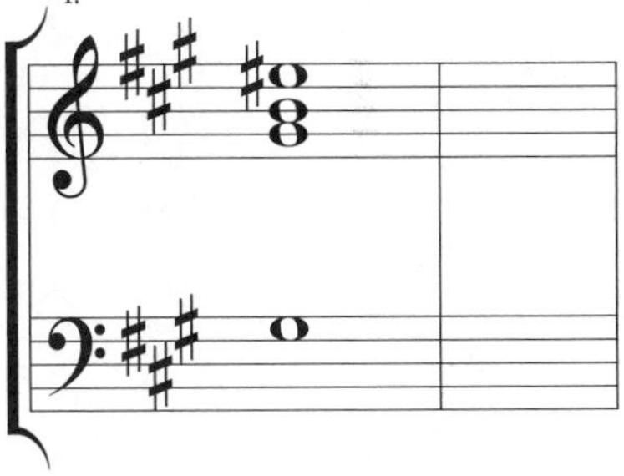

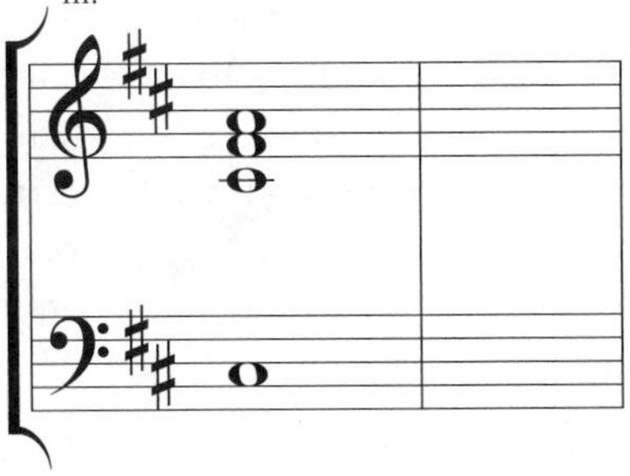

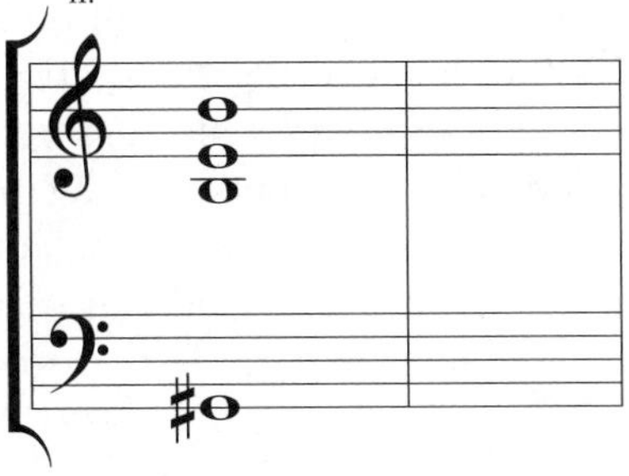

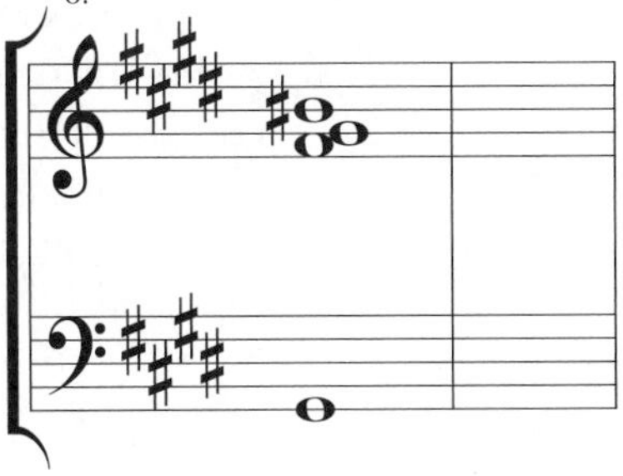

P12-4.

1. Below the key signature, indicate the minor key in which the phrase is written.
2. Analyze each chord of the phrase by writing down its figured-bass numbers and Roman numeral in the space underneath the system. Use care with accidentals and chord-quality designations (iv vs. IV, etc.).

    Hint: The Roman numeral is determined from the root, *not* the bass. If the chord is in $\frac{6}{3}$ or $\frac{6}{4}$ position, you must follow the procedure introduced in Chapter 9 to determine which of the upper-staff pitches functions as the root.

3. Indicate the type of cadence that ends each phrase: perfect authentic, imperfect authentic, perfect plagal, imperfect plagal, half, or deceptive.

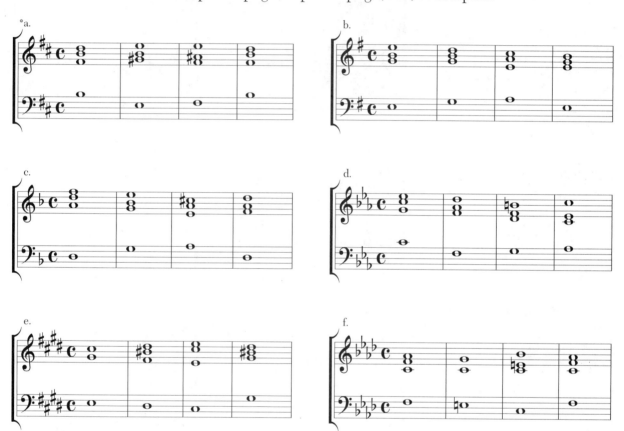

P12-5. Analyze the following examples from music literature in the same way you did the phrases of exercise P12-4. The chords of these examples are constructed using a variety of strategies that contrast the standard procedure of this text. Observe that composers often embellish a chord with "nonharmonic" pitches. The notes that form each chord are circled. The notes outside the circles should not be acknowledged in the chordal analysis, for their function is melodic, *not* harmonic. When a chord is repeated or expanded through arpeggiation, write down its analytical symbols only once, and use horizontal lines to indicate their duration.

Name: _____

Instructor: _____

Date: _____

°a.

Bach: Chorale No. 281, "Wo soll ich fliehen hin"

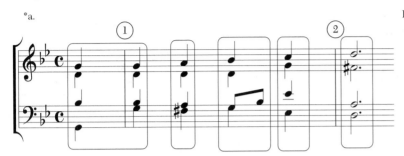

b.

Bach: Chorale No. 62, "Wer nur lieben Gott läßt walten"

c.

Schumann: *Scenes from Childhood,* Op. 15, No. 3, "Blindman's Bluff"

d.

Schubert: Waltz, D. 924, No. 3

Note: The chord in the second measure is in $\frac{6}{3}$ position, the first inversion of G♯–B♯–D♯–F♯. (You may explore inversions of seventh chords in the Appendix.)

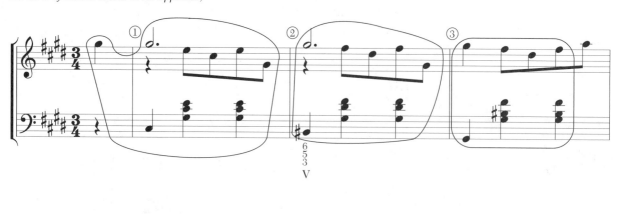

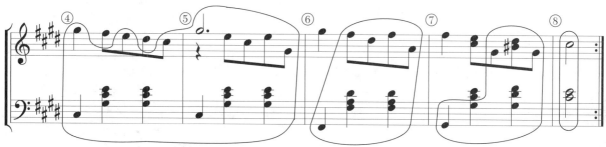

Rhythm Exercises

R12-1. For each of the rhythms in the left column, write an equivalent notation in the right column using the meter indicated.

Name: _____

Instructor: _____

Date: _____

e.

f.

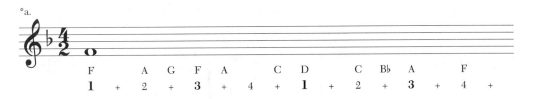

g.

R12-2. Create the melodies indicated by the positioning of the pitch names in relation to the counting numbers. From one note to the next, use only a unison, second, third, or fourth as a melodic interval. Do not add rests.

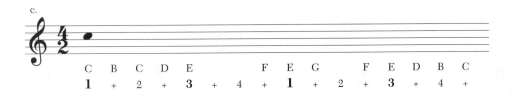

°a.

| F | | A | G | F | A | | C | D | | C | B♭ | A | | F |
| **1** | + | 2 | + | **3** | + | 4 | + | **1** | + | 2 | + | **3** | + | 4 | + |

b.

| E | | | G | | A | G | F♯ | G | A | C | | B | | A | G | F♯ | E |
| **1** | ee | + | ee | 2 | ee | + | ee | 3 | ee | + | ee | **1** | ee | + | ee | 2 | ee | + | ee | 3 | ee | + | ee |

c.

| C | B | C | D | E | | F | E | G | | F | E | D | B | C |
| **1** | + | 2 | + | **3** | + | 4 | + | **1** | + | 2 | + | **3** | + | 4 | + |

d.

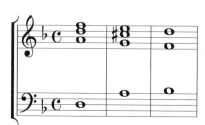

D	E		F	A	G	F			F	E	D	F		E			E	F	G	F		D
1	ee	+	ee	**2**	ee	+	ee	**1**	ee	+	ee	**2**	ee	+	ee	**1**	ee	+	ee	**2**	ee	+	ee

Audio Exercises

A12-1. One of two chord progressions—iv–i or V^7–i—is performed. Indicate which.

   *a. iv–i V^7–i   f. iv–i V^7–i

   *b. iv–i V^7–i   g. iv–i V^7–i

   c. iv–i V^7–i   h. iv–i V^7–i

   d. iv–i V^7–i   i. iv–i V^7–i

   e. iv–i V^7–i   j. iv–i V^7–i

A12-2. One of two chord progressions—V^7–i or V^7–VI—is performed. Indicate which.

   *a. V^7–i V^7–VI   f. V^7–i V^7–VI

   *b. V^7–i V^7–VI   g. V^7–i V^7–VI

   c. V^7–i V^7–VI   h. V^7–i V^7–VI

   d. V^7–i V^7–VI   i. V^7–i V^7–VI

   e. V^7–i V^7–VI   j. V^7–i V^7–VI

A12-3. Circle the music notation that corresponds to the pitches performed.

*a.

b.

c.

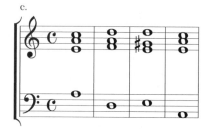

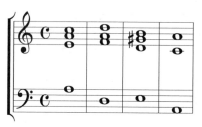

Name: _____

Instructor: _____

Date: _____

d.

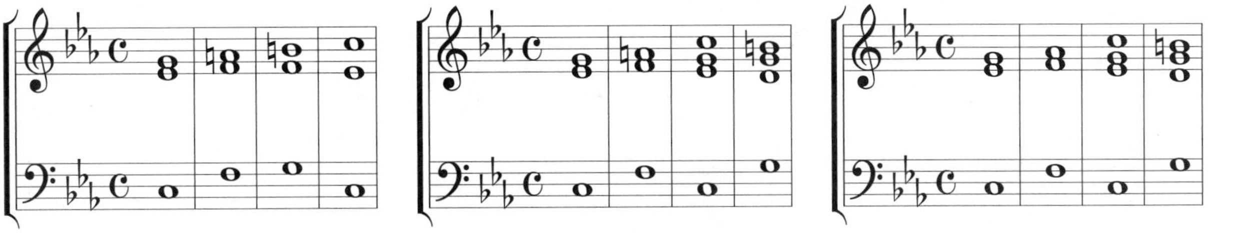

A12-4. Circle the music notation that corresponds to the rhythm performed.

°a.

b.

c.

d.

PRACTICE FINAL EXAM

A *Practice Final Examination* appears on the pages that follow. Complete this exam in an uninterrupted fifty-minute time period. You will need your CD-ROM for the listening questions, which will be performed twice each.

Do not consult any other section of your textbook when completing the exam. You will need to know from memory such concepts as note names in treble and bass clefs, key signatures, interval and triad qualities, and so on. Though the exam questions for the most part resemble homework exercises, they are stated without any hints regarding how to proceed.

You may use the space below as a work area. Staves and a keyboard diagram are provided.

When you have finished, check your solutions against the answer key on the text's website (http://music.wadsworth.com/damschroder_3e).

Use your CD-ROM for Questions 1–4.

1. Three pitches are performed. Indicate whether the chord they form is in root position, first inversion, or second inversion.

    a.   Root Position   First Inversion   Second Inversion

    b.   Root Position   First Inversion   Second Inversion

    c.   Root Position   First Inversion   Second Inversion

2. A scale is performed, ascending and descending. Identify it.

    a.   Major   Natural Minor   Harmonic Minor   Melodic Minor

    b.   Major   Natural Minor   Harmonic Minor   Melodic Minor

    c.   Major   Natural Minor   Harmonic Minor   Melodic Minor

3. Circle the music notation that corresponds to the pitches performed.

4. Circle the rhythm performed.

5. Create the scales requested. Employ the appropriate key signatures.

a. E Harmonic Minor, ascending   b. C Harmonic Minor, descending

c. D Melodic Minor, ascending   d. B Melodic Minor, descending

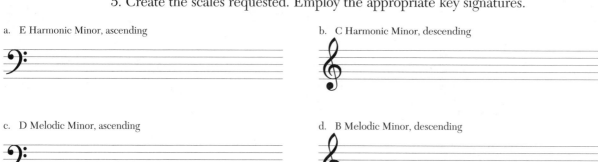

6. Create the chords indicated by each Roman numeral, figured bass, and key. Use three half notes in the upper staff and one half note in the lower staff.

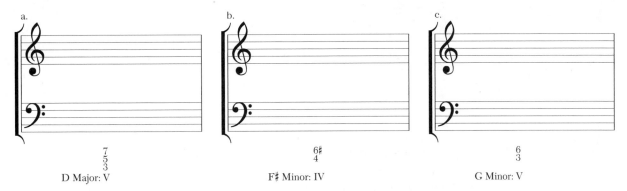

a.

$$\begin{matrix}7\\5\\3\end{matrix}$$

D Major: V

b.

$$\begin{matrix}6\sharp\\4\end{matrix}$$

F♯ Minor: IV

c.

$$\begin{matrix}6\\3\end{matrix}$$

G Minor: V

7. Indicate the major key indicated by the key signature. Then analyze each chord (Roman numeral and figured bass). Indicate which of the six basic cadence types ends the phrase.

a.

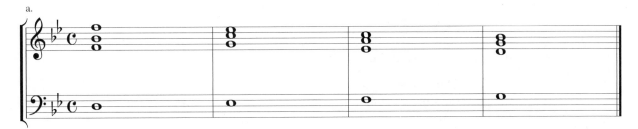

b.

8. Indicate the minor key indicated by the key signature. Then analyze each chord (Roman numeral and figured bass). Indicate which of the six basic cadence types ends the phrase.

a.

b.

9. Create the melody indicated by the positioning of the pitch names in relation to the counting numbers. From one note to the next, use only a unison, second, third, or fourth as a melodic interval. Do not add rests.

Eb	F		G	F	D	Bb		Bb	C	D	F		Eb
1	ee	+	ee	2	ee	+	ee	1	ee	+	ee	2	ee	+	ee

10. Draw each symbol requested.

   a. Flagged sixteenth note with stem pointing downwards

   b. Double whole note

   c. Time signature for a meter of three beats in which the half note represents the beat

   d. Sixteenth rest

Additional Meters

Though the meters introduced within the twelve chapters are among the most commonly employed, there are others. The following chart lists most of the meter symbols that you may encounter.

Simple Meters

Unit of the Beat	Two Beats	Three Beats	Four Beats
Eighth note	$\frac{2}{8}$	$\frac{3}{8}$	$\frac{4}{8}$
Quarter note	$\frac{2}{4}$	$\frac{3}{4}$, 3	$\frac{4}{4}$, 𝄴
Half note	$\frac{2}{2}$, 𝄵, 2	$\frac{3}{2}$	$\frac{4}{2}$

Compound Meters

Unit of the Beat	Two Beats	Three Beats	Four Beats
Dotted eighth note	$\frac{6}{16}$	$\frac{9}{16}$	$\frac{12}{16}$
Dotted quarter note	$\frac{6}{8}$	$\frac{9}{8}$	$\frac{12}{8}$
Dotted half note	$\frac{6}{4}$	$\frac{9}{4}$	$\frac{12}{4}$

Composers may occasionally use meters not listed above, such as the $\frac{5}{4}$ meter (five quarter notes per measure).

Exercise

Perform each of the following melodies at the keyboard.

a.   Bach: French Suite No. 6: Bourrée

b.   Tchaikovsky: Symphony No. 6

c.   Bach: *The Well-Tempered Clavier*, Vol. 2, Fugue 11

d.   Bach: French Suite No. 2: Gigue

Chromatic Scales

The major and natural minor scales assemble *all* the diatonic pitches within an octave, even if, in some melodies, not all of those pitches are employed. Likewise, when we create a chromatic scale, we include all of the chromatic pitches that fall within an octave, even if it is common for a melody to employ only some of them. Ascending and descending forms of the chromatic scale employ contrasting spellings for the chromatic pitches.

The example below demonstrates how to construct an ascending chromatic scale in the key of A Major. The process is broken down into the following three steps:

Step One: Place the key signature at the left edge of the staff and then write in all the diatonic pitches, using open noteheads. Leave extra space where there is a whole step in the scale. Since all major and natural minor scales contain five whole steps, there should be five positions where gaps occur.

Step Two: In each of the five positions where a chromatic note belongs, draw a filled-in notehead. Always use the same notehead as the one *to the left!*

Step Three: Carefully assessing the effect of the key signature upon the diatonic pitches, affix the appropriate accidental to each filled-in notehead. For ascending scales, if the preceding diatonic pitch is flat, affix a natural; if it is natural, affix a sharp; and if it is sharp, affix a double sharp.

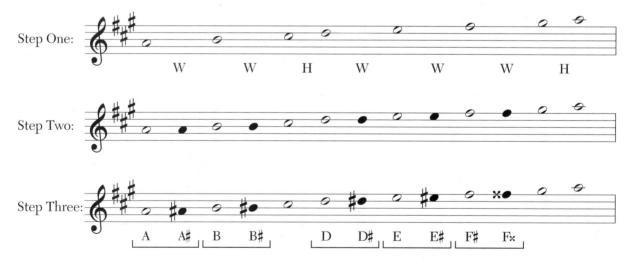

Observe that the chromatic pitch above B is B♯, *not* C. And the chromatic pitch above F♯ is F𝄪, *not* G.

The creation of a descending chromatic scale in the key of E♭ Major is shown on the next page. We follow the same procedure, but now with a revised third step:

Step Three: Carefully assessing the effect of the key signature upon the diatonic pitches, affix the appropriate accidental to each filled-in notehead. For descending scales, if the preceding diatonic pitch is sharp, affix a natural; if it is natural, affix a flat; and if it is flat, affix a double flat.

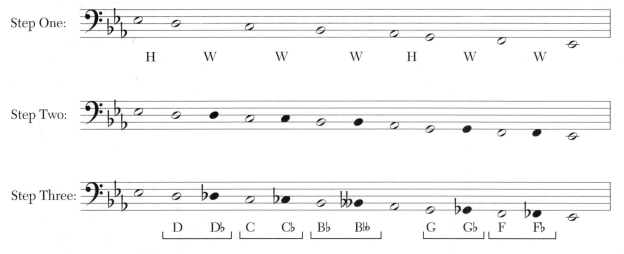

Remember that the descending major scale begins with a half step (Half-Whole-Whole . . .). There is no chromatic pitch between E♭ and D! Observe that the chromatic pitch below C is C♭, *not* B. And the chromatic pitch below B♭ is B♭♭, *not* A.

Chromaticism occurs in minor keys just as it does in major keys. The example below demonstrates the construction of a descending chromatic scale in the key of C♯ Natural Minor. Do not be alarmed that a flat is employed in a sharp key.

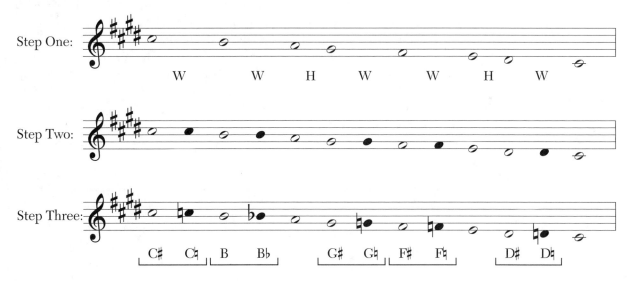

Exercise

Form the chromatic scales requested. Use open noteheads for the diatonic pitches and filled-in noteheads for the chromatic pitches. Employ the appropriate key signature.

a.   G Major, ascending chromatic

b.   F Major, descending chromatic

c.   D Natural Minor, ascending chromatic

d.   G Natural Minor, descending chromatic

Clefs

The treble clef is sometimes called the "G-clef," because its lower spiral surrounds the line of the staff that corresponds to the G above Middle C. The bass clef is sometimes called the "F-clef," because its two dots surround the line that corresponds to the F below Middle C. In past centuries, these clefs were sometimes positioned higher or lower on the staff, with corresponding adjustments in the location of G or of F.

Another clef, the C-clef (𝄡), is still used for some instruments today. Its center indicates the line that corresponds to Middle C. It is most commonly positioned on the middle line of the staff, in which case it is called the alto clef; or on the fourth line of the staff, in which case it is called the tenor clef. When used in writing for certain instruments (or even for voices), these clefs can reduce the need for ledger lines. The most frequently employed noteheads are displayed in their alto- and tenor-clef contexts below.

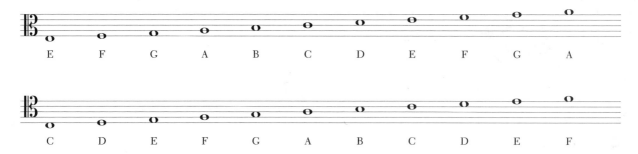

Exercise

Name each pitch.

a.   b.   c.   d.   e.

f. g. h. i. j.

Conducting Patterns

If you are called upon to lead an ensemble of musicians, or if you want to "feel" the rhythm more dynamically when you sing alone, you might want to conduct. Several standard patterns are displayed below. Wave your right arm, with your fingers pointing forward.

Two-Beat Meters   Three-Beat Meters   Four-Beat Meters

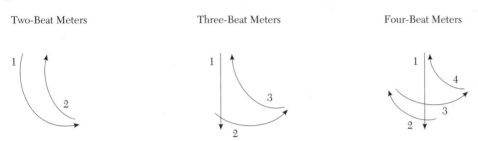

Keys with Five through Seven Sharps or Flats

Each of the nine key signatures with four or fewer sharps or flats corresponds to two relative keys—one major, one minor. Using those signatures, nine of the twelve pitches per octave function as tonic in a major key, and nine in a minor key. For the remaining three major and three minor keys, there is a surprise: each of these new keys may be constructed using either sharps or flats.

All six of the keys with two through four sharps that we explored in Chapter 5 have a parallel relationship with another key. Thus far, we have explored only three of those relationships. Locate the six keys with two through four sharps in the example below. (They appear in the fourth row of circles.) The major keys with two through four sharps—D Major, A Major, and E Major—have parallel minors with less complex key signatures, as we learned in Chapter 5. (These parallel relationships are represented by the parallel vertical lines that connect the third and fourth rows of circles in the example.) But what about the remaining keys with between two and four sharps: B Natural Minor, F♯ Natural Minor, and C♯ Natural Minor? Though those keys were introduced in Chapter 5, their parallel major keys were overlooked then because they require key signatures that are more complex, with five through seven sharps. These keys—B Major, F♯ Major, and C♯ Major—are presented in their rightful positions in the fifth row of circles in the example on the next page.

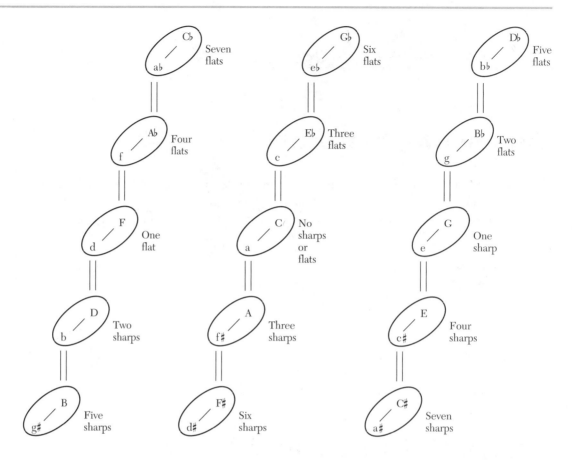

Likewise, though all six of the keys with two through four flats were introduced in Chapter 5, we have explored only three of their parallel relationships. (Those are represented by the parallel vertical lines that connect the second and third rows of circles in the example above.) What about the remaining keys with between two and four flats: B♭ Major, E♭ Major, and A♭ Major? Their parallel minor keys were overlooked in Chapter 5 because they require key signatures with five through seven flats. These keys—B♭ Natural Minor, E♭ Natural Minor, and A♭ Natural Minor—are presented in their rightful positions in the first row of circles in the example above.

In introducing the six remaining parallel keys, six new key signatures were required: those with five through seven sharps, and those with five through seven flats. Remember that every key signature corresponds to two relative keys—one major, one minor. Thus, the signatures for the three new major keys (B Major, F♯ Major, and C♯ Major) also correspond to three minor keys: G♯ Natural Minor, D♯ Natural Minor, and A♯ Natural Minor, respectively. These keys are included in the example above. They duplicate in sound (though not in visual appearance on the staff) the three new minor keys just introduced (A♭ Natural Minor, E♭ Natural Minor, and B♭ Natural Minor). The term for such a relationship is *enharmonic equivalence*. Whether one composes in G♯ Natural Minor or A♭ Natural Minor, it will sound the same.

Likewise, the signatures for the three new minor keys just introduced (B♭ Natural Minor, E♭ Natural Minor, and A♭ Natural Minor) also correspond to three relative major keys: D♭ Major, G♭ Major, and C♭ Major, respectively. These keys are included in the example above as well. They are the enharmonic equivalents of the three new major keys that were introduced previously (C♯ Major, F♯ Major, and B Major). All six pairs of enharmonic equivalents are displayed in the example on the next page.

Just as Chapter 5 offered a circular diagram and a listing of all the keys with their signatures to display the relationships among the eighteen keys you knew at that point, these same diagrams, now in an expanded and complete form, appear below. In both diagrams, relative keys are positioned near one another, with the major tonic indicated using a capital letter, and the natural minor tonic using a small letter.

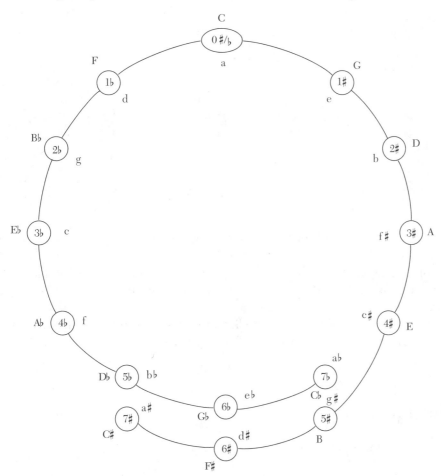

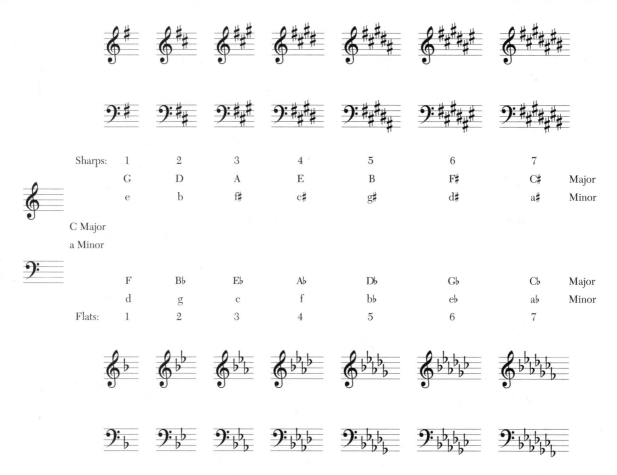

Sharps:	1	2	3	4	5	6	7	
	G	D	A	E	B	F♯	C♯	Major
	e	b	f♯	c♯	g♯	d♯	a♯	Minor

C Major

a Minor

	F	B♭	E♭	A♭	D♭	G♭	C♭	Major
	d	g	c	f	b♭	e♭	a♭	Minor
Flats:	1	2	3	4	5	6	7	

This gives us a total of thirty keys, including six pairs of enharmonic equivalents. Here we stop! Do not be too curious and, for example, wonder about the parallel minor of C♭ Major. Its key signature would require the use of double flats! That is more than most musicians care to think about. For our purposes, you could regard B Natural Minor as C♭ Major's parallel minor. In fact, you might imagine cutting out each of the three vertical strands in the first example and forming them into bracelets. If you "snap" the a♭-C♭ piece on top of the g♯-B piece, then you have a continuous loop.

Exercise

Perform each of the following melodies at the keyboard.

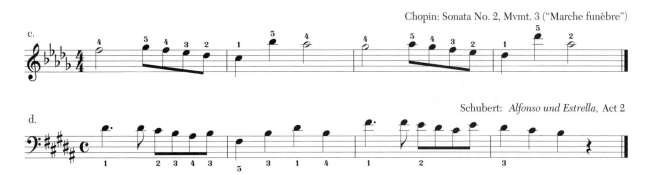

Chopin: Sonata No. 2, Mvmt. 3 ("Marche funèbre")

Schubert: *Alfonso und Estrella*, Act 2

Pop Music Symbols

If you perform popular music, you probably have encountered symbols such as "Fm" or "C⁷" printed above the melody line. These symbols indicate appropriate chords to harmonize the melody at that point. The exact positioning of the chord's pitches is at the discretion of the performer, and may vary from one instrument to another or from one performance to another. For example, a pianist may use a fuller texture when accompanying a group of singers than for a single voice. The following chart samples the principal symbols of this musical shorthand.

C   A **capital letter** indicates that the pitches of a **major triad** are to be employed.

Am   A **capital letter** followed by the letter **"m"** indicates that the pitches of a **minor triad** are to be employed.

G⁷   A **capital letter** followed by the number **"7"** indicates that the pitches of a **dominant seventh chord** (major triad with minor seventh) are to be employed.

Dm⁷   A **capital letter** followed by the letter **"m"** and the number **"7"** indicates that the pitches of a **minor seventh chord** (minor triad with minor seventh) are to be employed. (*See* "Seventh Chords and Their Inversions" in this Appendix.)

FM⁷   A **capital letter** followed by the letter **"M"** and the number **"7"** indicates that the pitches of a **major seventh chord** (major triad with major seventh) are to be employed. (*See* "Seventh Chords and Their Inversions" in this Appendix.)

All of the examples above are diatonic. However, one might also encounter situations in which an accidental is required. For example, in A Minor the symbol for the dominant seventh chord is "E^7", spelled E G♯ B D. You need to remember to sharp the G.

To indicate a specific inversion, the bass note will be indicated after a slash. For example "C/G" implies a C Major chord in second inversion (bass G), while "Dm/F" implies a D Minor chord in first inversion (bass F).

Exercise

Create the chords indicated by the pop symbols. First, write the required notes as a parent triad or chord on the lower staff, and then spread them out between the two staves, being especially careful in your choice of the bass pitch.

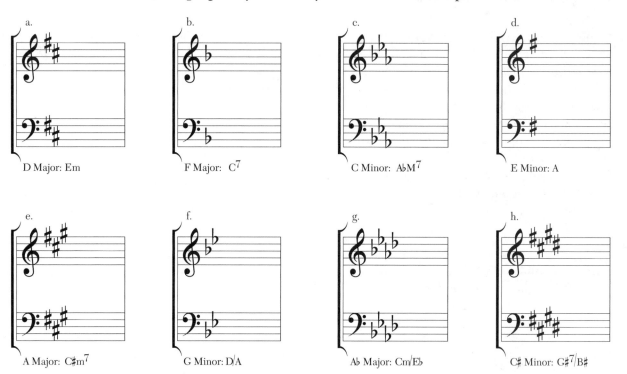

a.   D Major: Em

b.   F Major: C^7

c.   C Minor: A♭M^7

d.   E Minor: A

e.   A Major: C♯m^7

f.   G Minor: D/A

g.   A♭ Major: Cm/E♭

h.   C♯ Minor: G♯^{7}/B♯

Precise Pitch Designations

In this text we have used the label "C" for any C on the keyboard, with the special name "Middle C" for the one closest to center. Musicians can indicate individual pitches more precisely by using additional words or symbols when naming pitches. One common method is presented on the next page. Observe that one may write:

below or above a note to indicate that the pitch should be played an octave lower or higher than notated, respectively. Middle C corresponds to the symbol c' (pronounced "one-line C").

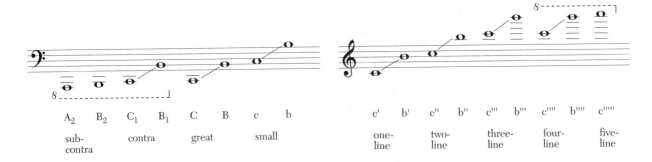

| A_2 | B_2 | C_1 | B_1 | C | B | c | b | | c' | b' | c'' | b'' | c''' | b''' | c'''' | b'''' | c''''' |
| sub-contra | | contra | | great | | small | | | one-line | | two-line | | three-line | | four-line | | five-line |

Exercise

Name each pitch both using a symbol ($E\flat_1$, $f\sharp''''$, etc.) and in words ("contra $E\flat$," "three-line $F\sharp$," etc.).

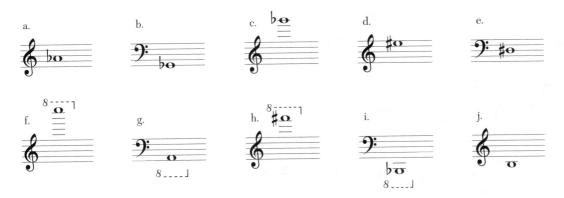

Seventh Chords and Their Inversions

In Chapter 10, we added a seventh to the dominant chord to create a dominant seventh chord. In fact, any triad may serve as the foundation for a seventh chord. The most commonly employed seventh chords fall into five categories: Major-Minor, Major, Minor, Half-Diminished, and Diminished. Each is described below, along with examples based on the triads introduced in this text.

Major-Minor Seventh Chords

Construction: Major triad with minor seventh

Roman numeral: Capital

Major Seventh Chords

Construction: Major triad with major seventh

Roman numeral: Capital

Minor Seventh Chords

Construction: Minor triad with minor seventh

Roman numeral: Small

Major-Key locations: C Major: ii   iii   vi

Minor-Key locations: C Minor: i   iv   v

Half-Diminished Seventh Chords

Construction: Diminished triad with minor seventh

Roman numeral: Small followed by a slashed degree circle (∅)

Major-Key location: C Major: vii∅

Minor-Key location: C Minor: ii∅

Diminished Seventh Chords

Construction: Diminished triad with dimished seventh

Roman numeral: Small followed by a degree circle (°)

Minor-Key location: C Minor: vii°

Just as triads and chords derived from triads may be inverted, seventh chords may be inverted. Because seventh chords contain four pitches, there are three inversions. All chord members must be present in inverted chords. Examples of each are presented below, along with appropriate analytical symbols.

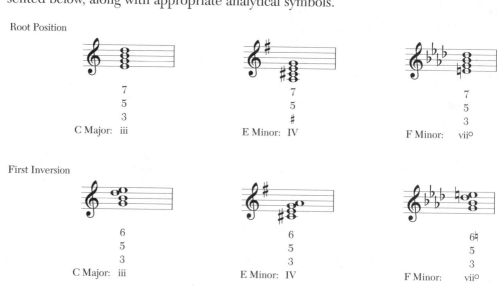

Root Position

7
5
3
C Major: iii

7
5
♯
E Minor: IV

7
5
3
F Minor: vii°

First Inversion

6
5
3
C Major: iii

6
5
3
E Minor: IV

6♮
5
3
F Minor: vii°

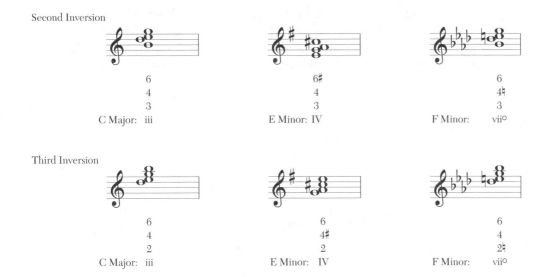

Second Inversion

C Major: iii   E Minor: IV   F Minor: vii°

Third Inversion

C Major: iii   E Minor: IV   F Minor: vii°

Exercise

Label each chord below with the appropriate Roman numeral and figured bass. Below these labels, indicate each chord's quality (Major-Minor, Major, Minor, Half-Diminished, or Diminished).

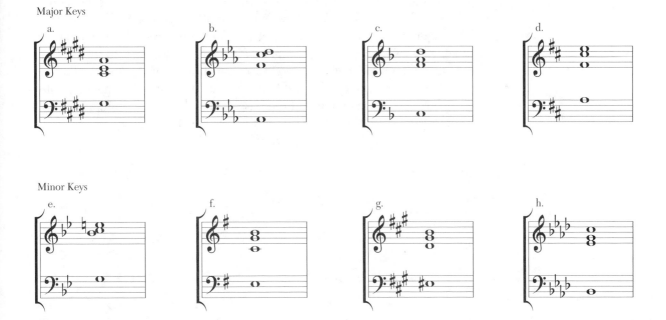

Major Keys

a.   b.   c.   d.

Minor Keys

e.   f.   g.   h.

Transposition

Not all melodies are written in a range that will ideally suit your voice. If a melody is written for a high range and you happen to have a low range (or vice versa), then you will need to perform the operation of transposition upon it before you can sing it comfortably. By doing so, you can tap a wider array of materials for your musical enjoyment.

In the example below, every pitch of the given melody is lowered by one octave. To avoid the excessive use of ledger lines, it is efficient to convert from treble to bass clef. (Due to the context of this song within the musical *Fiddler on the Roof*, the words change as well as the clef in this example.)

Harnick and Bock: *Fiddler on the Roof*, "Matchmaker"

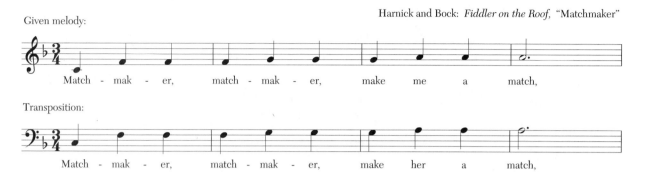

Sometimes moving a melody by an entire octave is not the appropriate transposition. The melody below is from Mozart's opera *Don Giovanni*. Certainly an opera company would hire a singer whose range matches this melody. But if you would like to sing it for pleasure, it might not fall within your range. Most people possess a range of at least an octave, but it might not extend to the higher D of this melody. Transposing the melody down by an octave might not help matters any, because then the lower D would likely be too low. In this situation it would be appropriate to transpose the melody from one key into another. Even though the tonic pitch shifts, each pitch of the melody will retain its position relative to the other pitches—that is, the succession of scale degrees will remain intact. The example below shows a transposition down a minor third, from the key of Bb Major to the key of G Major. Because key signatures take care of all the whole- and half-step relationships of both major keys, you do not need to worry about adding any accidentals when the given melody uses only the diatonic pitches of the key, as is the case here. You may find it helpful to create a conversion chart that correlates the two keys by juxtaposing the pitches of their ascending scales. For example, the following chart corresponds to the transposition displayed in the example:

	$\hat{1}$	$\hat{2}$	$\hat{3}$	$\hat{4}$	$\hat{5}$	$\hat{6}$	$\hat{7}$	$\hat{8}$
Bb Major:	Bb	C	D	Eb	F	G	A	Bb
G Major:	G	A	B	C	D	E	F♯	G

Mozart: *Don Giovanni*, K. 527, Act 1

Be aware not only of the scale degrees involved in a transposition, but also of the contour of the melody that is being transposed. For example, the succession of scale degrees $\hat{2}$–$\hat{5}$ might refer to an ascending fourth (for example, D up to G in C Major)

or to a descending fifth (for example, D *down* to G in C Major). Follow the contour of the given melody to ensure that the end result will be correct.

When you are comfortable with the two operations introduced above, you may combine them—shifting the clef and the key at the same time. In the example below, the "Matchmaker" melody from above is transposed down a major sixth, from F Major to A♭ Major. Use the following conversion chart to confirm that the transposition has been accomplished correctly:

	$\hat{1}$	$\hat{2}$	$\hat{3}$	$\hat{4}$	$\hat{5}$	$\hat{6}$	$\hat{7}$	$\hat{8}$
F Major:	F	G	A	B♭	C	D	E	F
A♭ Major:	A♭	B♭	C	D♭	E♭	F	G	A♭

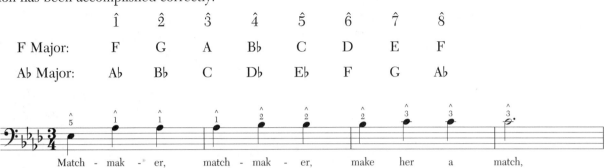

In transposing from one key into another, the key signature will always yield the correct set of diatonic pitches. But when chromatic pitches occur in the original melody, they must be tended to on an individual basis when transposing. A chromatic pitch always requires an accidental. This becomes tricky when transposing because the particular accidental that raises or lowers a scale degree may vary from key to key. For example, in F Major, $\hat{1}$ is F. To raise it, we use a sharp (F♯). But in A♭ Major, $\hat{1}$ is A♭. To raise it, we must instead use a natural (A♮). A natural, a sharp, or a double sharp may be required to raise a pitch, depending on the context. In the example below, the three versions of Verdi's melody will all sound correct in their respective keys. But the accidentals required for the chromatic pitches vary considerably. In each case, however, the chromatic pitches of the melody follow the principles articulated in the Chromatic Scales segment of the Appendix. Likewise, a natural, a flat, or a double flat may be required to lower a pitch.

Exercise

Transpose each melody below into the keys indicated. Begin by creating a conversion chart. Then mark all the pitches of the given melody with scale degree numbers ($\hat{2}$, $\uparrow\hat{4}$, etc.). Finally, complete the transposition. Because transposition moves notes higher or lower on the staff, change the stem directions where warranted.

a.

Puccini: *Madama Butterfly*, Act 2

D Minor:

B Minor:

F# Minor:

c.   Clementi: Sonata, Op. 40, No. 1, Mvmt. 4

^1   ^2   ^3   ^4   ^5   ^6   ^7   ^8

G Minor:

A Minor:

C# Minor:

Given melody:

G Minor:

A Minor:

C# Minor:

SCORES FOR MUSIC ANALYSIS

When not writing music textbooks, your author devotes most of his time to the study, teaching, and performance of classical music from the eighteenth and nineteenth centuries. This vast, varied, and wonderful musical heritage is widely available on CD, over the radio, and in concerts offered by college music departments and by professional music organizations. However, given the many choices young people confront nowadays, it often happens that a student of music fundamentals has never encountered works by composers such as Beethoven, Schubert, or Brahms before. That is like arriving at college never having read a word of Shakespeare or Dickens! One purpose of this text is to make the classical repertoire more accessible. For example, your Laboratory exercises include many melodies by classical composers. You may enjoy listening to the compositions from which your favorite exercise melodies are taken. In the following anthology of scores for analysis, several complete classical compositions are presented. Though they are shorter and simpler than most works by these composers, you will find many opportunities to apply knowledge gained from this text when studying them and listening to them on the text's CD-ROM. A series of questions, coordinated with the new material introduced in the text's chapters, accompanies each composition. Your instructor may want you to write down answers to these questions, or to be prepared for a class discussion that uses them as a starting point. Creating a course project based on one or several of these works (perhaps including a live performance) would be an ideal way to end your music fundamentals experience . . . and to begin a broader exploration of music that will last for the remainder of your life!

1. An Anonymous Menuet That J. S. Bach Included in his *Notebook for Anna Magdalena Bach* (1725)

Chapter 1

- Locate and mark examples of each of the following intervals between adjacent notes of the melody (the uppermost notes): an ascending second, a descending second, an ascending third, a descending third, an ascending fourth, a descending fourth, a descending fifth, an ascending sixth, an ascending seventh, a descending seventh. Note that a symbol such as "♯" or "♮" placed beside a notehead does not affect the calculation of an interval's size.

Chapter 3

- Locate and mark examples of each of the following intervals between adjacent notes of the bass (the lowest notes, governed by the bass clef): an ascending second, a descending second, an ascending third, a descending third, an ascending fourth, a descending fourth, an ascending fifth, a descending fifth, a descending sixth, an ascending octave, a descending octave. Note that a symbol such as "♯" or "♮" placed beside a notehead does not affect the calculation of an interval's size.

Chapter 4

- Apply scale degree numbers, in the context of D Natural Minor, to the bass (lowest) pitches in measures 1 through 4.

Chapter 5

- Sometimes a composer will employ a repeat sign even when the material to be repeated is not *exactly* the same as in the first instance. When the alteration is only in the ending, the composer may write first and second endings and place them under brackets labeled "1." and "2." This notation occurs both in the middle and at the end of this Menuet. How would you describe the difference in effect between the two endings in each case? Which one of each pair creates a greater sense of conclusion?

Chapter 6

- Mark all the intervals formed by adjacent *melodic* pitches in measures 1 through 4. Examine first the line governed by the treble clef, and then the line governed by the bass clef. For example, A to F is a . . . , F to E is a . . . , etc. (Indicate both quality and size: *perfect fifth* or *P5*, etc.)

Chapter 7

- A compound interval is formed by the two pitches that sound together at the downbeat of most measures of the Menuet. Mark the precise interval quality and size for all downbeat intervals. For example, the D and A of measure 1 form a *perfect twelfth (P12)*. If the interval is *dissonant*, circle it.

Chapter 10

- Compare the use of B♮, C, and C♯ in the D Melodic Minor and D Harmonic Minor scales with how the following pitches are used in this composition:

  C♯ in measure 3   C in measure 5   B♮ in measure 12   C♯ in measure 15

Chapter 12

- The cadence at measure 8 appears most awkward if one thinks in the key of D Minor. Often in music (though not so often in this anthology of very simple compositions), the composer will move from one key to another—often several times over the course of a work. That process is called *modulation*. Thinking in the key of F Major, what type of cadence occurs at the downbeat of measure 8? (Assume that the doubled pitch F implies an F–A–C triad.) At measure 16, does F Major still prevail, or has the composition returned to D Minor?

2. Beethoven's Harmonization of the Folk Song "God Save the King" (1803)

Chapter 1

- Mark an example of each of the following symbols within the score: bar line, double bar, ledger line, quarter note, treble clef.
- The uppermost notes (C C D | B C D | etc.) form the famous melody "God Save the King." Apply scale degree numbers to all of the melody's pitches, generally three or four per measure—always the top notes. (For example, above the melody notes of measure 1, write "1̂ 1̂ 2̂.")
- Locate and mark an example of each of the following intervals between adjacent notes of the melody: an ascending second, a descending second, an ascending third, a descending third. Do you think that the absence of larger intervals within the melody makes it easier or harder to sing?
- In measures 1 and 2, two notes at a time appear on the upper staff, governed by the treble clef. Mark the intervals formed by these note pairs. (For example, beat 1 of measure 1 contains $\frac{C}{E}$, the intervals of a *sixth*.)

Chapter 2

- Is the $\frac{C}{E}$ sixth in measure 1 (beat 1) a *major* sixth or a *minor* sixth? Is the $\frac{C}{A}$ third in measure 4 (beat 3) a *major* third or a *minor* third?
- For the most part, Beethoven employs pitches in a wider spacing than the triads we encounter in Chapter 2. Yet at two points—in measures 3 (beat 2) and 10 (beat 3)—the space-space-space or line-line-line arrangement of three noteheads characteristic of the triad occurs. Circle these triads, and indicate their qualities (*major, minor,* or *diminished*).

Chapter 3

- You circled two triads when completing the Chapter 2 questions. Examine these triads again, indicating their Roman numerals (I, ii, iii, etc.) in the context of C Major.

Chapter 4

- Add counting syllables (1 + 2 + 3 + 1 + 2 + 3 + . . .) below measures 1 through 6, being careful to align these syllables with the appropriate notes above.

Chapter 6

- Explain the melodic role of G♯ (bass) in measure 4, in relation to the G and A that precede and follow it. What interval is formed by bass G♯ and the F just above it? What interval is formed by bass G♯ and the melody note D that arrives on the second half of beat 2?

  (The natural beside G in measure 5 is a *cautionary* accidental. It is not required, since a bar line cancels the effect of the preceding sharp. Yet composers often add such accidentals to prevent accidents during performance!)

Chapter 8

- Compare the following pairs of chords, assessing their pitch content and inversional relationship.

measure 1, beat 1	and	measure 1, beat 2
measure 2, beat 1	and	measure 2, beat 3
measure 7, beat 1	and	measure 7, beat 3

  (*Note:* When numbering measures, musicians would number the first ending as 6a and the second ending as 6b. So measure 7 is the first measure of the second phrase.)

  (*Hint:* In context, measure 7, beat 3, will sound as if a C belongs with the other chord members, though now with bass G.)

Chapter 9

- In arithmetic, one needs to find a "common denominator" when dealing with unlike fractions. For example, to subtract ⅓ from ½, one converts to fractions that share the denominator six: 3/6 − 2/6 = 1/6. Examine what Beethoven wrote during beat 1 of measure 13! The right hand's notes each occupy one-third of the beat, while the left hand's notes each occupy one-half of the beat. Again here, the common denominator is six. Fill in the boxes below, perhaps using different colors of ink, to correctly represent how these notes fill that beat. (The entire diagram represents *one beat*.)

Right Hand:

Left Hand:

3. Brahms's Song "The Man," from *Children's Folk Songs* (1858)

Animated

1. Wil - le wil - le will, the man just got here,
2. Wil - le wil - le will, the man just got here,
3. Wil - le wil - le will, what more might he have?
4. Wil - le wil - le will, my child is kind - ly,

wil - le wil - le will, what has he brought? Wil - le wil - le will, some
wil - le wil - le will, what else has he? Wil - le wil - le will, some
wil - le wil - le will, a brand new rod! Wil - le wil - le will, he
wil - le wil - le will, my child is calm! Wil - le wil - le will, the

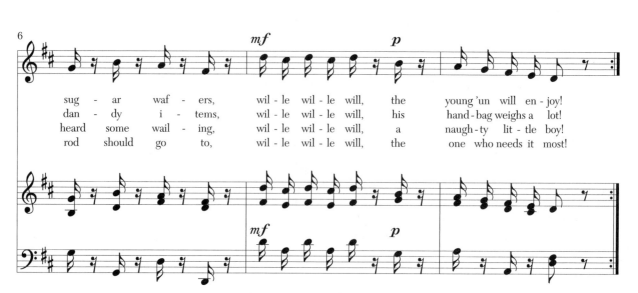

sug - ar waf - ers, wil - le wil - le will, the young'un will en - joy!
dan - dy i - tems, wil - le wil - le will, his hand - bag weighs a lot!
heard some wail - ing, wil - le wil - le will, a naugh - ty lit - tle boy!
rod should go to, wil - le wil - le will, the one who needs it most!

Chapter 5

- Apply scale degree numbers, in the context of D Major, to all of the vocal melody pitches—the notes in the top staff. (For example, above the melody notes of measure 1, write "$\hat{3}$ $\hat{2}$ $\hat{3}$ . . .")

Chapter 6

- The right-hand piano part contains many thirds. Label each harmonic third as a *major third (M3)* or as a *minor third (m3)*. (There are six thirds in measure 1, one in measure 2, one in measure 3, one in measure 4, one in measure 5, two in measure 6, one in measure 7, and four in measure 8.)

Chapter 7

- Add counting syllables (1 ee + ee 2 ee + ee . . .) below each measure.
- What are the names of the rests (⁊ and ⁊) employed?

Chapter 9

- Two different chords occur in alternation during measure 5, with bass D and E. Compare these two chords in three different ways:
    1. Which chord is in root position, and which chord is in an inversion? Which inversion?
    2. Which chord is consonant, and which chord is dissonant?
    3. Which chord falls in the stronger metrical positions, and which chord falls in the weaker positions?
    Do you notice any correlation between inversion, consonance/dissonance status, and metrical positioning?

Chapter 11

- The song contains four two-measure phrases. What cadence type ends each? (*Hint:* Measures 2 and 6 each contain the same two harmonies, the first of which is somewhat sparsely represented in measure 2 but more fully realized in measure 6. Both harmonies are reiterated. Regard the moment of cadence as the beginning of beat 2.)

4. Brahms's "Sailor Song," from *Children's Folk Songs* (1858)

Gracefully and with animation

1. There in the mead-ow stands a house, stands a house, stands a house, the maid sits at the
2. By morn' he plies the riv-er's flow, riv-er's flow, riv-er's flow, and sings to her his
3. The song bird in the li-lac bush, li-lac bush, li-lac bush, does sing a song that

win-dow sill, the win-dow sill! She _ looks up-stream, she looks down-stream, why
greet-ing fair, his greet-ing fair, by _ eve-ning when the glow-worms fly, his
I know, too, that I know, too; it _ says: a year from now I'll wed, and

has my beau not got here yet, the fin-est lad in all the land, I call him mine!
boat rocks on the riv-er bank, that's when I can to-geth-er be with my fine lad!
with my love a nest I'll make, where we'll be king and queen roy-al of this fair land!

Chapter 5

- Apply scale degree numbers, in the context of G Natural Minor, to all of the vocal melody pitches—the notes in the top staff. (For example, above the opening melody notes, write "$\hat{5}$ $\hat{1}$ $\hat{2}$ . . .")
- Explain why the last measure contains a quarter note and an *eighth* rest rather than a quarter note and a quarter rest.

Chapter 6

- The use of an upper neighbor, such as the E♭ within D–E♭–D in measure 2, is a pervasive feature of this melody. Mark all instances of this idea within the melody, and assess whether the same quality of second is used in all instances, or if instead some measures employ major seconds and other measures employ minor seconds.

Chapter 9

- First, determine the figured-bass numbers for the chords that occur on beat 1 of measures 9 through 14. Do you notice a pattern? Next, determine the root for the first four of these six chords. Do you notice a pattern? Develop a hypothesis concerning what you would expect the root of the next chords to be, and then analyze the downbeat chords of measures 13 and 14 to see if Brahms has done what you expect he has done. (Musicians call this sort of pattern a *sequence*.)

Chapter 12

- Create a careful Roman-numeral and figured-bass analysis of measures 1 through 8. Name the cadence type employed. (*Hint:* Only three harmonies occur during measures 1 through 6, corresponding to the bass succession G–C–G. Each harmony is prolonged through repeated statement and by embellishing passing and/or neighboring notes.)

5. Brahms's Song "Fairest Love, My Sweet Angel," from *German Folk Songs* (1893–94)

Chapter 2

- Mark an example of each of the following symbols within the score: time signature, dotted half note, half note, quarter note.

Chapter 3

- Apply scale degree numbers, in the context of G Major, to all of the vocal melody pitches—the notes in the top staff. (For example, above the melody notes of measure 1, write "1̂ 3̂.") Which scale degree does not appear? Does that scale degree ever appear in the upper piano line?
- Apply scale degree numbers, in the context of G Major, to the first bass note of each measure—in the staff governed by the bass clef. (For example, below the first bass note of measure 1, write "1̂.")
- For the most part, Brahms employs pitches in a wider spacing than the triads we first encountered in Chapter 2. Yet at two points—in measures 8 and 19 (beat 3, spread between the two keyboard staves)—the space-space-space or line-line-line arrangement of three pitches characteristic of the triad occurs. Circle these triads, and indicate their Roman numerals (I, ii, iii, etc.) in the context of G Major.
- Add counting syllables for the vocal melody (1 2 3 1 2 3 . . .).
- What are the names of the rests (𝄾 and ‑) in the final measures?

Chapter 7

- The ascending melodic lines that spread chord members over an entire measure are a characteristic feature of this song's piano accompaniment. (This is called *arpeggiation*. The unusual beaming of eighth notes, as in measures 5 and 6, tells the pianist which notes should be played by the left hand and which by the right hand.) Brahms may have been *mimicking* the typical manner of writing for the harp (an instrument traditionally associated with angels, mentioned in the song's text). For example, in measure 5, instead of a vertical chord as in measures 3 and 4, six notes gradually ascend, from a B below the bass-clef staff to a D a *minor seventeenth* higher. We will explore exactly what these chords are in Chapters 9 and 10. For now, assess the extent of each arpeggiation by measuring the interval formed by the first and last notes of each ascent in measures 5, 6, 7, 12, 15, 16, 17, 18, 21, 22, and, in slower motion, the two-measure first ending (inside the bracket marked "1."). (*Hint:* In some cases there is an overlap between hands. For example, in measure 7 the ascent begins in the left hand with G–D–G, but along with the D the right hand begins its ascent, B–D–G–B. The total ascent is from first-line G in the bass clef to third-line B in the treble clef.)

Chapter 9

- Write in the appropriate figured-bass numbers and Roman numerals, in the context of G Major, for the arpeggiated chords in measures 5, 7 (both hands), 15*, 16, 18, 21* (both hands), and 22* (both hands). For example, the chord arpeggiated in measure 5 is a *I* chord in $\frac{6}{3}$ position. (*In measures 15, 21, and 22, the bass shifts before the arpeggiation is complete. In these cases, provide two answers. For example, in measure 15 consider first the chord on beats 1 and 2, with bass G, and then the chord on beat 3, with bass E.) (*Hint:* In measure 22, disregard the G and B dotted quarter notes. They linger from measure 21, delaying the arrival of chord member A.)

Chapter 10

- The piano accompaniment in five measures contains, either in a vertical presentation or as a horizontal arpeggiation, the pitches of a V^7 chord. Identify these measures and, in each case, examine Brahms's treatment of the chordal third and seventh (scale degrees $\hat{7}$ and $\hat{4}$). Does he avoid doubling these pitches, or, given the special nature of "harplike" arpeggiation, does one of these pitches sound in two different octaves? In each case, mark the resolutions of these two pitches in the chord that follows.
- Now examine measure 12. This chord would be labeled vi^7. (See "Seventh Chords and Their Inversions" in the Appendix.) What interval is formed by its third and seventh? Is that interval consonant or dissonant? Does the seventh of this chord ($\hat{5}$) resolve downward by step?

Chapter 11

- In measures 7 through 11 and in measure 21 through the end, label each curved line as either a *slur* or a *tie*.
- The vocal line of this song is twenty-one measures long. It consists of three phrases. Mark the boundaries of each phrase, count how many measures each phrase contains (it is somewhat unusual!) and identify (after some harmonic analysis) the cadence that ends each phrase. (*Hint:* The melodic note that you should consult to determine whether a cadence is *perfect* or *imperfect* is the vocal note, not the highest piano note.)

6. Schubert's "Cradle Song" (1816)

Slowly

1. Sleep well, sleep __ well, love-ly, charm-ing, __ fine boy, gent - ly rock - ing
2. Sleep well, sleep __ well, in the co - zy __ hol - low, you're pro - tect - ed
3. Sleep well, sleep __ well, in the down - y __ cra - dle, where you hear __ the

pp

by your moth - er's __ hand; calm and si - lent, rest - ful com - fort you will have __ with -
by your moth - er's __ arm; all your wish-es, all _____ your treas-ures are watched o - ver
sound of love's _ sweet _ song; here's a li - ly, and _____ a rose bud, wait - ing for __ you

in this cra - dle __ bed.
in love's warm _ em - brace.
when you wake _ once _ more.

Chapter 5

- Apply scale degree numbers, in the context of A♭ Major, to all of the vocal melody pitches—the notes in the top staff. (For example, above the melody notes of measure 1, write "$\hat{3}\,\hat{5}\,\hat{2}$ . . .")

Chapter 6

- Explain the role of B♮ at the end of measure 6. What interval is formed by E♭ and this B♮?

  (Compare Schubert's use of a flat beside the B notehead in measure 7 and Beethoven's use of a natural in measure 5 of Selection 2, above.)
- Schubert employs three thirds prominently in the vocal melody of the opening two measures. Each is presented in a somewhat different manner. The first third, C–E♭, is presented as an ascending leap. The second third, B♭–D♭, is also ascending, but filled in with a passing note, C. The third third, C–A♭, descends and is likewise filled in with a passing note. Thus we hear:

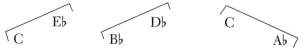

  Identify the quality (*major* or *minor*) of each of these thirds.

Chapter 7

- Add counting syllables (1 ee + ee 2 ee + ee . . .) above the vocal melody.

Chapter 8

- Explore the relationships among the following four chords, considering especially the notion of chordal inversion.

measure 5, fourth chord	measure 5, sixth chord	measure 6, first chord	measure 6, third chord

  Remember that, in terms of *intervals*, the minor sixth and the major third are inversionally related. These intervals are outlined melodically in the bass, highlighted by the slurs. (*Hint:* Schubert is using an especially light texture here. In the first chord of measure 6, the pitch A♭ is implied in the middle of the right-hand texture, continuing the A♭ sounded before the bar line.)

Chapter 10

- The first half of measure 9 (repeated in measure 10) contains a very interesting combination of pitches. On the one hand there is a persistent Ab and Eb on the bottom and top; on the other hand, the pitches Eb–G–Bb–Db mingle in the middle. Members of two chords are occurring at once! What are they?

Chapter 11

- Mark the boundaries of the four phrases that make up this song (excluding the two-measure interlude in measures 9 and 10). Identify (after some harmonic analysis) the cadence that ends each phrase. The first two phrases together form a larger unit. Use appropriate terminology to indicate the overall structure of these measures and the role of each component phrase. The form of the song is ternary (three-part). Musicians often call this the "ABA" form. In what measures does the contrasting B phrase occur? How does the concluding A section differ from the initial A section?

7. Schumann's Piano Piece "The Poor Orphan," from *Album for the Young* (1848)

Chapter 4

- Apply scale degree numbers, in the context of A Natural Minor, to all of the melody (highest) and bass (lowest) pitches in measures 1 through 8. (For example, above the opening melody notes, write "$\hat{1}$ $\hat{2}$ $\hat{3}$ $\hat{2}$ $\hat{1}$"; below the opening bass notes, write "$\hat{8}$ $\hat{5}$ $\hat{8}$.") Note that the treble clef replaces the bass clef for the bass notes of measures 3–4 and 7–8.

  The "♮" (*natural*) sign beside the G notehead in measure 2 does not affect the note's meaning. It simply reaffirms that G is G. Schumann wrote a G♯ in measure 1. (The reason for this will be explained in Chapter 10.) A performer who then sees a G in measure 2 might suspect a typographical error. To prevent any confusion, Schumann has used the "♮" sign as a precaution.

Chapter 6

- Schumann employs three thirds prominently in the melody of the opening three measures. All three are filled in with a passing note. We hear:

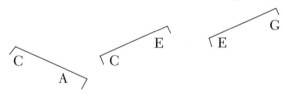

  Identify the quality (*major* or *minor*) of each of these thirds.

  Likewise three thirds occur in succession in the melody of measure 9 and the preceding upbeat:

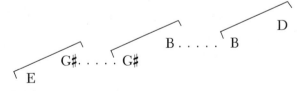

  Identify the quality (*major* or *minor*) of each of these thirds. What interval is formed by the initial G♯ and the final F?

  Below G♯–B–D–F another set of thirds occurs, in the lower staff:

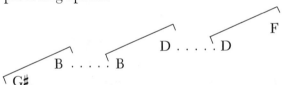

  Identify the quality (*major* or *minor*) of each of these thirds. What interval is formed by the initial E and the final D? Do the interval qualities of the upper and lower lines match, or are they contrasting?

Chapter 10

- Account for the occurrence of the pitches F♯ and G♯ within the score.

Chapter 12

- Create a careful Roman-numeral and figured-bass analysis of measures 1 through 8. Then describe the phrases (two) and their cadences, using appropriate terminology.

  (*Hint:* Heed the several changes of clef on the lower staff.)

- Compare the form of this piano piece with that of Schubert's "Cradle Song" (Selection 6, above). Label sections using the letters "A" and "B." Schubert's song is in "ABA" form. How would you employ these letters to display the form of Schumann's piece?

SOLUTIONS TO PRACTICE EXERCISES

Chapter 1

Practice Exercises 1-1.

h. F   i. B   j. B   k. D   l. D   m. A   n. A   o. G

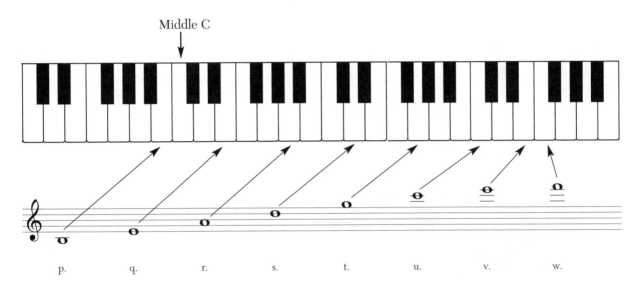

Middle C

p.   q.   r.   s.   t.   u.   v.   w.

Practice Exercises 1-2.

a. A–F, 6   b. B–C, 7   c. D–E, 2   d. D–G, 5   e. B–E, 4   f. B–D, 3

g. *G D*

h. *E D*

i.  *A D*

j. *C D*

k.  *F D*

l. *E C*

Practice Exercises 1-3.

a. $\hat{6}$ b. $\hat{3}$ c. $\hat{1}$ (or $\hat{8}$)   d. $\hat{5}$ e. $\hat{2}$ f. $\hat{7}$

Practice Exercises 1-4.

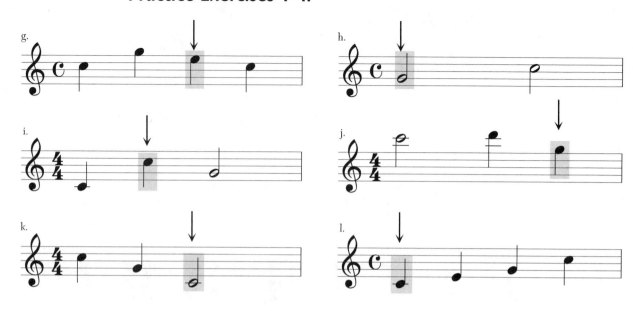

Chapter 2

Practice Exercises 2-1.

a. Î–4̂, P4, circle   b. Î–6̂, M6   c. Î–3̂, M3

d. Î–7̂, M7, circle   e. Î–5̂, P5   f. Î–2̂, M2, circle

Practice Exercises 2-2.

a. 8̂–6̂, m3   b. Î–6̂, M6   c. 7̂–Î, M7, circle   d. Î–2̂, M2, circle

e. Î–Î (or 8̂–8̂), P1   f. 8̂–4̂, P5   g. 5̂–8̂, P4, circle   h. 8̂–2̂, m7, circle

i. 3̂–8̂, m6   j. 5̂–Î, P5   k. 4̂–Î, P4, circle   l. Î–3̂, M3

m. M7   n. P4   o. m7   p. m6   q. M3   r. M2

Practice Exercises 2-3.

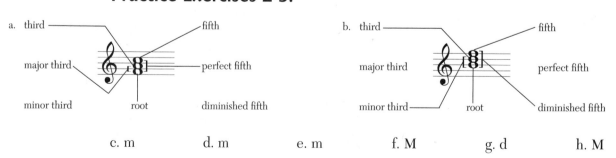

c. m   d. m   e. m   f. M   g. d   h. M

Practice Exercises 2-4.

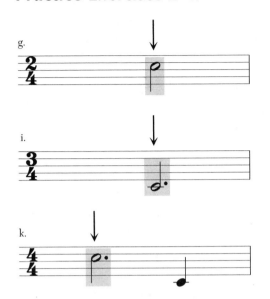
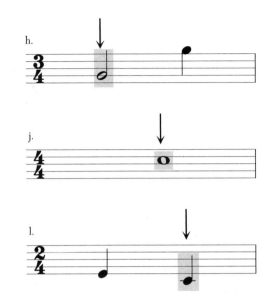

Chapter 3

Practice Exercises 3-1.

c. $\hat{4}$ d. $\hat{1}$ (or $\hat{8}$)   e. $\hat{7}$ f. $\hat{6}$ g. $\hat{3}$ h. $\hat{6}$ i. $\hat{5}$ j. $\hat{4}$ k. $\hat{1}$ (or $\hat{8}$)   l. $\hat{7}$

Practice Exercises 3-2.

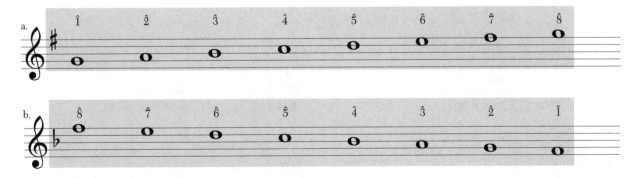

Practice Exercises 3-3.

a. F Major: $\hat{1}$–$\hat{8}$, P8   b. G Major: $\hat{8}$–$\hat{7}$, m2   c. G Major: $\hat{7}$–$\hat{1}$, M7   d. F Major: $\hat{4}$–$\hat{1}$, P4

e. G Major: $\hat{8}$–$\hat{3}$, m6   f. F Major: $\hat{1}$–$\hat{5}$, P5   g. G Major: $\hat{8}$–$\hat{2}$, m7   h. F Major: $\hat{8}$–$\hat{6}$, m3

Practice Exercises 3-4.

a. F Major: V   b. G Major: IV   c. G Major: vii°   d. F major: I   e. G major: vi   f. F major: ii

g.

F Major: vi

h.

G Major: V

i.

F Major: vii°

j.

G Major: iii

k.

F Major: IV

l.

G Major: ii

Practice Exercises 3-5.

f. G   g. D   h. C   i. C   j. F   k. F   l. F   m. C

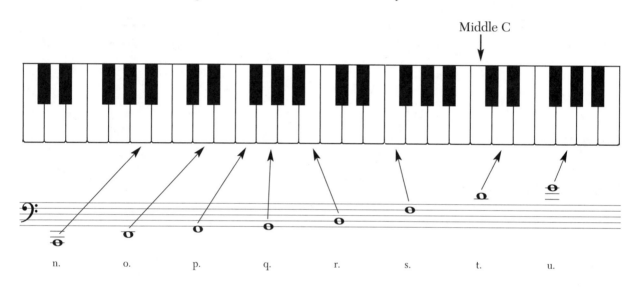

n.   o.   p.   q.   r.   s.   t.   u.

Practice Exercises 3-6.

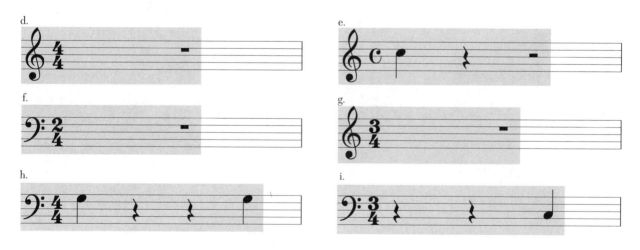

Chapter 4

Practice Exercises 4-1.

a. $\hat{2}$ b. $\hat{7}$ c. $\hat{4}$ d. $\hat{3}$ e. $\hat{6}$ f. $\hat{1}$ (or $\hat{8}$)   g. $\hat{4}$ h. $\hat{5}$ i. $\hat{3}$

j. $\hat{6}$ k. $\hat{4}$ l. $\hat{1}$ (or $\hat{8}$)   m. $\hat{6}$ n. $\hat{5}$ o. $\hat{2}$

Practice Exercises 4-2.

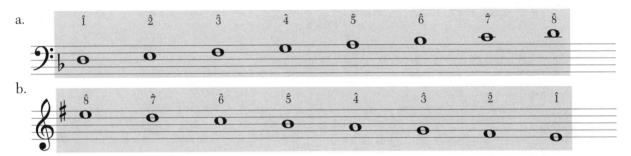

Practice Exercises 4-3.

a. D Natural Minor: $\hat{8}$–$\hat{4}$, P5

b. A Natural Minor: $\hat{1}$–$\hat{4}$, P4

c. E Natural Minor: $\hat{8}$–$\hat{2}$, m7

d. D Natural Minor: $\hat{1}$–$\hat{7}$, m7

e. E Natural Minor: $\hat{1}$–$\hat{6}$, m6

f. E Natural Minor: $\hat{8}$–$\hat{5}$, P4

g. A Natural Minor: $\hat{1}$–$\hat{3}$, m3

h. D Natural Minor: $\hat{8}$–$\hat{7}$, M2

Practice Exercises 4-4.

a. E Natural Minor: iv   b. D Natural Minor: ii°   c. A Natural Minor: VII   d. E Natural Minor: VI

e. D Natural Minor: v   f. E Natural Minor: i   g. A Natural Minor: III   h. D Natural Minor: VII

D Natural Minor: III

E Natural Minor: ii°

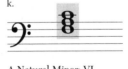

A Natural Minor: VI

D Natural Minor: iv

E Natural Minor: VII

A Natural Minor: v

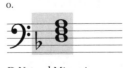

D Natural Minor: i

E Natural Minor: III

Practice Exercises 4-5.

l.

m.

n.

o.

Chapter 5

Practice Exercises 5-1.

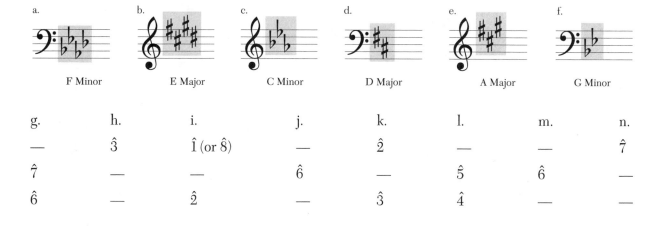

a.   F Minor

b.   E Major

c.   C Minor

d.   D Major

e.   A Major

f.   G Minor

g.	h.	i.	j.	k.	l.	m.	n.
—	$\hat{3}$	$\hat{1}\,(\text{or } \hat{8})$	—	$\hat{2}$	—	—	$\hat{7}$
$\hat{7}$	—	—	$\hat{6}$	—	$\hat{5}$	$\hat{6}$	—
$\hat{6}$	—	$\hat{2}$	—	$\hat{3}$	$\hat{4}$	—	—

Practice Exercises 5-2.

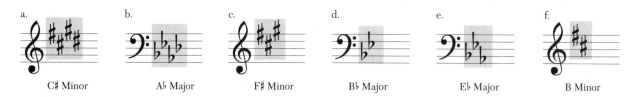

a.   C♯ Minor

b.   A♭ Major

c.   F♯ Minor

d.   B♭ Major

e.   E♭ Major

f.   B Minor

Practice Exercises 5-3.

a. D Major, B Minor   b. E♭ Major, C Minor   c. A♭ Major, F Minor   d. E Major, C♯ Minor

e. B♭ Major, G Minor   f. A Major, F♯ Minor

Practice Exercises 5-4.

a.
D Major: vi

b.
F Minor: iv

c.
E♭ Major: iii

d.
E Major: vii°

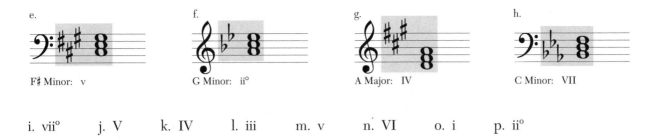

e. F♯ Minor: v f. G Minor: ii° g. A Major: IV h. C Minor: VII

i. vii°　　j. V　　k. IV　　l. iii　　m. v　　n. VI　　o. i　　p. ii°

Practice Exercises 5-5.

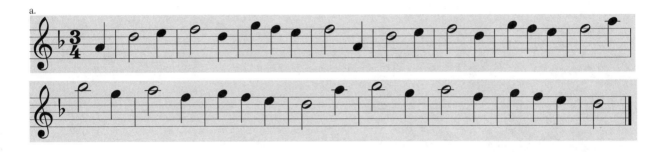

a.

b.

c.

d.

Chapter 6

Practice Exercises 6-1.

a. A♭　b. F♯　c. F♯　d. B♭　e. F♯　f. C♯　g. D♯　h. E♭　i. D　j. C　k. F♯　l. E♭

Practice Exercises 6-2.

a. m6　　b. m3　　c. M6　　d. M7　　e. m7　　f. M3　　g. m7　　h. M6

Practice Exercises 6-3.

a.
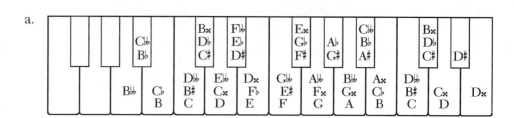

b.

c.

d.

e.

f.

g.

Practice Exercises 6-4.

a. A5 b. d7 c. d5 d. A6 e. M3 f. A6

g.

h.

i.

j.

k.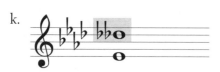

l.

Practice Exercises 6-5.

a.

b.

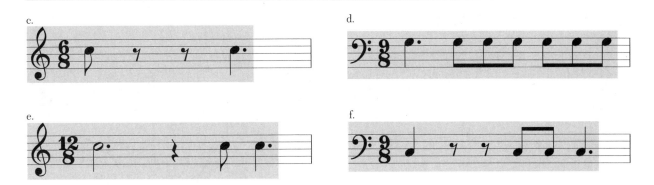

Chapter 7

Practice Exercises 7-1.

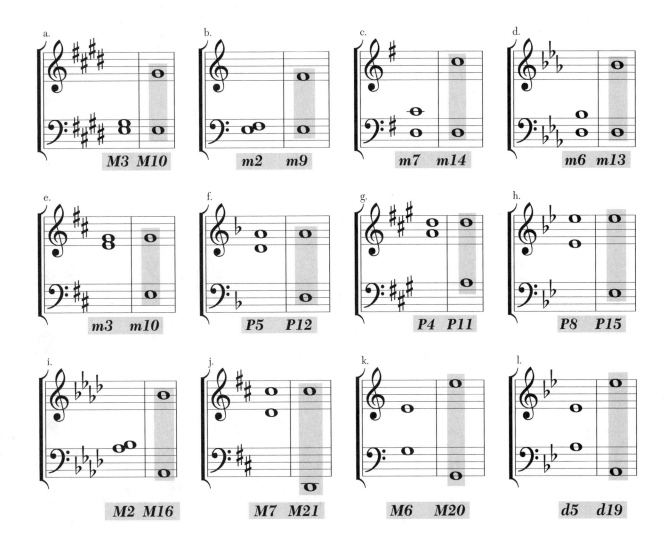

Practice Exercises 7-2.

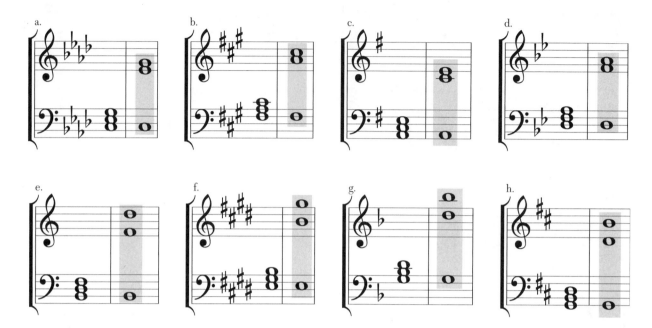

Practice Exercises 7-3.

a. The three upper notes span more than an octave.

b. The A is missing. The stemming in the upper staff is incorrect.

c. D appears instead of C. F♯, G Major's leading tone, is doubled.

d. The bass stem should point upward, not downward. The stemming in the upper staff is incorrect. The three upper notes span more than an octave.

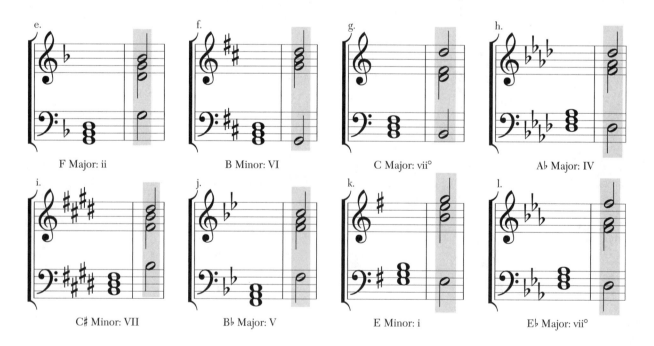

Practice Exercises 7-4.

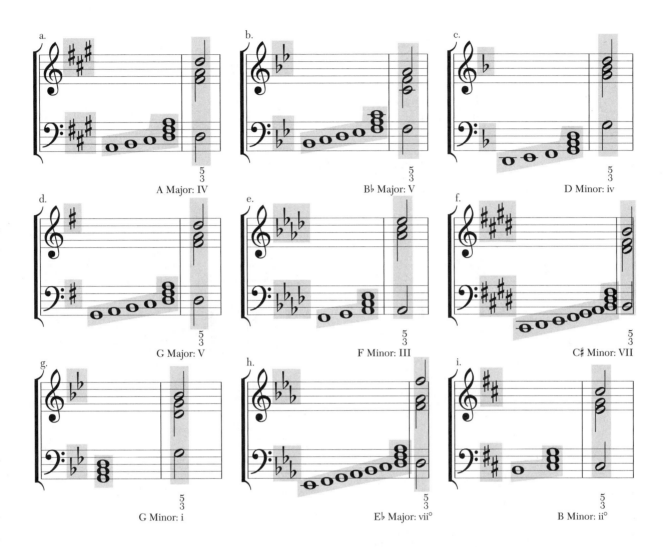

a. A Major: IV

b. B♭ Major: V

c. D Minor: iv

d. G Major: V

e. F Minor: III

f. C♯ Minor: VII

g. G Minor: i

h. E♭ Major: vii°

i. B Minor: ii°

Practice Exercises 7-5.

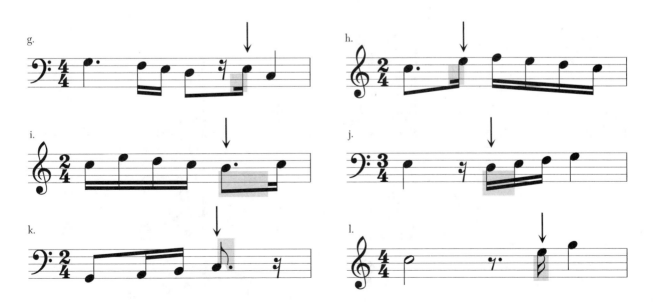

g.

h.

i.

j.

k.

l.

Chapter 8

Practice Exercises 8-1.

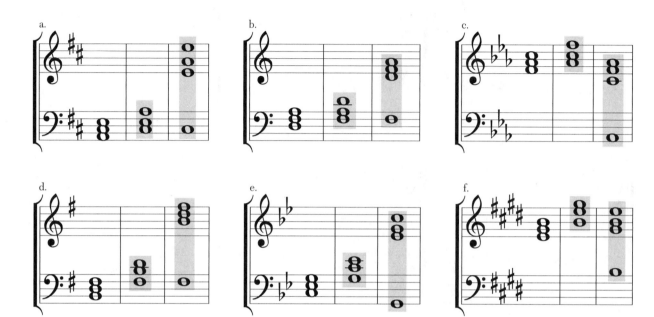

Practice Exercises 8-2.

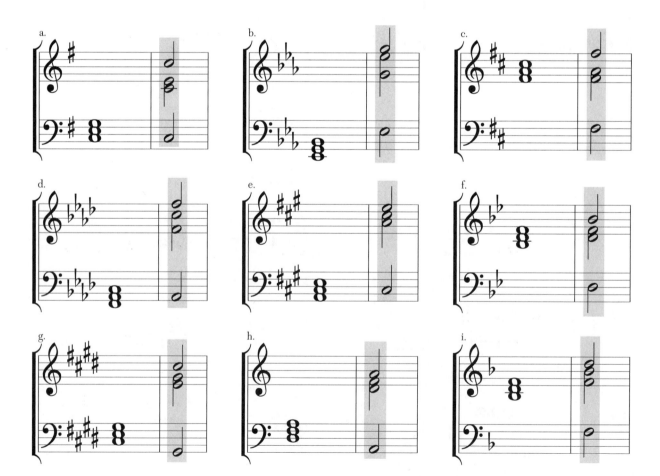

Practice Exercises 8-3.

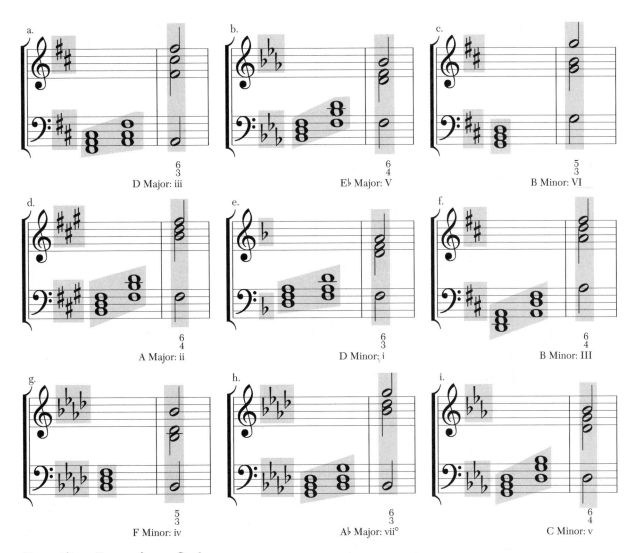

Practice Exercises 8-4.

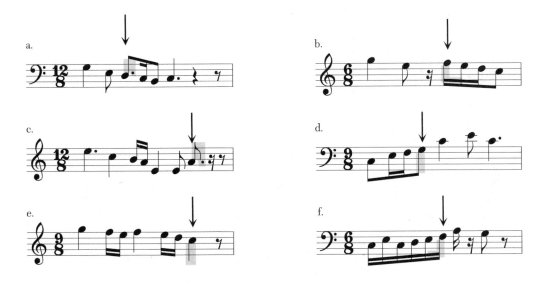

Chapter 9

Practice Exercises 9-1.

a. $\frac{6}{3}$ b. $\frac{5}{3}$ (5th omitted)   c. $\frac{6}{4}$ d. $\frac{6}{3}$ e. $\frac{6}{4}$ f. $\frac{6}{3}$ g. $\frac{5}{3}$ (5th omitted)   h. $\frac{6}{4}$

Practice Exercises 9-2.

a. D Major: $\frac{6}{3}$, iii   b. E♭ Major: $\frac{5}{3}$, V   c. A Major: $\frac{6}{4}$, vii°   d. F Minor: $\frac{6}{4}$, VI

e. E Minor: $\frac{6}{3}$, ii°   f. G Minor: $\frac{5}{3}$, iv

Practice Exercises 9-3.

a. mediant   b. dominant   c. leading tone   d. submediant   e. supertonic   f. subdominant

Practice Exercises 9-4.

Chapter 10

Practice Exercises 10-1.

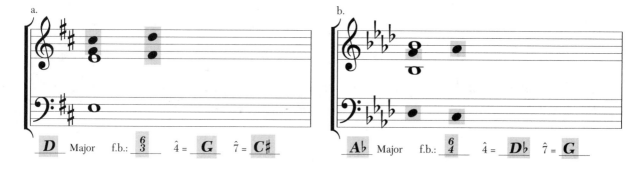

c. **G** Major   f.b.: $\frac{6}{3}$ $\hat{4}$ = **C** $\hat{7}$ = **F♯**

d. **E♭** Major   f.b.: $\frac{5}{3}$ $\hat{4}$ = **A♭** $\hat{7}$ = **D**

e. **A** Major   f.b.: $\frac{6}{3}$ $\hat{4}$ = **D** $\hat{7}$ = **G♯**

f. **B♭** Major   f.b.: $\frac{5}{3}$ $\hat{4}$ = **E♭** $\hat{7}$ = **A**

Practice Exercises 10-2.

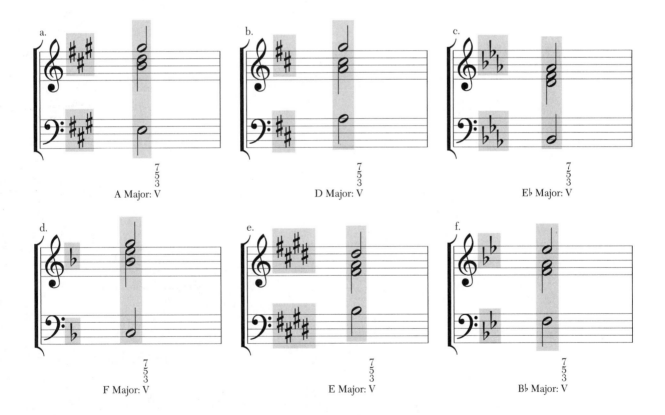

a. $\begin{smallmatrix}7\\5\\3\end{smallmatrix}$ A Major: V

b. $\begin{smallmatrix}7\\5\\3\end{smallmatrix}$ D Major: V

c. $\begin{smallmatrix}7\\5\\3\end{smallmatrix}$ E♭ Major: V

d. $\begin{smallmatrix}7\\5\\3\end{smallmatrix}$ F Major: V

e. $\begin{smallmatrix}7\\5\\3\end{smallmatrix}$ E Major: V

f. $\begin{smallmatrix}7\\5\\3\end{smallmatrix}$ B♭ Major: V

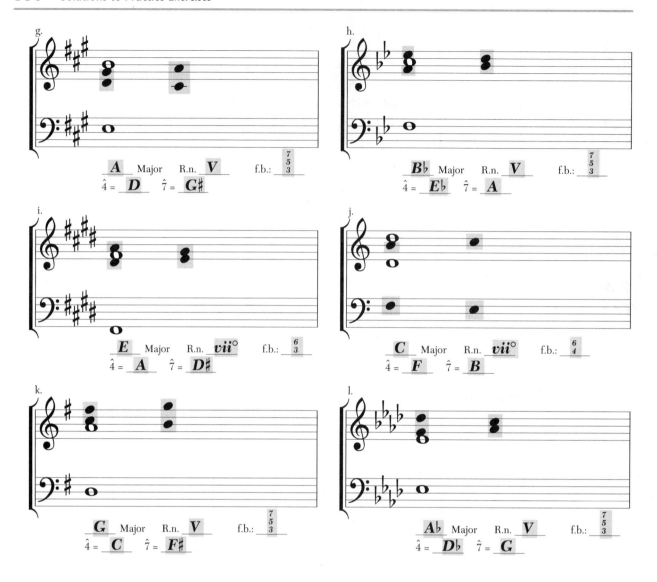

g.

A Major   R.n. **V**   f.b.: $\begin{smallmatrix}7\\5\\3\end{smallmatrix}$

$\hat{4}$ = **D** $\hat{7}$ = **G♯**

h.

B♭ Major   R.n. **V**   f.b.: $\begin{smallmatrix}7\\5\\3\end{smallmatrix}$

$\hat{4}$ = **E♭** $\hat{7}$ = **A**

i.

E Major   R.n. **vii°**   f.b.: $\begin{smallmatrix}6\\3\end{smallmatrix}$

$\hat{4}$ = **A** $\hat{7}$ = **D♯**

j.

C Major   R.n. **vii°**   f.b.: $\begin{smallmatrix}6\\4\end{smallmatrix}$

$\hat{4}$ = **F** $\hat{7}$ = **B**

k.

G Major   R.n. **V**   f.b.: $\begin{smallmatrix}7\\5\\3\end{smallmatrix}$

$\hat{4}$ = **C** $\hat{7}$ = **F♯**

l.

A♭ Major   R.n. **V**   f.b.: $\begin{smallmatrix}7\\5\\3\end{smallmatrix}$

$\hat{4}$ = **D♭** $\hat{7}$ = **G**

Practice Exercises 10-3.

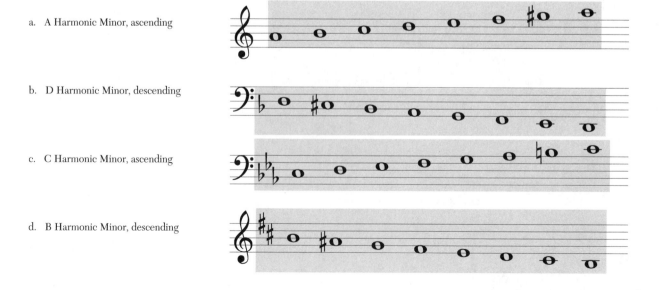

a. A Harmonic Minor, ascending

b. D Harmonic Minor, descending

c. C Harmonic Minor, ascending

d. B Harmonic Minor, descending

e. C♯ Harmonic Minor, ascending

f. F Harmonic Minor, descending

Practice Exercises 10-4.

a. F Major, ascending

b. F Natural Minor, ascending

c. F Harmonic Minor, ascending

d. F Melodic Minor, ascending

e. E Major, descending

f. E Natural Minor, descending

g. E Harmonic Minor, descending

h. E Melodic Minor, descending

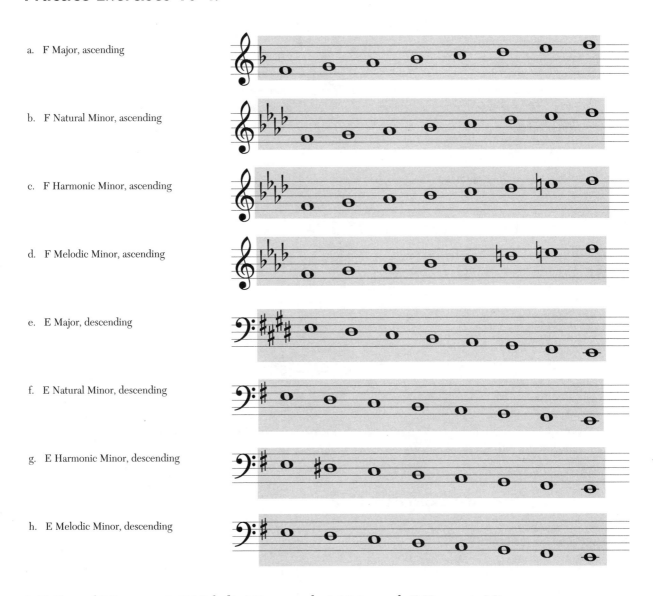

i. D Natural Minor   j. G Melodic Minor   k. A Major   l. F Harmonic Minor

m. B Melodic Minor   n. C Harmonic Minor

Practice Exercises 10-5.

a.

1 ee + ee 2 ee +ee 3 ee + ee 4ee+ee 1 ee + ee 2 ee + ee 3 ee + ee 4ee+ee

b.

ee 1ee+ ee 2 ee + ee 3ee+ ee 1 ee + ee 2 ee + ee 3 ee +

c.

1ee+ee uh ee 2 ee +ee uhee 1ee+ee uhee 2ee+ee uhee 1 ee + ee uhee 2ee+ ee uh ee 1ee+eeuhee2ee+eeuhee

Chapter 11

Practice Exercises 11-1.

a.

		7					
5	5	5	6	6	———		5
3	3	3	3	3	———		3
I	V	vi	I	ii	———		V

		7				7	
5	5	5	6	6	——	5	5
3	3	3	3	3	——	3	3
I	V	vi	I	ii	——	V	I

b. phrases   half   antecedent phrase   perfect authentic   consequent phrase
parallel period

Practice Exercises 11-2.

a.

					7	
5	6	6	6	5	5	5
3	4	3	3	3	3	3
I	———————————		ii	V	———————	vi

					7	
5	6	5	6	5	5	5
3	3	3	3	3	3	3
I	———————		IV	ii	V	——————— I

b. deceptive   imperfect authentic

Practice Exercises 11-3.

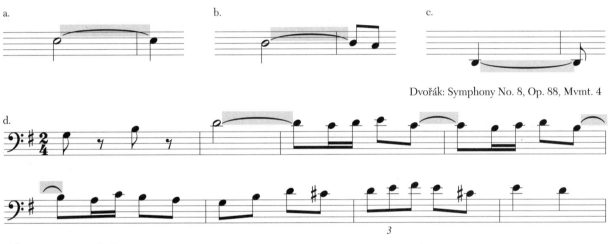

Practice Exercises 11-4.

Dvořák: Symphony No. 8, Op. 88, Mvmt. 4

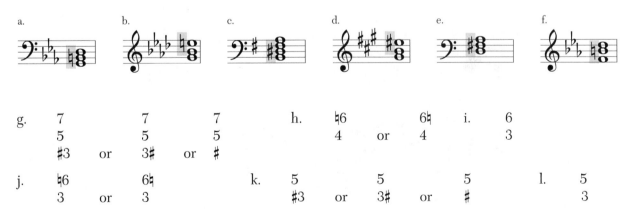

Chapter 12

Practice Exercises 12-1.

a. b. c. d. e. f.

g.	7		7		7	h.	♮6		6♮	i.	6
	5		5		5		4	or	4		3
	♯3	or	3♯	or	♯						

j.	♮6		6♮	k.	5		5		5	l.	5
	3	or	3		♯3	or	3♯	or	♯		3

Practice Exercises 12-2.

a. E Minor: iv, subdominant

b. G Minor: vii°, leading tone

c. D Minor: v, dominant

d. B Minor: IV, subdominant

e. F Minor: vii°, leading tone

f. F♯ Minor: V, dominant

g. C Minor: V, dominant

h. C♯ Minor: VII, subtonic

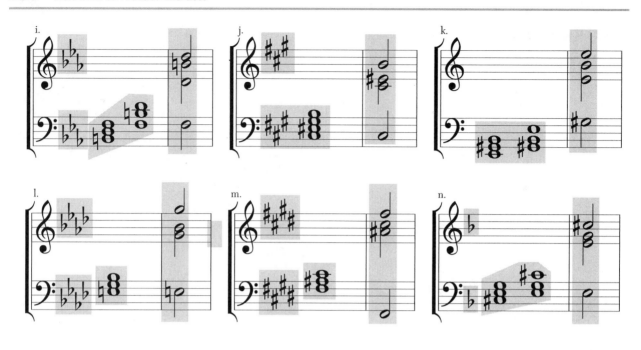

o. E Minor: $\frac{6}{4\sharp}$, vii°, leading tone   p. C Minor: $\frac{6}{3}$, IV, subdominant   q. C$\sharp$ Minor: $\frac{5}{3\sharp}$, V, dominant

r. D Minor: $\frac{6\sharp}{3}$, vii°, leading tone   s. F$\sharp$ Minor: $\frac{6}{3}$, V, dominant   t. G Minor: $\frac{6\natural}{4}$, IV, subdominant

u.

	5	6$\sharp$	6	5	6	7 5	5
	3	3	3	3	3	3$\sharp$	3
D Minor:	i	vii°	i	———	ii°	V	i

perfect authentic cadence

Practice Exercises 12-3.

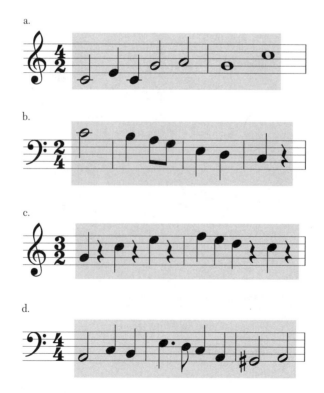

Practice Exercises 12-4.

GLOSSARY

Accidental   Any symbol that modifies the letter name of a pitch or its notehead within the body of a composition. Accidentals applied to individual noteheads retain their effect until the next bar line unless superseded by another accidental. *See* SHARP, FLAT, NATURAL, DOUBLE SHARP, and DOUBLE FLAT.

Alla breve   A name applied to the $\frac{2}{2}$ meter, often notated with a symbol (¢) in place of the $\frac{2}{2}$ time signature. Also called cut time.

Antecedent and consequent phrases   A pair of phrases, the first ending in a half cadence, the second in an authentic cadence. Antecedent and consequent phrases together form a period.

Arpeggiate   To sing or play the pitches of a chord successively.

Augmentation dot   A dot placed after a notehead or rest to increase its value by one half.

Augmented   (1) An interval quality applied to all interval sizes. Augmented intervals are a half step larger than major or perfect intervals. (2) A triad quality. The augmented triad has a major third between its root and third, and an augmented fifth between its root and fifth.

Authentic cadence   A complete closure, consisting of the chord succession from a root-position dominant chord to a root-position tonic chord. If the tonic pitch appears in both the soprano and the bass, the cadence is called a perfect authentic cadence. If only in the bass, it is called an imperfect authentic cadence.

Bar lines   The vertical lines that extend from the first to the fifth line of a staff, or the bottom to the top line of a system, to show the divisions between measures.

Bass   The lowest note of a chord.

Bass clef   A symbol ($\mathcal{9}$) used in the notation of pitches in the low to middle range on a staff.

Beam   A horizontal or diagonal line used in forming the eighth- and sixteenth-note symbols.

Beats   A continuous flow of regular pulses, forming the basis of meter. Beats may follow one another at a slow, moderate, or fast rate. Also called pulses.

Cadence   A succession of chords that invokes a sense of closure at the end of a phrase.

Chord   Any combination of three or more simultaneously sounding pitches.

Chromatic   *See* DIATONIC.

Chromatic neighboring note   A note from the chromatic scale that is employed to embellish a single diatonic pitch, such as F♯ in the succession G F♯ G.

Chromatic passing note   A note that comes between two adjacent diatonic pitches, such as C♯ in the succession C C♯ D.

Chromatic scale   A scale that includes all the pitches within an octave, such as C C♯ D D♯ E F F♯ G G♯ A A♯ B C, or C B B♭ A A♭ G G♭ F E E♭ D D♭ C.

Clef   A symbol placed at the left edge of a staff to give meaning to the noteheads drawn on that staff. The most commonly used clefs are the treble clef and the bass clef.

Common time   A name applied to the $\frac{4}{4}$ meter, often notated with a symbol (C) in place of the $\frac{4}{4}$ time signature.

Compound interval   Any interval larger than an octave.

Compound meter   A meter whose beats tend to divide into thirds.

Consequent phrase   *See* ANTECEDENT AND CONSEQUENT PHRASES.

Consonance   The classification of two or more pitches sounding in a stable relationship.

Cut time   *See* ALLA BREVE.

Deceptive cadence   A last-moment prevention of closure when an authentic cadence is expected, created through the harmonic progression from dominant, to submediant, to subdominant in $\frac{6}{3}$ position, or to some other substitute for the tonic.

Diatonic   A description of the seven pitches per octave that form the scale for a given major or natural minor key, in contrast to the five chromatic pitches, which are absent from this scale.

Diminished   (1) An interval quality applied to all interval sizes. Diminished intervals are a half step smaller than minor or perfect intervals. (2) A triad quality. The diminished triad has a minor third between its root and third, and a diminished fifth between its root and fifth.

Dissonance   The classification of two pitches sounding in an unstable relationship. Dissonant pitches invoke a tendency toward motion or resolution.

Dominant   The triad whose root is the fifth scale degree of the prevailing key.

Dominant seventh chord   A four-note chord built on the fifth scale degree, consisting of the root, third, and fifth of the major triad, plus a minor seventh above the root. Occasionally the fifth is omitted so that the root may be doubled.

Dotted eighth note   A symbol (♪.) denoting a pitch lasting three-quarters of a beat in simple meters such as $\frac{2}{4}$, $\frac{3}{4}$, and $\frac{4}{4}$, or half a beat in compound meters such as $\frac{6}{8}$, $\frac{9}{8}$, and $\frac{12}{8}$.

Dotted eighth rest   A symbol (ɤ·) denoting silence lasting three-quarters of a beat in simple meters such as $\frac{2}{4}$, $\frac{3}{4}$, and $\frac{4}{4}$, or half a beat in compound meters such as $\frac{6}{8}$, $\frac{9}{8}$, and $\frac{12}{8}$.

Dotted half note   A symbol (𝅗𝅥.) denoting a pitch lasting three beats in simple meters such as $\frac{3}{4}$ and $\frac{4}{4}$, or two beats in compound meters such as $\frac{6}{8}$, $\frac{9}{8}$, and $\frac{12}{8}$.

Dotted quarter note   A symbol (♩.) denoting a pitch lasting one and one-half beats in simple meters such as $\frac{2}{4}$, $\frac{3}{4}$, and $\frac{4}{4}$, or one beat in compound meters such as $\frac{6}{8}$, $\frac{9}{8}$, and $\frac{12}{8}$.

Dotted whole note   A symbol (𝅝·) denoting a pitch lasting three beats in compound meters such as $\frac{3}{2}$ and $\frac{4}{2}$.

Double bar   Two vertical lines, the second of which is thicker than the first, which appear at the end of a composition.

Double flat   An accidental (♭♭) that instructs the performer to lower the pitch of the notehead or the pitch name to which it is applied by two half steps.

Double sharp   An accidental (×) that instructs the performer to raise the pitch of the notehead or pitch name to which it is applied by two half steps.

Double whole note   A symbol (𝅜) denoting a pitch lasting one full measure in $\frac{4}{2}$ meter.

Double whole rest   A symbol (𝄺) denoting a silence lasting one full measure in $\frac{4}{2}$ meter.

Doubling   Reinforcing a pitch by positioning it in two or more of the four voices of a chord.

Downbeat   The first beat of a measure.

Eighth note   A symbol (♪ or, when two or more eighth notes appear beside one another, ♫) denoting a pitch lasting one-half of a beat in simple meters such as $\frac{2}{4}$, $\frac{3}{4}$, and $\frac{4}{4}$, or one-third of a beat in compound meters such as $\frac{6}{8}$, $\frac{9}{8}$, and $\frac{12}{8}$.

Eighth rest   A symbol (ɤ) denoting a silence lasting one-half of a beat in simple meters such as $\frac{2}{4}$, $\frac{3}{4}$, and $\frac{4}{4}$, or one-third of a beat in compound meters such as $\frac{6}{8}$, $\frac{9}{8}$, and $\frac{12}{8}$.

Embellishing note   A note that either connects two harmonic notes or temporarily substitutes for a harmonic note. Common embellishing notes include the PASSING NOTE, NEIGHBORING NOTE, and INCOMPLETE NEIGHBORING NOTE.

Enharmonic equivalent   A different name that may be applied to a given pitch, such as C♭ in place of B.

Fifth   (1) An interval of size five. *See* INTERVAL SIZE. (2) The highest pitch of a triad.

Figured bass   The use of figures (numbers) such as $\frac{5}{3}$, $\frac{6}{3}$, $\frac{6}{4}$, and $\frac{7}{5}$ to indicate the intervals that occur above a chord's bass pitch.

First inversion   The positioning of the notes of a triad or chord such that the triad's third is the lowest-sounding pitch. Also called $\frac{6}{3}$ position.

$\frac{5}{3}$ position   *See* ROOT POSITION.

Flag   A flowing, curved line ( ) attached to a stem in forming the symbols for eighth notes and sixteenth notes.

Flat   An accidental (♭) that instructs the performer to lower the pitch of the notehead or pitch name to which it is applied by one half step.

Fourth   An interval of size four. *See* INTERVAL SIZE.

Half cadence   A partial closure, created by a harmonic motion to a root-position dominant chord.

Half note   A symbol ( ) denoting a pitch lasting two beats in simple meters such as $\frac{2}{4}$, $\frac{3}{4}$, and $\frac{4}{4}$, and one beat in simple meters such as $\frac{2}{2}$, $\frac{3}{2}$, and $\frac{4}{2}$.

Half rest   A symbol (—) denoting a silence lasting two beats in $\frac{4}{4}$ meter, and one beat in simple meters such as $\frac{2}{2}$, $\frac{3}{2}$, and $\frac{4}{2}$.

Half step   The distance between adjacent keys on the keyboard, considering both white and black keys.

Harmonic minor scale   A variant of the natural minor scale in which the raised seventh scale degree (leading tone) takes the place of the diatonic seventh scale degree (subtonic).

Harmonize   To supply appropriate chords for the pitches of a melody.

Imperfect authentic cadence   *See* AUTHENTIC CADENCE.

Imperfect plagal cadence   *See* PLAGAL CADENCE.

Incomplete neighboring note   *See* NEIGHBORING NOTE.

Inner voices   The notes that sound between the soprano and the bass in a chord.

Interval   A relationship between any two pitches, measured both in terms of interval size and interval quality.

Interval size   The numerical measure of how close or far apart an interval's two pitches are from one another. For example, an interval written on adjacent lines has size three because three positions (line, space, and line) separate the two noteheads.

Interval quality   A qualifier, such as major, minor, perfect, augmented, or diminished, to distinguish among various intervals that, though of the same interval size, are not identical.

Inversion   (1) Exchanging the positions of a simple interval's two component pitches, so that the lower pitch becomes the higher pitch. For example, the inversion of the major third $\frac{E}{C}$ is the minor sixth $\frac{C}{E}$. (2) When applied to a triad or chord, *see* ROOT POSITION, FIRST INVERSION, and SECOND INVERSION.

Key   (1) Each of the black or white levers on a piano keyboard. (2) Each of the twenty-four collections of diatonic pitches used in music. Any pitch within the octave may serve as the key's tonic, or tonal center. Some keys have two alternative spellings (such as F♯ or G♭). A key may be in either of two modes. (*See* MAJOR and MINOR.)

Key signature   A symbol that designates an automatic application of sharps or flats to noteheads on specific lines and spaces, in order to establish a specific major or minor key. The key signature appears near the left edge of the staff, just after the clef.

Leading tone   The pitch that serves as the seventh scale degree of the major, harmonic minor, and ascending melodic minor scales; and the triad built using this pitch as its root.

Ledger line   A short horizontal line that serves as a temporary extension of the staff. Also spelled *leger line.*

Lines   The five straight horizontal constituents of a staff, numbered from the bottom upward.

Major   (1) An interval quality applied to seconds, thirds, sixths, sevenths, and their compounds. Major intervals are a half step larger than minor intervals, and a half step smaller than some augmented intervals. (2) A triad quality. A major triad has a major third between its root and third, and a perfect fifth between its root and fifth. (3) A mode. A major key contains as diatonic pitches a major second, major third, perfect fourth, perfect fifth, major sixth, and major seventh above its tonic pitch. (4) A scale quality. An ascending major scale contains the following steps between adjacent pitches: whole step, whole step, half step, whole step, whole step, whole step, half step.

Measure   Each of the groupings of beats in a specific meter, set off in staff notation by bar lines.

Mediant   The triad whose root is the third scale degree of the prevailing key.

Melodic minor scale   A variant of the natural minor scale in which the sixth and seventh scale degrees are raised in the ascent and diatonic in the descent.

Meter   The segmenting of uniform pulses into groups, and the organization of the pulses within each group into strong and weak beats.

Metronome   A mechanical device that can be adjusted to tick from forty to over two hundred times per minute, used as an aid in the performance of rhythm.

Middle C   A pitch corresponding to the first ledger line below the staff using the treble clef, or the first ledger line above the staff using the bass clef. The key for Middle C is found in vertical alignment with your left eye when you are sitting well-centered at the keyboard.

Minor   (1) An interval quality applied to seconds, thirds, sixths, sevenths, and their compounds. Minor intervals are a half step larger than some diminished intervals, and a half step smaller than major intervals. (2) A triad quality. A minor triad has a minor third between its root and third, and a perfect fifth between its root and fifth. (3) A mode. A minor key contains as diatonic pitches a major second, minor third, perfect fourth, perfect fifth, minor sixth, and minor seventh above its tonic pitch. (4) A scale quality. An ascending natural minor scale contains the following steps between adjacent pitches: whole step, half step, whole step, whole step, half step, whole step, whole step.

Modes   The two ways in which the diatonic pitches of a key may be arranged. *See* MAJOR and MINOR.

Natural   An accidental (♮) applied to a notehead, canceling any accidental previously applied to that notehead within the measure or indicated by the key signature.

Natural minor   A term applied to the minor mode and to its scale, to distinguish them from the variants called harmonic minor and melodic minor.

Neighboring note   An embellishing note that sounds temporarily in place of a single pitch that appears both before and after it. If the note that is embellished appears on only one side of the neighboring note, the embellishing note is an incomplete neighboring note.

Note   *See* NOTEHEAD.

Notehead   A symbol (◦ or •) placed through a line or in a space on a staff (or using ledger lines) to represent a specific pitch.

Octave   An interval of size eight. *See* INTERVAL SIZE.

Parallel keys   Two keys that share the same tonic pitch but are of different modes. Parallel keys do *not* share the same key signature.

Parallel period   *See* PERIOD.

Parent triad   The triad from which a chord is derived.

Passing note   An embellishing note that connects two harmonic notes in stepwise ascending or descending motion.

Perfect   An interval quality applied to unisons, fourths, fifths, octaves, and their compounds.

Perfect authentic cadence   *See* AUTHENTIC CADENCE.

Perfect plagal cadence   *See* PLAGAL CADENCE.

Period   Two phrases that form a pair. When the two phrases begin identically, the period is called a parallel period.

Phrase   A coherent segment of music shaped by a clearly perceptible beginning and ending, usually two, four, or eight measures in length.

Pickup   *See* UPBEAT.

Pitch   A musical sound, named according to its position within a range from low to high.

Plagal cadence   A cadence that attains closure through the harmonic progression from a root-position subdominant chord to a root-position tonic chord. If the tonic pitch appears in both the soprano and the bass, the cadence is called a perfect plagal cadence. If only in the bass, it is called an imperfect plagal cadence.

Pulses   *See* BEATS.

Quality   *See* INTERVAL QUALITY.

Quarter note   A symbol (♩) denoting a pitch lasting one beat in simple meters such as $\frac{2}{4}$, $\frac{3}{4}$, and $\frac{4}{4}$, or two-thirds of a beat in compound meters such as $\frac{6}{8}$, $\frac{9}{8}$, and $\frac{12}{8}$.

Quarter rest   A symbol (𝄽) denoting a silence lasting one beat in simple meters such as $\frac{2}{4}$, $\frac{3}{4}$, and $\frac{4}{4}$, or two-thirds of a beat in compound meters such as $\frac{6}{8}$, $\frac{9}{8}$, and $\frac{12}{8}$.

Relative keys   Two keys—one major, one minor—that use the same collection of diatonic pitches. The distance separating the tonics of two such keys is always a minor third. Relative keys share the same key signature.

Repeat sign   Either of two symbols (‖: and :‖) that instruct a performer to repeat the section of a composition they enclose. If only the latter sign is present, the performer is to go back to the beginning of the work.

Rest   A period of silence, notated by various symbols representing specific durations.

Rhythm   How music unfolds over time, notated in relation to the underlying pulse of a meter.

Roman numerals   Analytical symbols that indicate both the scale degree of a chord's root in the context of a specific major or minor key and the chord's quality.

Root   The lowest pitch of a triad.

Root position   The positioning of a triad or chord such that the root is the lowest-sounding pitch. Also called $\frac{5}{3}$ position.

Scale   The arrangement of the seven pitches of a key in a linear succession, with the tonic pitch appearing at both the beginning and end of the succession. A scale may ascend or descend. *See* DIATONIC.

Scale degree An Arabic number topped by a circumflex, such as $\hat{3}$, indicating the numerical position of a pitch within an ascending scale.

Score notation Music's visual representation, in which a variety of symbols indicate the pitches that are to sound at each moment of a musical work.

Second An interval of size two. The two noteheads of a second appear on an adjacent line and space. *See* INTERVAL SIZE.

Second inversion The positioning of a triad or chord such that the triad's fifth is the lowest-sounding pitch. Also called $\frac{6}{4}$ position.

Seventh An interval of size seven. *See* INTERVAL SIZE.

Sharp An accidental (♯) that instructs the performer to raise the pitch of the notehead or pitch name to which it is applied by one half step.

Simple interval Any interval that falls within the span of an octave.

Simple meter A meter whose beats tend to divide into halves.

$\frac{6}{3}$ position *See* FIRST INVERSION.

$\frac{6}{4}$ position *See* SECOND INVERSION.

Sixteenth note A symbol (♪ or, when two or more sixteenth notes appear beside one another, ♬) denoting a pitch lasting one-fourth of a beat in simple meters such as $\frac{2}{4}$, $\frac{3}{4}$, and $\frac{4}{4}$, or one-sixth of a beat in compound meters such as $\frac{6}{8}$, $\frac{9}{8}$, and $\frac{12}{8}$.

Sixteenth rest A symbol (𝄿) denoting a silence lasting one-fourth of a beat in simple meters such as $\frac{2}{4}$, $\frac{3}{4}$, and $\frac{4}{4}$, or one-sixth of a beat in compound meters such as $\frac{6}{8}$, $\frac{9}{8}$, and $\frac{12}{8}$.

Sixth An interval of size six. *See* INTERVAL SIZE.

Size *See* INTERVAL SIZE.

Slur A curved line connecting noteheads that represent different pitches. It implies legato (smooth) connections among pitches in performance or indicates phrasing (the grouping of notes into coherent units).

Soprano The highest note of a chord.

Spaces The four positions between the long horizontal lines of the staff, numbered from the bottom upward.

Staff (pl. *staves*) The standard format for score notation, consisting of a set of five evenly spaced horizontal lines.

Stem A vertical line added to one side of a notehead in music notation to form half notes, quarter notes, eighth notes, and so on.

Subdominant The triad whose root is the fourth scale degree of the prevailing key.

Submediant The triad whose root is the sixth scale degree of the prevailing key.

Subtonic The triad whose root is the seventh scale degree of the prevailing natural minor key.

Supertonic The triad whose root is the second scale degree of the prevailing key.

Syncopation A temporary contradiction of the prevailing meter.

System Two staves bound together at the left edge and at each bar line.

Tempo The speed at which the beats of the meter follow one another.

Third (1) An interval of size three; the two noteheads of a third appear on adjacent lines or adjacent spaces. *See* INTERVAL SIZE. (2) The middle pitch of a triad.

Tie A curved line connecting two noteheads that represent the same pitch, indicating a single pitch whose duration equals the sum of the durations of the notes thus connected.

Time signature A symbol, such as $\frac{4}{4}$ or $\frac{6}{8}$, that appears near the left edge of the staff to indicate the meter.

Tonal center *See* TONIC.

Tonic   The most stable pitch of a key, serving as the first and last pitches of its scale; and the triad whose root is the first scale degree of the prevailing key.

Transposition   The operation of moving a melody higher or lower, either with or without a change of key.

Treble clef   A symbol ($\&$) used in the notation of pitches in the middle to high range on a staff.

Triad   A combination of three simultaneously sounding pitches notated on three adjacent lines or three adjacent spaces. A triad contains a root, a third, and a fifth. The interval between the root and third is a third, and between the root and fifth is a fifth. The most common triad qualities are major, minor, and diminished.

Triplet   A group of three notes that divide the quarter-note beat of a simple meter into three equal parts.

Unison   An interval of size one; the two noteheads of a unison appear on the same line or space. *See* INTERVAL SIZE.

Upbeat   A note or notes preceding a downbeat. Also called pickup.

Voice leading   The principles by which each of the four voices, or pitches, of a chord move in relation to one another.

Whole note   A symbol ($\circ$) denoting a pitch lasting four beats in simple meters such as $\frac{4}{4}$, and two beats in simple meters such as $\frac{2}{2}$, $\frac{3}{2}$, or $\frac{4}{2}$.

Whole rest   A symbol ($-$) denoting a silence lasting one full measure in all meters except $\frac{4}{2}$.

Whole step   The combination of two half steps.

INDEX

A

accidentals, 47–50, 99–101, 125–27, 255–56, 339
alla breve meter, 256–59, 339
antecedent phrases, 234, 339
arpeggiations, 236, 339
augmentation dot, 35, 36, 339
augmented intervals, 127–31, 211, 339
authentic cadences, 234, 339

B

bar lines, 12, 339
bass clef, 52–54, 153, 339
bass pitch, 155, 178, 197
beams, 80–81, 339
beats, 11, 339

C

cadences, 233–38, 339
choral music notation, 156
chordal analysis, 193–98
chords, 30, 339
    compound intervals, 153–54
    double pitches, 156
    four-note chords, 156–60
    inversions, 173–78, 289–91
    leading tones, 211–14
    major key cadences, 233–38
    minor key progressions, 251–56
    naming, 196–97
    pop music symbols, 287–88
    root position, 154–55, 175
    roots, 31
    See also intervals; triads
chromatic intervals, 127–30, 339
chromatic pitches, 125–29
chromatic scales, 280–81
clefs, 4, 12, 52–54, 153, 282–83, 339
C Major, 8–9, 27–34
common time, 11–13, 55–56, 339
compound intervals, 153–54, 339
compound meters, 131–33, 178–81, 279, 339
conducting patterns, 283
consequent phrases, 234, 339
consonance, 27, 174–75, 340
counting. *See* rhythm
cut time, 256–59, 340

D

deceptive cadences, 236, 237, 340
diatonic pitches, 9, 340
dictionaries of musical terms, 36
diminished intervals, 31–32, 127–29, 211, 340
diminished triads, 33
dissonance, 27, 174–75, 211–14, 340
dominant chords, 197, 211–19, 340
dotted notes, 340
    eighth notes, 160–61
    half notes, 35
    quarter notes, 81–82, 178–79
    whole notes, 258–59
double bars, 12, 340
double flats, 125–27, 340
double pitches, 156
double sharps, 125–27, 340
double whole notes, 258–59, 340
downbeats, 107–8, 340

E

eighth notes, 80–83, 160–61, 340
embellishing notes, 341
enharmonic equivalents, 101, 284–87, 341

F

fifth intervals, 6–7, 27, 31, 341
fifth pitch, 31
figured bass, 155, 193–94, 197, 251–52, 341
final exam, 275–78
first inversion, 173–74, 341
$\frac{5}{3}$ position, 155, 341
flags, 81–82, 341
flats, 47–48, 99–101, 105, 125–27, 341
F Major, 47–48, 50–52
$\frac{4}{2}$ meter, 256–59
$\frac{4}{4}$ meter, 11–13, 55–56, 339
four-note chords, 156–60
fourth intervals, 27, 160, 341

G

G Major, 47–48, 50–52

H

half cadences, 234, 237, 341
half notes, 12–13, 35, 55–56, 256–59, 341
half steps, 9, 341